THE PROFESSIONAL AMATEUR

The Cricketing Life of Bob Barber

COLIN SHINDLER

Max Books

A CIP catalogue record for this title is available from the British Library

ISBN: 978-0-9562224-8-0

Typeset and Design by Andrew Searle

Jacket Cover Design and Artwork by David Valentine

Printed and bound in Great Britain by
CPI Group (UK) Ltd, Croydon, CR0 4YY

MAX BOOKS
Epworth House
34 Wellington Road
Nantwich Cheshire CW5 7BX
Tel: 01270 625278
Email: maxcricket@btinternet.com

FOREWORD

by GEOFFREY BOYCOTT O.B.E.

THE FIRST TIME I met Bob Barber was the day before we walked out together to open the innings against Australia at The Oval in 1964. I had no idea what to expect but I soon realised that he was a very straight sort of guy.

Having played county cricket for a few years before I started, Bob was obviously more experienced and worldly-wise than me. He soon took me under his wing and behaved much like an older brother, particularly that winter on our first tour together to South Africa, when he put himself out to look after me.

In those early days I was a very introverted young man but on the field we soon became good foils for each other. Bob played in an expansive, free-spirited, almost carefree manner which was very different from how I had been raised in Yorkshire. He was also a superb, athletic fielder and a useful leg spinner. In that era cricket coverage was still in its infancy and it is sad that his best batting performances were never captured or retained on film.

DEDICATION

This book is dedicated to the memory of Jack Barber 1907-1972

His scrupulous integrity and unwavering support provided his
son with everything he needed in life

ACKNOWLEDGEMENTS

MY GREATEST DEBT is of course to Bob Barber himself who generously provided not just his time and total co-operation but the scrapbooks carefully compiled by his three maternal aunts and the files assembled in chronological order by his secretary. To be confronted by such well-organised material is a historian's delight.

I am also indebted to Bob's playing colleagues who were happy to recall their times together. They included Jack Bond, Jim Stewart, Mike Smith, Jim Parks, Geoffrey Boycott, John Murray, Alan Smith, Bob Bennett and Edward Craig as well as the Sage of Longparish, John Woodcock. I am extremely appreciative of the trouble Geoffrey Boycott took to provide the foreword to this book.

I am grateful to Stephen Chalke for his helpful comments on the manuscript and for permission to reprint his article on Bob's seventieth birthday celebrations; to Jonathan Coy for his gift of Barber-related *Wisden*s and to Malcolm Lorimer for allowing me to choose a Lancashire hero to contribute to his excellent series. Ken Grime at Old Trafford provided me with access to the committee's minute books for the relevant years.

Katherine Fisher accompanied me to Switzerland when I went to interview Bob at his home there and provided me with her reliably sharp analysis and constant support for which I am daily grateful.

I also want to acknowledge my late cousin Ronnie Weidberg with whom I saw so many innings played by the young Bob Barber at Old Trafford. Ronnie wanted to bowl like Brian Statham and I wanted to hit sixes like Peter Marner but after the experience of researching and writing this book, I think I would now like to return to the late 1950s and become Bob Barber. I can think of no higher compliment that any biographer can pay his subject than actually to want to become him!

PROLOGUE

IN 2012 I WROTE an article for the *Wisden Almanack* on the fiftieth anniversary of the abolition of the distinction between amateur cricketers and their professional counterparts. There were a number of men who had been playing in 1962 to whom I would have been delighted to have spoken, but my first call was to the man whose knowledge of county cricket at that time probably exceeds that of most of the surviving players. Stephen Chalke had written a delightful article for *The Wisden Cricketer* magazine on the occasion of Bob Barber's seventieth birthday in 2005 when R.W. Barber's XI took on a team captained by M.J.K. Smith, each side containing men who had played before 1962 as either amateurs or professionals. They had all played with Bob at some point in the various stages of his life, either at school, at university or in first class and international cricket. Having read the piece again, it was Bob Barber who I immediately thought would provide the best insight into the extraordinary social rift created by cricket's anachronistic perpetuation of the Gentlemen v Players division.

I learned from Stephen that Bob was now living in Switzerland, so one evening I rang the number he gave me and began what was for me a very special relationship that has found its fulfilment in this book. Despite never having met each other, within minutes we had established an easy rapport and we were ensconced in Bob's memories of the Oval Test match in 1966, and where he was fielding when the all-conquering West Indies captain Garry Sobers was caught first ball off bat and pad at short leg by Brian Close off a delivery from John Snow. The easy familiarity of references to "Closey", "Garry" and "Snowy" never seemed less fraught with embarrassment.

A few weeks later I was driving to the small Cotswold village where Bob frequently stays when he is in England. On the way I saw very clearly in my mind's eye the young man, in a peaked Lancashire cap adorned with the red rose, clattering his way down the pavilion steps at Old Trafford followed by those fabled heroes of my childhood – Brian Statham, "Noddy" Pullar, Ken Grieves, Peter Marner, Tommy Greenhough and the rest of them. Bob's voice on the telephone had sounded strong but I had been researching a book on National Service and I was aware from the men I had interviewed how capricious the ageing process can be.

He was standing in the driveway as I arrived, casually dressed, his shirt collar turned up as I had remembered he and Garry Sobers (later slavishly copied by Tony Greig and Eric Cantona) had always worn it. He was light on his feet, friendly and open-faced, looking a good ten years younger than the men of his age I had been talking to about conscription. From the moment the talking started it would have taken a military operation to have stopped the conversation.

I knew well enough that the days of his captaincy at Lancashire in 1960 and 1961 had not been happy ones. They were miserable enough just being an eleven-year-old supporter. The county cricket club was experiencing a turmoil that would not subside until the end of the decade when Jack Bond took control of a side now including Clive Lloyd and Farokh Engineer. I knew too, that Barber's cricketing fortunes changed radically as soon as he left Lancashire and started playing for Warwickshire. The received wisdom, contested by the man himself, is that the stodgy, poky, cautious batsman who was clearly using about a tenth of his potential at Old Trafford was miraculously transformed at Edgbaston into a confident, upright batsman who stood tall at the crease and began, from the first ball of every match, to seize the initiative from the bowling side by clean, powerful hitting. This was the man who made 113 for his new county against the powerful 1963 West Indians, when nobody else made more than 22, who smashed a hundred before lunch against the Australians the following year and eighteen months after that went to Sydney and made 185 in a Test match there that became one of cricket's legendary innings.

Bob Barber disappeared from first-class cricket in a slow fade out at the end of the 1960s, his business career and future life proving more challenging and important to him than the need to show the world that he was good at games. Every player who speaks of Bob Barber talks of him in tones of the warmest friendship and professional admiration. It was going to be a labour of love to re-introduce Bob Barber to the readers of the twenty-first century.

Long before Kevin Pietersen decided the best way to get to a hundred was with a lofted drive for six or four, Bob Barber was doing just that, getting himself bowled three short of his first Test century at The Wanderers in Johannesburg, after an enormous cross-batted slog aimed at the distant mid-wicket boundary that had completed a two hundred degrees arc before the ball crashed into the unprotected stumps off a thick inside edge. "Six or out" he had cheerfully informed the slack-jawed Ted Dexter, his dilatory partner at the other end who had made only forty out of their stand of 136 before the fatal ball had been bowled. "You're mad!" exclaimed the man whose time as Chairman of Selectors in the 1990s gave a whole new meaning to the word "eccentric".

The media in 1964 effectively meant the written press and they did not excoriate him for failing to achieve those extra three runs. Charles Fortune, the chronicler of the MCC tour of South Africa in 1964-65, merely observed that bookings for the remaining three Tests of the series increased substantially once the crowd had seen what Barber was likely to do.

As they walked out to bat in the first innings of the first match of the 1965-6 Ashes tour, the state match against Western Australia in Perth, Barber confided to his astonished partner John Edrich that he was going to hit the first ball he received for four over extra cover. In fact the outfield was slow and it only went for three but this is the nature of the man. No bowler was going to tie him down and the spectators who came to watch Barber would be guaranteed more than their money's worth, whatever his final tally. This was the amateur of popular folklore, the man who played to entertain the crowd, free from the grinding responsibilities of the professional.

Except that the man I met was the most studious and cerebral of cricketers. He was a man who took his cricket as seriously in his own way as any gnarled old professional who played for Yorkshire in the inter-war years. How could the amateur and the professional co-exist in this manner? How could a man who thrived in the steely world of international cricket, who told Geoffrey Boycott to run less selfishly or he would run him out be reconciled with the man of whom his contemporaries talk in such glowing terms of his thoughtfulness and his sensitivity?

This is what interested me at the start of the preparation for this book. Bob Barber's time coincided with the death of the amateur cricketer and the emergence of the paid cricketer with no exceptions. It was a fascinating pattern of social change in English history and it would be fascinating, I thought, to see how Bob Barber's life as a cricketer fitted into, or even somehow symbolised, that change in English social history. Bob Barber's career in cricket finished over forty years ago. He has, until now, for a variety of reasons which will become clear as the book progresses, never wanted to talk about those distant times. Nevertheless, as we sat on the couch in his quiet comfortable lounge in Gloucestershire, Bob started to recall the road that led to fame, to notoriety, to celebrity and eventually to a much delayed retirement from cricket though assuredly not from life.

CHAPTER ONE

MY BIRTH CERTIFICATE says I was born in Didsbury in September 1935, but it was probably a nursing home in Wythenshawe. My parents at the time were living in Cheadle Hulme, only a few miles from Old Trafford. Six months after I was born, my father took a job in North Wales. He was an accountant, not a chartered accountant but a certified accountant. He took a position as Company Secretary in a small public company that was involved in fuels like coke, so we went to live in a village in Flintshire called Hawarden, where Gladstone's wife's family came from. We always thought of the Hawarden estate as the Gladstone estate. There was never any mention of any other name.

Bob's father, Jack, had been born in the early years of the twentieth century in Almondbury near Huddersfield and he remained a Huddersfield Town and Yorkshire CCC supporter all his life, which meant that Roses battles were integral to the household. His mother, born Mabel Payne, came from Manchester. The fact that Bob played the first half of his career as an amateur might have led some people to make an incorrect supposition about his origins.

I was certainly not born with a silver spoon in my mouth. My father's father died when he was about 47. He worked in a grocery shop in Huddersfield before he set up his own shop in Almondbury. His wife came from a reasonably well off family but when she married him she was shunned by her family, who thought she had married beneath her. When he died young, my grandmother and her children moved to Manchester. My father, Jack Barber, had won a scholarship to the well-regarded Almondbury Grammar School and somewhere I have a letter from the headmaster recommending that he take the scholarship over to Manchester Grammar School. However, he was now the man of the family at the age of 13, so he left school and went out to work. He worked very, very hard all his life. He was a very disciplined Yorkie. He passed on to me the principle of recording every single half-penny he ever spent. It taught me to save money even though I didn't earn very much. I told my children about it because if you know exactly how much you are spending you tend not to over-spend.

Bob's later discovery of one of his father's notebooks, in which he had recorded buying the *Evening Chronicle* for a half-penny, confirms that Jack practised what he preached.

For all the fact that his boyhood was spent in North Wales, culturally the Barbers did not move far from their birth places in the North of England.

My father, don't forget, was a Yorkshireman and we used to have all those arguments about Roses matches and Huddersfield Town versus Manchester City. My uncle was a season ticket holder at City and he used to adore Peter Doherty.

The wilful introduction of such enmity into family life, frequently to the despair of the women for the unnecessary arguments it creates, is a phenomenon most of us recognise as having a parallel in our own lives.

If Jack Barber's financial background had been tough, Bob's maternal family, the Paynes, didn't come from comfortable circumstances either. Mabel's grandfather had been a friend of C.P. Scott, the Editor of the *Manchester Guardian* in its great days. Bob has in his possession a copy of his great-grandfather's will in which he writes with reference to his grandfather essentially, "I've given him enough and I'm not giving him any more."

It's my understanding that my grandmother took the children and left my grandfather which was very rare in those days. I've no idea if they divorced or not but my grandfather continued to live in the family house and she moved into a small house in Didsbury. I didn't feel under-privileged growing up but money was certainly tight.

Curiously, there was another marriage between the Barber and Payne families. Mabel Payne's brother was teaching Maths at Almondbury Grammar when he met and married Jack's younger sister. This presumably meant that his uncle married his aunt before they were in fact his uncle and his aunt, which sounds very much like a plot from a Gilbert & Sullivan opera.

Bob's first real memory is the declaration of war in 1939, just before his fourth birthday. Like so many others, the whole family gathered round the wireless for the broadcast. Neville Chamberlain solemnly intoned to a resigned Sunday morning audience, that the British Ambassador in Berlin had handed the German government a note, stating that unless he heard from them by 11 o'clock that they were at once prepared to withdraw their troops from Poland, a state of war would exist between them. Unaware of the profound nature of the broadcast Bob was playing football with pins, flicking matches for shots, the significance and the emotion of the occasion not leaving much of a mark on the boy, not quite four years old.

Indeed, if anything, life immediately got better. The following morning, September 4th 1939, their parents told Bob and his brother Tony that they were going to take a holiday, because it would be the last for a long time and they all drove up to Scotland. It was a long journey and one with a long remembered discomfort.

We had a small car, a Vauxhall or something and there was a hump in the back that covered the transmission. Being the younger brother, I had to sleep on that while Tony was on the seat. I remember waking up in Scotland and I could hear pipers playing. I loved porridge as a boy and I was not very happy because in Scotland they put salt on it whereas I'd been used to sugar and top of the milk cream with my porridge.

When Jack Barber took his medical at the outbreak of war it was discovered that he wasn't as fit as he should have been and so he ended up looking after gas and water services in North Wales. He lived at home and he was the one who pretty much kept Hawarden Cricket Club going during the war. He and his boys used to walk to the ground through the park because there was no transport and, from the age of five or so, Bob was allowed to hold one handle of the bag with the equipment. It is memories of the impact of such a responsibility that reveal how important a role, any kind of a role, within the game and the club must have been to the young boy.

Jack had been born in 1907 so he was too young for the First World War and unfit for World War II which depressed him because he had been very anxious to join the Royal Navy on the outbreak of war in 1939. Bob acknowledges that it is difficult to be sure of his parents' inner feelings because children were not expected to ask questions about them in those days. This inability to challenge authority was to have particularly unfortunate consequences during his years at Lancashire, but it can be seen that such attitudes were integral to the general society in which he grew up.

War itself, for most children of Bob's age, was rather like cricket, with periods of boredom interspersed with violent action. Living in Flintshire meant that they were safe from direct bombing but they were near enough to Liverpool docks, a prime target for the Luftwaffe's relentless nightly raids, to be on the flight path on occasions. Bomber Command was at Broughton and Fighter Command was at RAF Sealand, but it was an even bigger risk to spend Christmas 1940 at Mabel's sisters' house in Parrs Wood, Didsbury, given its proximity to the Trafford Park engineering factories and the Manchester docks which were equally the target of relentless German bombing.

I can remember there were invariably raids, so when we were there, we slept under the mahogany hard wood dining room table. There was blackout material attached to the curtains and I can remember getting up, pulling the curtains aside and looking at what looked a firework display. I never felt the remotest fear. It was just very exciting. We were all given gas masks and we found that if you blew into them in a certain way they made a rude noise. It was all great fun.

John Boorman's *Hope & Glory*, a film about the director's schooldays in south west London during this time, seems to capture much of the spirit that Bob recalls. There is of course the added similarity that the boy in the film is taught by his grandfather how to bowl leg breaks and in particular how to deceive with a carefully disguised googly. The difference between the two however was emphasised by the fact that, whereas the boy in the film was "taught" by the actor Ian Bannen, Bob was shown how to bowl a googly by George Tribe, Northamptonshire's Australian import from the Lancashire Leagues and generally reckoned to be one of the finest left arm wrist spinners in the history of the game. John Boorman had to settle for becoming a very good film director with what one can only assume was a decent googly.

It was Jack who first got to know George Tribe and he invited the Australian to stay with the Barbers.

George Tribe was a huge influence. He showed me, with a tennis ball, how to bowl and that's why I started to bowl leg spinners. Boys at that age just tried to bowl fast, so my hero at that stage was the chap who opened the bowling for Hawarden Park. I think I started scoring there when I was five or six and Alec Reidford bowled fast, so I bowled fast. George showed me how to bowl leggies and I used to go to see him for coaching, both at Rawtenstall and Milnrow when he was the pro. George gave me a book on spin bowling called **How To Bowl Them Out** *by Christopher Sly and I've still got it at home. That book was very instrumental in my learning leggies. It got me to think about bowling, altering the speed of the ball and changing the field. I didn't hold the ball like Eric Hollies. I held it between two fingers. Did you ever see Washy [Cyril Washbrook] trying to play George? The lads all raced to the window to watch, because he had no idea at all which way it was turning. George used to bring a team to play against us at school. He was a good batsman and did the double every year.*

The two Barber boys were together for most of the war and they were good sporting company for each other. Tony was two years and three months older than Bob, with whom he had a normal fraternal relationship in which the older brother was occasionally forced to remind his younger sibling of the traditional deference due to age. Tony was a good all-round sportsman, in particular a very good wicket keeper. During his days as a National Serviceman, he got into the final RAF trial but there he found himself up against Roy Swetman, the future Surrey and England keeper, an experience that appears to have upset him so much that, sadly, he hardly bothered to play cricket after that.

Tony batted right handed but I batted left because my father did. I think many people today finish up standing the wrong way round. We all have an arm and an eye that are dominant. My right eye is significantly more dominant than the left so I have to stand left handed. The right arm was dominant and you were always coached that the top hand holding the bat is the key so it came naturally to me standing left handed that the right hand was the top hand and controlled the bat. I also learned to throw with my left hand, because at Cambridge in my first year I damaged my elbow when I was throwing the javelin. I couldn't throw the ball that first cricket season and so to be able to play, I practised throwing left handed until I could do it reasonably well. I could threaten a batsman trying to steal a run if I picked it up in my right hand but he didn't know if I was going to let it go like that. I always played lots of sports so that if I made three ducks in a row, it didn't matter if I scored a try or a goal.

Sport, not just cricket, was the dominant passion of Bob Barber's early life and athletics in particular became almost as important to him as cricket at one stage. Like many other men and women of his age he can still recall the start of the 1948 Olympics in London and the handsome blonde quarter-miler, John Mark, running into Wembley Stadium with the torch to light the flame. Sport runs through the Barber family. His wife, Anne, was a fine county standard tennis player. His middle daughter, Janny, was, at the various ages, the Welsh junior champion and played the major junior tournaments, acquitting herself well during her two years on the circuit, after coaching from Harry Hopman. His eldest daughter, Sandy, was one of the rare North Walians to be picked at that time for the Wales junior hockey teams.

Apart from the occasional newsreel in the local cinema which showed a couple of minutes of frequently inexplicable action from a recent FA Cup match or rugby international and, in the summer, the fall of a Test Match wicket, most sporting moments in the immediate post-war years were relayed to their audiences, who couldn't see them live, by means of the wireless. It was through the crackling unreliable radio transmission that Bob heard the unfolding of Freddie Brown's 1950-1 tour of Australasia, and in particular the famous final Test victory at

Melbourne where Simpson and Hutton batted England to their first Ashes victory since 1938, after Alec Bedser had heroically bowled himself into the ground, taking ten wickets in the match.

Even when he was away at school, Bob remained close to cricket at Old Trafford. His headmaster at Ruthin used to arrange for a charabanc full of the boys from the school to go to Old Trafford to watch Test matches there. Some of the memories are indelible.

I saw the 1948 Australians and I saw Dick Pollard pull one into Sid Barnes at short leg. I saw Bradman batting and Cyril hooking Lindwall. My memories go back to watching the Australian services matches in 1945 with Carmody, Hassett, Cristofani, Miller, Cec Pepper and Jack Pettiford. I also remember going to Old Trafford in the first season after the war and Charlie Barnett hit Dick Pollard into the seats where we were sitting, just to the left of the pavilion. It was very close and what made it even more impressive, it was in the first over of the match.

That sort of bold hitting clearly made a significant mark on the mind of the young opening batsman.

In those days, boys did not grow up obsessing exclusively about international cricket as they do now because they see it all the time on television. Test cricket lasted, at most, for twenty-five days each summer. First class cricket was really county cricket and Bob retained strong feelings for county cricket.

*We used all the names when we played those cricket games like **Howzat** and we studied the scores, and of course Lancashire was my team.*

It's charming to imagine the fifteen-year-old Bob Barber with his ear glued to the wireless for the latest news of Freddie Brown's men, learning that two of his heroes, Roy Tattersall and Brian Statham, were being flown out as late replacements. Less than ten years later, Bob was to be their captain.

On Mabel's side of the family, there were three sisters and one brother who were all teachers so education was clearly important in the family. Unsurprisingly, it seems apparent that, having to leave Almondbury Grammar at the age of 13 had profoundly affected Jack Barber, who was determined that his two sons should not be cruelly deprived of a good education in the way that he had been. He decided that the boys were going to be sent away to school. At first, Jack's intention was to send Tony to Sedbergh near Kendal, in what was then Westmorland on the edge of the Lake District, because Tony used to suffer from bronchitis. Mabel disagreed with her husband quite strongly, believing that Sedbergh was too far north and far too cold. Jack took Mabel there in an attempt to convince her but she was aghast to find the boys walking around in shorts in the middle of winter. It was clearly a Spartan existence too far.

Tony eventually ended up at Ruthin School in north Wales. He went when he was eleven and Bob, much to his delight, followed him there just before his tenth birthday in September 1945.

I pestered my parents so much, because I was desperate to go there. It looked to be a lot of fun but I wasn't at all unhappy at home. My relationship with my parents was very good. I was particularly close to my father because of the sporting connection. He loved football and cricket and he passed on that love to his sons. Going to Ruthin just looked like a new step in life and I wanted to take it.

Bob arrived at Ruthin a year after Tony. There were consequences for both of them, not always fortunate ones, because, in his first year, Bob was picked to open the batting for the junior cricket team. The previous year, Tony had been entrusted with that responsibility. He still played as wicketkeeper but it probably didn't help their relationship that his young squirt of a brother was quickly identified as outstanding. He himself was talented but being outshone by your younger brother when he is only ten years old is rarely going to make for an easier fraternal relationship. It also happened with their academic work. By the time Tony got to school certificate level, he found Bob was in the same class and, in the days when schoolchildren were regularly informed of their exact position in class in every subject, Tony was having to cope with the excruciating torment of seeing his younger brother frequently being identified as first or second in the class, which couldn't have greatly helped the harmonious growth of their relationship either.

After they went their separate ways, Tony eventually became the junior of three senior partners and became a very successful estate agent but unfortunately he developed a heart problem and he died ten years ago. When Tony passed away, he was only a few years older than his father had been; Jack had been taken by cancer when he was 60. The boys' paternal grandfather had died at 47. Bob shakes his head ruefully and confesses that no serious breeder would pay much for him at the Newmarket sales. Fortunately, there was one relative, his Great Uncle Henry, who lived to a ripe old age and who used to cycle around the Yorkshire Dales when he was over 80.

Much as he was looking forward to life at Ruthin School, since he wasn't yet ten when he left the warm familiarity of the home in Hawarden, it was inevitable that he also found the experience initially to be a little daunting. With a September birth date, everyone was older than he was and therefore most of them were also much bigger and stronger and Tony did not see it as his role to look after his younger brother in an overly protective manner.

It could certainly be argued that Bob had little need of that sort of protection. He was in the first eleven at school in his second year there. At the start of the 1951 season, the fifteen-year-old schoolboy had forced his way into the first team at Boughton Hall in Chester and was attracting the sort of gushing praise that followed him for the next few years, as his prodigious talents were revealed to a wider public gaze. His form for school and club was such that he was selected to play for Welsh Schools against English Schools at Old Trafford. That match provided his first sight of the equally talented but temperamentally opposite Peter Marner of Crompton, who was to feature significantly in Bob's future life in cricket. This early taste of representative cricket ended in a tame draw but Bob showed his qualities to the assembled judges at Old Trafford with a stylish 50 not out in the second innings. Among these judges was the Lancashire batting hero of the inter-war years, Ernest Tyldesley, who was now a Lancashire committee member. R.W. Barber's card was marked.

Also playing for Wales in that match was Robert Duray-Aiyar, the son of Anglo-Indian parents, who took 5-55 including the wicket of Ken Taylor, the future Yorkshire and England opener. Aiyar was fast and accurate enough to have made a considerable impact in first class cricket but he was on his way to Oxford University and his father, a distinguished ENT surgeon, clearly had other plans for his son that did not include uprooting stumps. Facing the fearsome Aiyar in the nets taught Bob not to be afraid of fast bowling and the courageous manner in which he took on Hall and Griffith in his later career shows that Aiyar's impact was entirely successful.

By the middle of that 1951 season, Arthur Booth, the old Yorkshire spinner and now coach at Manchester Grammar School, had seen enough of young Barber to write a glowing letter of recommendation.

Dear Sir,

I have assisted in the coaching of Robert W Barber at Ruthin School for many seasons. I have played league cricket with his father and known Robert since he was a toddler. Robert, in my view, has only to develop normally to be assured of a first class career. He played in the first XI at school when he was only eleven years of age and has kept his place ever since.

For his age he is a brilliant batsman, left hand with an excellent defence and a wide range of strokes. He is a very fine fielder particularly near the wicket and he also bowls a very good leg break mixed with googlies and top spinners. He spins the ball both quickly and prodigiously. …

Unquestionably, Robert has all the makings of a first class player and I am recommending him to Harry Makepeace for a selective trial at Old Trafford. My own County, unfortunately, cannot entertain Robert who was born in Manchester and is therefore not eligible for Yorkshire.

Yours faithfully,

Arthur Booth
ex-Yorkshire C.C.C.

At the start of the 1952 season, Aiyar, Barber and Taylor were among the 34 boys chosen by Jack Hobbs and Herbert Sutcliffe to take part in one of the first organised coaching courses, sponsored by the *News Chronicle* at Lilleshall, deep in the glorious Shropshire countryside. Among the former players who coached the boys were Freddie Brown who was then the current England captain, Gubby Allen, Tom Dollery the captain of Warwickshire, the previous season's county championship winners and Harry Altham, the Winchester School master and MCC Treasurer who took a special interest in the young Barber, and who proved particularly helpful at this stage of his career.

Despite being only 16 years old, Bob was finding in that season that schools cricket was becoming increasingly easy for him. Playing for Ruthin School against Old Ruthinians, Bob scored 124 not out and, being captain, declared the innings closed at 198 for 1 before putting himself onto bowl to take four Old Boys wickets for 25. He clearly needed a bigger challenge. When school finished, in the summer holidays of 1952, he was chosen to play for Cheshire in the Minor Counties competition against Northumberland. Returning to play for Boughton Hall alongside Robert Aiyar against Liverpool, Bob top scored and then ran through the opposition claiming 6-41.

A few weeks later, he made his debut at Lord's, playing for The Rest against Southern Schools, who included A.C Walton later of Middlesex, (bowled Barber 20) A.B.D. Parsons later of Surrey and E.R. Dexter of Radley (bowled Barber 44). Because he batted in the lower middle order but took wickets with his big spinning leg breaks, Bob was being seen by the press at this point as primarily a bowler. Barber, Dexter, Walton and Bob Gale, who was also later to play for Middlesex, were all chosen to represent the Public Schools to play the Combined Services who, thanks to National Service, could regularly field a side composed almost entirely of young county players.

In 1952, Bob was facing a team containing Micky Stewart and Keith Andrew, as well as future touring companions Fred Titmus and Jim Parks and his future Cambridge and Lancashire team mate, Colin Smith. It was captained by Colin Ingleby-Mackenzie and it was too strong for the schoolboys who collapsed in their second innings, despite a fine 43 by Dexter. Bob was bowled for 20 by Jim Parks, who was playing essentially as a batsman and spin bowler, the start of his wicket keeping days being some six years distant. There is an irony in seeing Bob dismissed in this manner since Parks was to spend so many days in the following decade keeping to Bob's leg spin.

1953 might have been the year that Everest was "conquered", Stanley Matthews won his coveted FA Cup-winners medal, the Queen was crowned and the Ashes were regained after nineteen long years but, in north Wales, 1953 was the year of the young Bob Barber. Playing for Ruthin School, he attained "the double" of a thousand runs and a hundred wickets in twenty-one matches, only the third time in the history of schools cricket that such a feat had been achieved. When he returned to Lord's that summer to play for The Rest against Southern Schools, it was as an opening batsman. *The Times* called him "a batsman of presence and distinction – one of the two outstanding all-rounders of this year's cricket – his leg breaks and googlies were vicious and coming quickly off the pitch".

Bob's sporting success insulated him somewhat from traditional schoolboy persecution and his academic success led to a discussion with his father and his Headmaster, when he was about 16, as to what Bob would do, once he had graduated. Bob's own preference was to become a barrister but this was immediately shot down by the headmaster because he was studying sciences and therefore it was decided very quickly, without much reference to Bob himself, that he was to read medicine. Dictatorial decisions of this nature were frequently made in that peremptory fashion in the early 1950s.

In the sixth form, Bob studied Physics, Chemistry and Biology for A level but, to go to Cambridge, students needed "matric" which included a language. As a potential medical student, the language was, by default, Latin. His rapid academic advance, however, was not without its negative consequences.

I went into the School Certificate form just before my 14th birthday. However, the government had introduced a rule, stating that you needed to be 16 at the start of the school year to take the O level exam, so although I was one of the top two in my class, I could not take it for three years. This could have meant that I would be kicking my heels in the O level form for three years. I did repeat a year but after that I moved up to study for the A level, taking the O level whilst I was studying the A level syllabus. I remember doing Geography as my fifth ordinary subject without going to any classes, which infuriated the Geography master.

To redress the balance slightly, it can be recorded that when Bob took the Cantab 1st MB paper in Organic Chemistry paper to keep himself occupied between being accepted at Cambridge and leaving school, he failed. It was one of the very few times he encountered that experience but he only knew he had failed because the message was conveyed verbally. It seemed a strange state of affairs then and still does.

The Headmaster of Ruthin School was J.R.T. Russell, although he had been born a Jew in Poland, where he was known by the less Anglo-Saxon name of Levi. Escaping the endemic anti-Semitism of Eastern Europe just in time, he had been to Brecon College and thence to Oxford where he played rugby for the Authentics. He loved his cricket, although he was not particularly good at the game. He was a strong, dominant character; a man much feared and respected by pupils and parents alike for the thirty-one years he remained in charge of Ruthin from 1936 to1967. Bob retained the respect he had felt for him as a youth and was honoured to be asked to go down to Swansea to carry the coffin at his funeral.

There are probably two or three people in my life I owe an enormous debt of gratitude to. My father first, Russell second and somewhere down the line I have a very soft spot for Harry Altham, who was hugely encouraging from the age of 15.

Russell got a lot of his pupils into Oxford and Cambridge in the days before league tables came to dominate the parents' choice of schools. It helped of course that Ruthin, like other schools, had a relationship with a particular college. In Ruthin's case it was Pembroke at Oxford and Magdalene at Cambridge. Again, it appears as if Bob didn't have much say in the matter. No doubt had he objected violently, notice would have been taken, but essentially he understood that his father and Russell had his best interests at heart and there seemed no point in opposing them, since they had a far more detailed knowledge of the world than he had, as a teenager.

The first time he saw Cambridge was when he went there for an interview at Magdalene College. Russell gave him excellent advice and Bob was grateful to be the beneficiary of it, although the Headmaster's advice went beyond university. Before he had even matriculated at Magdalene and begun his study of Medicine, Russell was busy organising his post-Cambridge life as a trainee doctor at St Bartholomew's Hospital in London, known as Bart's. Jack and Mabel made no objection. Their intention was for Bob to become independent, to have a life that gave him freedom, status and money; essentially not to have the life that Jack had been forced into by the abrupt termination of his formal education at the age of 13. There was no pressure on Tony or Bob to leave school and get a job. Their parents believed in the power of education to transform lives. Although they went to a public school, Bob and Tony were both part of that post-war generation who benefited from the reforms that followed the passing of R.A. Butler's 1944 Education Act. It was a more meritocratic society than had existed pre-war, and the Barber boys were well prepared to make the best of it.

In the 1945 general election, Bob suspects that Jack and Mabel would have voted for Churchill. To them, as to so many grateful British people, the prime minister was The Man Who Had Saved Us From Hitler. Like nearly everyone who voted for the Conservatives, the landslide election result in favour of Labour must have looked to them, as it did to Churchill, as a lack of gratitude. On the other hand, Mabel's sisters, the *Manchester Guardian* reading Payne women, would certainly have voted for the Liberal candidate although Manchester Withington, the constituency in which they lived, re-elected the Conservative Edward Fleming to Parliament, as it had done at every election since 1931. Jack's suspicions of what might happen to the gas and water industries he was working in were confirmed, when they were eventually nationalised under the Attlee government's policies.

Jack had owned the semi-detached house in Cheadle Hulme where his children were born but, Bob discovered later, the house in Hawarden was only rented. He couldn't sell the house in Cheadle Hulme during the financially depressed 1930s, so he rented it out, although he remained anxious to dispose of it. The cost of repairs he faced as a landlord turned out to be greater than the income in rent that he received, which had been frozen under wartime legislation. About the time Bob went away to school, Jack bought a house in Carrick Road in the Curzon Park district of Chester, a decent area by the river, close to the racecourse. There was enough space for the creation of a cricket pitch and Bob, with his customary dedication to the cause, claims to have put in as much work on that pitch as ever Bert Flack did at Old Trafford.

In October 1954, he left his home in Chester and went up to Cambridge to read Medicine. He arrived with something of a sporting reputation, having already made his debut for Lancashire in the County Championship as an eighteen-year-old schoolboy. Chester was to be Bob's home for the next twenty or so years. He moved there as a schoolboy. He left as a married man and an international cricketer. It sounds like the stuff of romance but, as he was to discover,, the transition did not come without considerable attendant difficulties.

CHAPTER TWO

MOST BOYS, WHEN unexpectedly summoned to the Headmaster's study, arrive there with some trepidation. At the start of the summer term at Ruthin School in 1954, the 18 year-old Bob Barber made the trip to Mr. Russell's office to be informed, to his astonishment, that he was to make his first class debut for Lancashire in the first match of the county championship season at home to Glamorgan. John Ikin was injured and would not be available until June, whilst Peter Marner was off to do his National Service, so Lancashire were two middle order batsmen down and Bob Barber was clearly in prime position to take one of the slots. Lancashire's Secretary, Geoffrey Howard, told the *Daily Dispatch*,

> *"We think he is a useful player. We will know better after the opening matches." Robert's father, Mr J. H. Barber, a Chester businessman said last night, "Robert is very bucked about it and the last person in the world to become swelled-headed."*

Not becoming "swelled-headed" was regarded as very important in 1954.

The letter of confirmation, from Geoffrey Howard to Bob, arrived a day or so later. It must be one of the few examples of a County Secretary informing a player that, "You will of course have to approach your Headmaster before accepting the invitation". The letter ends with a hope that, "You not only play successfully, but enjoy playing; as I am sure you will, under Cyril Washbrook, who will look after you as well as anybody I know".

I wonder too, how many County Secretaries express a wish for enjoyment when writing a similar letter sixty years later.

Looking at Bob's remarkable achievements as a young sportsman, it comes as little surprise to us that the county should have wanted to see what this talented young man was made of. To Bob, the whole thing was inexplicable, although he had played for Cheshire in the Minor Counties competition and for Welsh Schoolboys against England Schoolboys at Old Trafford. In addition, he had been invited for a session of pre-season training with the Lancashire staff, who had been so impressed by the boy's talents that Lancashire had written to Russell enquiring about his star pupil's birthplace, for the rules in those days meant that nobody could play for a county in which he had not been born, unless specially registered to do so by the MCC. Russell told Bob that he had been selected to play the first four games of the season – home and away championship matches against Glamorgan and matches at the two universities.

Bob knew from an unofficial conversation with Harry Altham, the Winchester schoolmaster, that Hampshire were interested in the prospect of his playing for them, which had presumably prompted Lancashire's decision to move quickly. He had played just that one representative schools game at Old Trafford, so that when he arrived at the ground on the day before he was to make his first class debut, he was quite sure that nobody would know who he was.

He was, despite his youth, far from overawed at the prospect of playing with seasoned professionals and Test cricketers.

When I played for Chester as a young schoolboy, most of the team had played for Cheshire. There was no one within ten years of my age. They must have all been in the war so I was used to playing with older men and therefore I didn't think much about the invitation when it arrived. The first game of cricket I played at Hawarden Park, I was about 11 but everyone else was ancient with grey hair.

In 1954, the young professionals at Lancashire and other counties were expected to earn the pittance they were paid, in addition to playing second eleven games and helping to maintain the ground, by bowling at the members, their social superiors, in the nets. It was the 1950s, the Nuclear Age, the mines had been nationalised and the National Health Service had begun but cricket still behaved as if it were stuck in a time warp of Edwardian England, its so-called "Golden Age".

The 1954 county championship season was due to start with a home game against Glamorgan on Saturday 8th May. On the Friday morning, Bob took the train to Warwick Road station and ventured into the indoor nets (the practice ground being too wet to play on) to get the feel of bat on ball. Amongst the Second XI bowlers waiting to bowl at the members was Tommy Greenhough, the wrist spinner from Rochdale with the famous loping run, with whom Bob was to share many a day's spin bowling in the years to come. Tommy clearly thought that Bob was one of the members' sons it was his duty to bowl at. He was soon offering the batting prodigy some helpful tips.

I played three or four balls and Tommy Greenhough, who didn't know me and I didn't know him, walked up to me and said, "You can't hold a bat like that". Next day I was batting at six for the first team and he's still batting at 11 in the seconds.

Bob, being the polite, shy, young man that he was, listened carefully to a lecture on the art of batting from Tommy Greenhough, whose career batting average terminated at 8.39. He tried to play in the net much as the googly and top spinning bowler had instructed, but decided that when he went out to make his debut the following day he would probably revert to the natural style that had served him well enough so far.

The match against Glamorgan was Cyril Washbrook's first match as the official Lancashire captain. Since the war Lancashire had had three captains; Jack Fallows (1946), Ken Cranston (1947-8) and Nigel Howard (1949-53) who, at the age of 28, had found the demands of the family's textile business too great to be able to juggle with the responsibilities of being Lancashire captain. There was simply no amateur available of any standing and the committee turned with some reluctance to the inevitable appointment of their senior professional, Cyril Washbrook.

There was over twenty years difference in age between the gruff veteran and his new, young all-rounder but Washbrook, conscious of the capricious ways of the committee, was as anxious as his junior to make a good impression. Fortunately for both of them, the match could scarcely have gone better, despite a 45 minute delay so that the first ball was not bowled until 12.15pm on the Saturday morning. When the teams eventually took the field, the weather was still grey and overcast, cold with the occasional blustery shower – in other words, a conventional May day in Manchester, in what would turn out to be one of the wettest summers on record.

On an uncovered pitch that was drying slowly in the pale spring sunshine, Glamorgan were put in to bat and bowled out for 81 in 32 overs by Malcolm Hilton and Roy Tattersall. Bob made two excellent catches, one from a lofted shot by Allan Watkins off the bowling of Tattersall, which was caught in the swirling wind but he clung on to it gratefully. He also ran out Jim McConnon with an athletic piece of fielding and a swift return. When Lancashire batted, after an uncertain start against Wilf Wooller and Don Shepherd, sound batting by the new captain in partnerships with Alan Wharton and Ken Grieves soon took Lancashire into a healthy lead. By close of play on Barber's first day of first class cricket, Lancashire had reached 192 for 3 with Washbrook five short of his century.

It was just after noon on the Monday morning when Grieves was caught behind by Haydn Davies off Wooller and the young schoolboy made his way out to the middle, with the Lancashire score on 215 for 4. He was not nervous, he never was. This was just another step up a ladder he had so far negotiated faultlessly. It probably helped that there wasn't a separate changing room for amateurs where he would have had to sit alone. He scored his first run in the county championship with a push for one off Wooller. It wasn't until many years later that Don Shepherd told him that the legendary competitor had informed his side that he was giving the debutant one to get off the mark. Shepherd never knew him to accord such generosity to any other batsman in his career. Bob attributed it to his Welsh connections.

Washbrook, thankfully for all concerned, had already completed his century before Bob took strike. Bob's first class education started immediately after Washbrook's departure, when Sid Smith, recently returned from National Service and playing only his sixth match for his county, came out to join Bob and immediately began to strike the ball fiercely.

Wilf Wooler was getting extremely exasperated with Sid. It was a wet wicket where the ball was doing a bit. Sid had nicked it and it had gone down and that was the very first time I heard the "f" word. It was a different world in those days. Wooller followed down the pitch a lot, despite being only medium pace and he was a big, towering fellow. He stood in the middle of the pitch with his hands on his hips glaring at Sid and he said, "If you're the best effing number 7 in Lancashire, God effing well help them" and I just thought, "What is he on about?"

At lunch, Washbrook declared the Lancashire innings closed on 311 for 6. Bob walked back to the pavilion, raising his bat in acknowledgement of the polite applause from the crowd for his very promising 41 not out, made with what *Wisden* called off drives of "skill and assurance". The press pounced on the "good news" story of the talented schoolboy. The *Evening Chronicle* reported that he "was given a rousing reception" for his innings and the *Daily Express* told its readers that the Glamorgan players had joined in the applause as Barber led the players off the field. The *Daily Mail* headlined its report on the game "Bob Barber big name of the future" and went on to tell the public eager for such information.

He is willowy. His back is straight as a flag pole and his left-handed batting is full of style – a style from which runs must flow sweetly. And so they did.

Denys Rowbotham in the *Manchester Guardian* wrote of the

polished promise of young Barber, a tall beautifully built left-hander who uses every inch of his height to play right over every ball and, joy of joys, has a back-footed basic technique as if the old lbw law had never been revised... Such shots, combined with a cut, played late as Macartney played it, suggest a batsman out of common in the making.

Second time round, Glamorgan put up more of a fight but Statham ripped out the heart of their batting and they subsided before the close of the second day for a total of 173 to give Lancashire victory by an innings and 57 runs. In conditions that did not favour leg spinners, it was hardly surprising that Bob did not get a bowl in either innings. It didn't matter. Spectators and press alike were convinced that Lancashire had unearthed a gem. Cyril Washbrook told the *Evening Chronicle*

> *I have seen today one of the most promising young players I have had the good fortune to see in a number of years. He wears his flannels like a cricketer and I am sure he will go a long, long way.*

Indeed he would, although it took a little while for the flannels to be ironed so that their creases were as immaculate as they had been so widely predicted.

Washbrook, who recognised his own difficulties with wrist spin, asked Bob to bowl to him in the nets which the young man found akin to a Royal Command Performance. On the Tuesday night they travelled down to Oxford, where they were to play the next day in The Parks against a university side captained by Colin Cowdrey and containing future internationals M.J.K. Smith and the South African J.P. "Pom Pom" Fellows-Smith. This time Bob did get a bowl and some words of advice from his captain.

> *I can remember Washy saying to me 'When you bowl at Cowdrey make sure you pitch it up.' Well, I pitched it up to Cowdrey and every time I did so, Cowdrey hit me for four.*

Bob bowled eight fruitless overs for 56 runs. Cowdrey made 94 before he was caught by Winston Place off Tattersall and Charles Williams, later to become a distinguished biographer and Labour Peer, scored 115, the two of them sharing a stand of 173 in less than three hours. Cowdrey declared just before the close, so Washbrook responded by dropping himself down the order and sending in the wicket keeper Alan "Ranji" Wilson as the nightwatchman opener. It proved not to be a stroke of tactical genius as Wilson was out for 0 in the first over.

Next day, Lancashire crawled to 255 for 9 with Bob contributing 12 before Cowdrey, in the days when he might have been considered an enterprising captain, declared, leaving Lancashire three hours to score 229 to win. Bob went in during the final over with six still needed for victory. He managed three but regained the bowling with two now needed off the last ball. He tried to loft Fasken over the head of Fellows-Smith at mid off but the South African jumped as he did in the line out during the winter months and caught the ball one-handed at full stretch, leaving Ken Grieves marooned on 94 at the other end. A good, exciting game and a comfortable championship win left Bob feeling delighted to be part of the first class cricket scene and he travelled to Cambridge with the rest of the party in high spirits. What awaited him was a perfect example of how fate in professional sport can turn on a sixpence.

Both university sides were still strong in the 1950s, and though Peter May and David Sheppard had gone down two years before and E.R. Dexter was not to arrive until two years later, Cambridge could still field future first-class cricketers in Dennis Silk of Somerset, Brian Parsons of Surrey, John Pretlove of Kent, Gamini Goonesena of Nottinghamshire and C.S. Smith of Lancashire (no relation to Sid) who was to become the distinguished architect Professor Sir Colin Stansfield Smith. In 1954, however, he was a quick and decidedly hostile seam bowler.

Lancashire bowled out Cambridge University for 256 (Barber 16-6-29-0) to give themselves three-quarters of an hour batting at the end of a bitterly cold and cheerless day in Cambridge, where the wind sweeps directly from the Urals straight across Parker's Piece and into Fenner's. The forty-year-old Washbrook opened the batting and was subjected to a relentless barrage of short pitched bowling in unfriendly conditions from the mischievous Colin Smith, who was clearly determined to show his future captain what he was capable of. Washbrook, a bruised and battered 19 not out overnight, stormed back into the pavilion muttering imprecations about the future Professor of Architecture, which no doubt vastly amused the rest of his team mates who would have silently applauded such *lese-majesty*. The following day, Bob made only twelve before he was bowled by Colin Smith but the triumphant bowler extended the hand of magnanimity by inviting his victim to dine in hall at Christ's College, whilst the rest of the Lancashire team no doubt made their way to the nearest bar.

Undergraduate food, especially in the year when rationing ended, was no great gastronomic feast, even if the company was enjoyable. On the way back to the hotel where the Lancashire team was staying, Bob tripped over some uneven paving. An X-ray revealed a fracture of a bone in his foot which ended Bob's cricket until late in the summer and, since he couldn't play before the end of the school year, he ended that final season at Ruthin School with a mere 17 wickets at 8.58. His batting, though restricted to 6 innings, included a highest score of 100* and left him with the Bradman-esque average of 149.00.

He returned to cricket at the end of July, captaining the Public Schools against the Combined Services and The Rest against the Southern Schools at Lord's. Opening the batting in the latter game with Ian Gibson of Manchester Grammar School, they put on 76 in 70 minutes with batting which *The Times* noted "would have done credit to a county side". Bob went on to make 70 before taking 5-32, the gentleman from *The Times* calling his bowling "a terror". *Wisden* noted that his bowling, except against the Combined Services, was admirably steady for a young practitioner of such a difficult art. The future England opener Peter Richardson was the batsman who hit him off his length in a calculated assault. Terry Spencer, who became the mainstay of the Leicestershire bowling for many years, then gave the partnership of Barber and Gibson a torrid time.

Bob's return to county cricket unfortunately produced fewer headlines than his debut but that he had made a significant impression on the cricket world was undeniable. Despite a run of low scores, he batted particularly well against Kent at Old Trafford. Pat Ward-Thomas, the golf correspondent of the *Manchester Guardian,* was on duty at Old Trafford to see Bob play an innings of outstanding maturity. As wickets tumbled at the other end, so carefully did Bob farm the bowling that Tommy Greenhough, batting at number 11, faced only eight balls in six overs. Ward-Thomas like the other judges rhapsodised about Barber's grace and style. He also spotted the true hallmark of a potentially great player – the speed at which Bob assessed the correct stroke to play, giving him the time to get his feet and hands in the right position to play it.

Desmond Hackett in the *Daily Express* gave him a warm welcome back with an article that managed to get his name wrong. Three times. He also related how, during an enforced break for rain in the match against Hampshire at Portsmouth, Bob persuaded John Ikin to coach him. Bob was conscious of his youth and immaturity in the game, polite and respectful to those senior to him but with a strong sense of cricket's proper place in the scheme of his life.

I have so much to learn about this game he told Hackett in the middle of August but cricket will have to take second place when I go up to Cambridge to read Medicine in October.

The match at the United Services Ground in Portsmouth also saw the debut of Roy Collins, a big-hitting all-rounder, who could bowl useful off spin and seam. On the first day twenty wickets fell, five ducks were recorded, one of which belonged to Bob Barber but Roy Collins kept on hitting. It was yet another auspicious debut by a talented young all-rounder. It is depressing to know, when looking back at the events of sixty years ago, that Lancashire were to mishandle so many talented young players. An example was in evidence in that match, as Bob recalls.

It was a turning wicket and I was out on the slog between deep mid-wicket and long on. Roy Collins was bowling and he wanted me in different positions for different batters and [Cyril Washbrook]on that occasion made a point by stopping the game and signalling me over as if I were in the wrong position, though I knew perfectly well I wasn't. The lads thought he was cross because there was some drunken sailor in the crowd giving Cyril stick and he wanted to take it out on someone.

The last match of the 1954 season took place at Hove and was won comfortably by Lancashire to provide a symmetrical end to a rain-ruined season in which the county won six matches, lost three but suffered from twelve draws and seven in which rain curtailed play so drastically that no result at all was possible. After the third place finish in 1953, a position of tenth was a disappointment but the general tenor of response from the excessively critical members was that the county was progressing in the right direction, with a strong batting line up of Washbrook, Place, Edrich, Grieves and Wharton and a bowling attack comprising Statham, Tattersall and Malcolm Hilton. Young players like Peter Marner, Geoff Pullar, Jack Dyson, Tommy Greenhough and Roy Collins had already broken through to the first team but above all, the mists of autumn for the cricket-deprived public of Lancashire were lifted by the prospect of Bob Barber, the brightest all-rounder to debut for the county in thirty years. For Bob Barber in the autumn of 1954, the cricket season of 1955 seemed far distant. What faced him now was a new phase of his life as a student of Medicine at Magdalene College, Cambridge.

CHAPTER THREE

IN 1954, MOST young men aged 18 were called up for National Service. A fellow Freshman in October 1954, David Bray, who was to remain a life long friend, observed that despite the fact that it was usually easy to distinguish between the mature twenty-one year olds who had done National Service and the callow eighteen-year old youths who had not, in Bob Barber's case, such a distinction was impossible to make.

> *Bob never seemed young to me when we met, even though I'd done two years in the RAF. He was a very sober, measured young man, not at all wild.*

To an extent, this must have developed from all those times when he was playing with people older than himself. In the 1st XI at school at the age of eleven, in the Boughton Hall 1st XI at pretty much the same age, playing with men he remembered only as having grey hair and in the Lancashire first team at 18, Bob had spent much of his life in a state of accelerated maturity.

Bob was excused National Service because he was going to university to read Medicine, but the reprieve looked like it might be short-lived. He had been concerned for a while about the state of his father's health, although as was the case in those days, it was never discussed even inside the family. The prospect of three years as an undergraduate, followed by many more years in a teaching hospital earning next to no money, meant that Bob feared he would be living off his father for years to come. He worried that the strain would adversely affect Jack's already fragile health, although he admits that he never discussed the situation with his parents. They never knew of his decision to give up Medicine until the matter was settled. If they felt any disappointment, they never expressed it to Bob. He talked to his father about sport rather than matters of great emotional concern. That was the way it was in most families in 1954.

> *I wasn't committed to my studies. I didn't believe I was going to be a successful doctor because otherwise I would have hung on longer but my father wasn't well at the time and it did weigh heavily on me and that was why I went to see the Senior Tutor and told him I wanted to change from Medicine. It was about a month into my first term. He said, "Barber, we accept two Medics a year and you have got one of the two places. What do you want to do?" I said, "Would it*

be possible to do Economics, sir?" and he said, "If you want to do Economics you'd better go into the military" - in other words go and do your national service. He didn't regard Economics as a high enough calling to be worthy of exemption so I asked what I would have to study to stay out of it and he said "Natural Sciences" so I became a Natural Scientist. I did Chemistry, Geology and the history and philosophy of science.

Once that change had been ratified, he settled quickly and easily into Cambridge life.

I was very happy to be in Cambridge. It was a wonderful step up from being in a small school in a small town in north Wales. I noticed the gap between those who had done National Service and those who hadn't, but I was always used to being with people who were older than I was. A third of the undergrads at Magdalene were either Etonians or Wykhamists, so it was a very upmarket college. I got the feeling they looked down on the rest of us.

David Bray was quick to agree.

Some Etonians treated me like a brother, but not all of them did. Magdalene was full of Etonians and Wykhamists. Some of those people used to push burning newspapers underneath the door of the clever grammar school boy. Not all of them, but that's how some of them behaved. I never experienced anything like that and I was treated very nicely by most people. There was an edginess about the place and I was very aware of these things. There was one chap from the landed gentry who said we were lucky because we could marry whoever we wanted, but people like him had to marry the "right gal". It was like something out of P.G. Wodehouse.

Perhaps then it was no wonder that David Bray concentrated successfully on getting his boxing Blue and he and Bob spent much of their time at Fenner's, the university sports centre, which housed not only the well known cricket ground but also the limited facilities that existed for athletics which was Bob's other principal interest. Although he enjoyed rugby and badminton and football, he excelled as much as a javelin thrower than as a cricketer.

The culture of the time permitted talented sportsmen a great deal of latitude and "good chaps" in the right colleges, if they were lucky with their tutors, could enjoy a life of some ease. Bob's good friend Owain Howell was one such.

The Master of Emmanuel had been at college with Owain's father. He called him in and asked, "Howell, are you bright like your father?" and Owain said, "I'm afraid not, sir." "In that case, settle for a Third and enjoy yourself". That was how things were then.

The influx into the Oxbridge colleges of comparatively hard-working grammar school boys, aspiring to the promise held out by R.A. Butler's 1944 Education Act, was still a trickle in 1954. The financial pressure exerted on the colleges by the government, and consequently the demand for academic excellence from all undergraduates to justify their privileges, had not yet overwhelmed the two ancient universities.

For Bob Barber, the first term at Cambridge was spent training for the athletics match against Oxford University.

I loved athletics and I nearly went with athletics rather than cricket. In my first week at Cambridge I met a wonderful athlete called Gwilym Roberts. He was also reading Natural Sciences. Gwilym had come from Newport Grammar and he'd already played on the wing for Newport as a schoolboy and displaced the great Ken Jones, Welsh god. He didn't know the system and he didn't even know there were Rugby Freshers trials. After talking for a few days, we went down to Fenner's for the athletics. He said he was thinking of going in for the sprints after I said I wanted to throw the javelin. He said, "I did it in the Army but there's a fellow over there called Bill Weale who was the Army champion and he beat me every time so I don't want to go through all that again." I remember very well saying to him, "If that's your attitude he'll always beat you" and Gwilym was very cross with me and stamped off but ran against the champion and beat him for the first time in the 100 yards. For the next two years Gwilym was great but he didn't want to win prizes because the front room of his parents' house was already full of the trophies he'd won. The best you could win was usually a voucher for seven guineas. He didn't stick to it because his heart wasn't in it. We went to Brighton in 1956 for a meeting and Gwilym comfortably beat whoever was going to the Olympics that year in the 220 yards. I won the javelin and we were the only two who won. Once he'd finished at Cambridge, that was it for Gwilym. He disappeared off to Canada as a geologist.

Inevitably, Bob's circle of friends was composed of sportsmen. The people he knew before going up in October 1954 were Colin Smith, who was at Christ's, and Gamini Goonesena, who was at Queen's. Going to see them in their rooms meant that he met their friends and so his own circle of friends widened. It was as well that he mixed mostly with impecunious sportsmen because there was a clear financial as well as social divide in Magdalene.

> *There were a lot of people from very wealthy families and I couldn't associate with people like them. On a Friday or Saturday night, it was rare to be able to afford anything more than a half a pint of bitter. Anyone who could afford a pint was probably on a scholarship.*

In the mid-1950s, social life at university was limited. There wasn't the range of diversions on offer then that there are now. Bob's life quickly fell into the routine of lectures in the morning, sport in the afternoon and half a pint of bitter in the college bar after dinner in hall.

Despite his status as an elite sportsman, Bob did not find that such a position inevitably brought with it a great deal of respect at Magdalene which, within Cambridge, has never been seen as a particularly "sporty" college. "It was the sort of college where you only played cricket if you borrowed someone else's whites", remembered David Bray. Bob agreed with the observation but found the corollary even more demeaning.

> *If you were a sportsman, the received wisdom is that you must be a bit thick. One night I was a bit late for dinner at Magdalene because I'd been playing cricket at Fenner's. It must have been close to exam time because they were all talking about a Geology question when I arrived to join them. I listened for a while and then I said that the answer was such and such. One chap turned to me and said scornfully, "What do you know about it? You're only a cricketer". That was not an atypical view of the time. I had no wish to dedicate my life to playing sport and to get a reputation like that.*

Field events in athletics started in November and the Varsity match took place in April, just before the cricket season began.

> *You trained in the snow and ice. One year some American intercollegiate fellow turned up and he said, "I ain't no polar bear". It was very primitive. I threw the javelin once over the wall into Hughes Hall next door. I held the Fenner's ground record for throwing the javelin. I loved the training. There was a nice fellow called Alan Malcolm who was our coach in the gym. I loved athletics up until I realised there were too many people fiddling with drugs. First there were the iron curtain countries and then everyone was at it.*

1955 was a good time to be involved in Athletics at Cambridge. What he saw from the top athletes confirmed his belief that it was possible to bring a professional attitude to an amateur sport without sacrificing an amateur's status. The former Cambridge athlete, Chris Brasher, one of the founders of the London Marathon and initial pacemaker for Roger Bannister's historic sub-four minute mile, did a lot of his training at Fenner's before he won the 3,000 metres steeplechase at the Melbourne Olympics the following year.

*The running track there went round the cricket field. It was 500 yards, bigger than 440. Brasher ran 440 then walked to the start line and ran again. He really pushed himself. When we used weights we had to use them quickly. If you moved them slowly that meant they were too heavy for you and all you would do is to boost the size of your muscles. It was **Chariots of Fire** stuff in those days. I competed in an event at the White City in London. I stayed at a friend's house in London overnight. I had my javelin with me. I had a friend who was a pole vaulter and he carried his pole and I carried my javelin with us to the White City on the tube!*

Bob could throw the javelin further than almost every other athlete in Britain so his Freshman Blue was certain but, early in the Lent term, he damaged his elbow which kept him out of the Varsity athletics match in the Lent term and had consequences for his cricket. When the summer term started in the usual Arctic conditions of April in Cambridge, Bob was still hampered by the injury he had sustained throwing the javelin two months earlier. It didn't affect his batting and his bowling was not going to be called upon too often because Goonesena was the first choice leg spinner, having already bowled for Nottinghamshire for three seasons. However, he couldn't throw with his right hand but, with typical dedication, he taught himself to throw left handed although he could, if the ball came towards his right hand, pick up and threaten to throw with it.

Exams for Natural Scientists came early so that it was important that Bob started well in the few first class games he would be available to play for the university. In the Freshman's match, he was run out for 2 but in the second innings he scored a pulsating 89 before he was officially "retired out". A week later he was in the Cambridge team for the first daunting match against Surrey. The university was no match for the champions for the past three seasons and lost by an innings. In those days, county sides tended to play their best teams at Oxford and Cambridge. Fred Trueman always regarded it as a chance to start off with forty cheap first class wickets and Tony Lock's attitude was similar. Bob's first innings ended in the reverse of the traditional dismissal when he was caught Laker bowled Lock for

5 and in the second innings he jumped out to drive and was easily stumped off Laker for 3. He wasn't the only batsman who would take guard against an attack of Laker, Lock, Bedser and Loader and wonder how anyone ever scored a run.

As far as Surrey were concerned, you thought you'd had a good game if you got into double figures. The Surrey close fielding was so tight. They had Stewart and Lock and Locky didn't bowl half volleys so where were you going to hit the ball? Jim Swanton might have said, "Just put your foot down the wicket and hit him over the top", but that's when you get caught Laker bowled Lock. Don't forget that, because of where you could legitimately deliver a ball from, bowlers were roughing up the wicket where the ball would land for a left handed batsman on or just outside the off stump. Lock and Laker were both a problem for left-handers at that point. Jim made the ball dip just before it arrived and it made the ball difficult to judge. Maybe they bowled the occasional bad ball but I don't remember any. If Locky let it go, you might get an edge that got you a run somewhere but it was very difficult to see how to get a run in front of the wicket.

Further matches against Yorkshire, Essex and Sussex followed before exams claimed the attention of the science students and the Fenner's season closed at the end of May. However, the coveted Freshman Blue was to remain tantalisingly out of reach after an injury sustained against Middlesex. He was opening the innings and had made 21 against an attack including John Warr, Don Bennett and Fred Titmus when he tried a pull shot. His feet were not in the right position and he damaged his foot again causing him to retire hurt. He still wonders today what would have happened had he played on through the pain. By the end of June, he had recovered and was fit for selection for the match against Oxford which would have given him the highly prized Freshman Blue. The team was always announced in traditional fashion, the team sheet being simply displayed in the shop window of Ryder & Amies, the outfitters on King's Parade. That was why the acceptable form for seeing if you were selected was to sidle quietly past the shop in case anyone was looking and glance quickly, with some anxiety, to see if your name was down there. In June 1955, R.W. Barber (Ruthin School & Magdalene) was nowhere to be seen.

I'd done nothing much that summer for Cambridge. In three years, I played a total of thirteen games of cricket for Cambridge at Fenner's. Before the Varsity match, Cambridge went on tour but I wasn't picked. Dennis Silk chose Peter Croft instead and I know they had a dressing room discussion just before they played Oxford and people like Colin Smith and John Pretlove said, "For goodness sake, you've got to bring Bob Barber back for the Varsity match" [Croft scored 9 and 1 and did not bowl]. Of course I was disappointed but Peter was a nice man, though I thought I was probably the better cricketer. Don Smith, who also played in the match, wrote me a nice letter about it and told me that it was Dennis who didn't want me on that tour. That letter upset me. It would probably have been better if I hadn't known but you sometimes learn from disappointments in life.

Returning to his parents' house in Chester, Bob was naturally keen to resume his Lancashire career in the face of the temporary rejection by Cambridge University but this time he didn't walk straight back into the first eleven and he was sent off to distant parts to continue his education in the second XI. He succeeded well enough to earn a recall to the county side at the start of August but, almost inevitably, the first match was against Surrey and the champions were no more inclined to be charitable in midsummer in Manchester than they had been in the late spring in Cambridge. It was a significant improvement that he managed to keep his wicket intact in both innings but Lancashire succumbed rather tamely by seven wickets to a Surrey side intent on clinching a fourth successive title.

I was once asked about my most memorable innings and I think that second innings against Surrey was it. I think I said I finished 4 not out but it was actually 10 not out. I was 4 not out overnight before we lost comfortably.

Although he played in all Lancashire's remaining matches in 1955 he rarely got into double figures and his only innings of note was a half century against the Combined Services in which he was dismissed caught and bowled by Peter Marner, whose place he had arguably usurped. First class cricket was a hard school and though Bob was learning, it could not be said that the figures he produced indicated anything like the stellar career he had enjoyed as a schoolboy prodigy. He was now competing on equal terms against highly motivated professional cricketers who didn't care that he was still 19 and learning the game. Few counties showed an interest in nurturing the talent of their youngsters with an arm round the shoulder and a cup of tea and sympathy. Life was hard, cricket was hard and if you couldn't stand the heat, you were well advised to stay out of the pavilion.

Bob remained positive in the difficult summer of 1955 because he always saw cricket as an enjoyable diversion. At Lancashire, over the next few years, the enjoyment factor was sometimes hard to find but he knew that his life would include more than cricket and it must have given him a way of dealing with a run of low scores. At close of play, it was just a game, a game that he thought he would continue to play until, probably when he was 28 years-old or so, which he would be at the end of the 1963 season.

What appealed to Bob from an early age was a life in business. It wasn't an ambition that was shared by many on the county circuit and it certainly marked him out as an amateur in the strictest sense of the word. He speaks today very kindly of the men in that dressing room whom he admired in many ways but looking in from the outside one can't help seeing a striking resemblance between Bob Barber's early days with those hard-bitten professionals and Michael Atherton's time when he too spent his summers with Lancashire after a hard term keeping Cambridge cricket going. The notorious FEC scrawled across Atherton's locker might have happened to Bob but in both cases natural talent, allied to sheer bloody mindedness, eventually won out as they each emerged to open the batting for England with considerable distinction.

The Cambridge terms are short (56 nights according to the Statutes) but extremely intense and, by the start of the cricket season in 1956, Bob Barber was a far more mature and confident cricketer than he had been a year earlier. It probably helped that this year he safely secured his Athletics Blue and remained free from injury. Dennis Silk had graduated and Michael Melluish, the wicket keeper, had assumed the captaincy. Ted Dexter had arrived and Bob was promoted to open the innings with Robin O'Brien who was to die three years later at the tragically young age of 26. As usual, the university began the season with three difficult games – Surrey, Yorkshire and Lancashire. The Surrey match ended in traditional fashion with a defeat by an innings but in the second innings of the Yorkshire game and facing an attack comprising Trueman, Appleyard, Wardle and Close, Cambridge battled their way to a draw with Bob Barber resisting unbeaten with 68 hard earned runs.

In the first innings he strode out to the middle deliberately wearing his red rosebud cap, the one given to Lancashire players who had not yet been "capped" when they would be presented with the full red rose article. It was a provocation of course to Trueman and the other jingoistic Yorkies. Barber had made only seven when he played forward to a full length ball from Trueman, heard a noise and, as the ball zipped into the gloves of Jimmy Binks, the entire Yorkshire side with one notable exception from square leg to mid off went up in unison. It was the only time Bob thought about whether to go of his own volition or not. He wasn't sure if the ball had hit the bat or the bat had hit the ground at the same moment. Helpfully, Johnny Wardle, who always wanted desperately to finish the season with more wickets than Trueman, called out from short leg, "Don't walk for that booger!" The umpire, however, raised his finger and Bob marched off without a backwards glance.

The third match of the season was against Lancashire and, as usual, the county played its strongest team. Having fought off Statham's opening burst, Bob had made 20 when he was run out by a smart return from the England fast bowler. O'Brien made 107 out of a Cambridge total of 217 and when they began their second innings they were seventy five runs in arrears. Cambridge lost wickets at regular intervals against the formidable attack of Statham, Tattersall, Hilton, Marner and Collins. Bob however, in a repeat of his dogged defensive display against Yorkshire, batted for over three hours for 58 until he was caught by Collins off Tattersall but he had again done enough for the university to claim an honourable draw. In his report for the *Manchester Evening News,* John Kay called him "a future England captain". It seemed as inevitable then as it does to us looking back at those times.

By the end of the month, and despite the pressures of Part I exams, Bob's form had continued to blossom. Against Middlesex, he fell just nine runs short of his maiden first class hundred. This time there was to be no question about his selection for the Varsity match and the *Chester Observer* hailed the triumph of the local prodigy in somewhat strangulated prose.

Congratulations to Mr "Bob" Barber, son of Mr and Mrs J.H. Barber of Carrick-Road Curzon Park who has been invited to play for Cambridge, where he is reading for an honours degree in Natural Sciences, against Oxford University on 7 July. "Bob" Barber is popular with local cricket enthusiasts, who for some seasons have taken an interest in his progress since he first played for Chester (Boughton Hall) 1st XI at the age of 14.

Cambridge warmed up with an encouraging nine wicket win at Lord's over a decent MCC side, including Ken Barrington and Robin Marlar but the Varsity match itself was a disappointment. O'Brien and MJK Smith traded centuries and the match was drawn. Bob made a trademark 35, looking more likely than O'Brien to go on and dominate the day's play until he played a loose shot at a full toss and was caught and bowled. It was to be symptomatic of the manner in which he played his cricket. As far as Bob Barber was concerned, if he made a bright and breezy 35 and the bowler felt enormously relieved when he got out, he had done his job as an opener. The man coming in first wicket down would be facing bowlers who had been given a torrid time by the departed opener. The side was off to a good start and whether Bob had scored 50 or 100 seemed to him of little importance. The team was better off than if he had stayed in all day and compiled 102 very boring runs. It was a philosophy that was to remain with him for the rest of his life.

He returned to Lancashire, after saying goodbye to his Cambridge team mates, but inevitably there was some resentment amongst the professionals. Jack Bond remembers

I would fight my way into the team in the early part of the season but when Bob came back from Cambridge and someone had to make way for him, more often that not, it would be me. I wasn't a capped player until 1961 when I'd played over 70 matches. I was a bed and breakfast sort of player, a solid pro but I didn't have Bob's ability or Peter Marner's. They were naturals. I didn't resent Bob because I was on a learning curve and I thought myself lucky to be playing as much first class cricket as I did when you looked at the people who were vying for places in the batting order – people like Geoff Pullar also started in 1954. D.M. Green was another Oxbridge lad but he and Bob were like chalk and cheese because David liked the booze. He batted the ball about like he didn't have a care in the world. He'd turn up for an away trip with the second XI with just a toothbrush in a brown paper bag. He was another one down from university who could take the place of a pro – like Eddie Craig and Duncan Worsley. That all bred professional jealousy. There were only so many places and you lost your match fee. I was on £10 a week which was a lot of money to me because I'd only been earning £6 a week at the electricity board. Then you would get £1 for a minor county game but you could play two of those in a week and get £2. But if you played in the first team some times you'd walk away with £30 in your wage packet.

It's easy to see why struggling professionals would resent losing that sort of money but the relationship between Jack and Bob grew out of mutual respect and liking. Fifty years later, when Bob held his famous seventieth birthday celebrations, Jack Bond was one of only two former Lancashire professionals who travelled to Broadhalfpenny Down.

In 1956, Bob came straight back into the first team at Old Trafford but he failed to adjust immediately to the demands of 1st XI county cricket and, after two undistinguished innings, he was dropped. Again Bob was asked by Lancashire to resume his county career by making runs in the second XI. The first time he had been asked in 1955, he had thought it a reasonable request but returning north having played a three day first class fixture at Lord's at a time when the Varsity match was still regarded as a major fixture in the summer calendar, he felt much more resentful. After rain ruined the first match against Cumberland in Barrow-in-Furness, he approached Geoff Edrich for advice. Edrich was particularly sympathetic to the problems of the young cricketers and the following year he was sent off to captain the Second XI which he did outstandingly well for three seasons until the committee abruptly cancelled his contract. Bob continued to play for the seconds until the end of the 1956 season but that, to his relief, was the end of his association with cricketing outposts in Wallingford and St. Helens.

The 1956 cricket season concluded with two much more enjoyable events. In a competition in Liverpool Bob retuned to play for Chester with familiar results – an innings of 114 followed by six wickets for 47. Additionally, he was selected to play for a Commonwealth XI against an Indian XI at the Colwyn Bay Festival in a side that included Frank Worrell, Everton Weekes, Sonny Ramadhin and Hugh Tayfield and he then made 50 for the Colwyn Bay Presidents XI against Sir Leonard Hutton's XI, after dismissing the recently knighted but now retired Yorkshire maestro for 32. Hutton returned the favour by catching him off the bowling of Brian Bolus. First class cricket might be tough but he was only twenty years of age and his raw talent had not deserted him; it just needed to be honed to the standard required to succeed in the professional game.

In his final year at Cambridge, Bob was a returning double Blue and his performances reflected the ease with which he moved from athletics to cricket. In March 1957, he broke the undergraduate record for the javelin with a throw four feet longer than the previous mark and although Cambridge lost to Oxford, as they did throughout his undergraduate career, Bob won his individual event comfortably. The previous November, the British Olympic team had warmed up for the Melbourne Olympics with a match against the best athletes of Oxford and Cambridge. Bob won the javelin with a throw of 176'1", over twenty feet further than his Cambridge team mate, John Kitching, with the British Olympian Tucker, trailing both the students, managing only 149 feet. The fourth thrower was Peter Cullen, who had recently beaten the Commonwealth javelin record; he was expected to be a strong candidate for gold in Melbourne. Beating the talented Cullen into fourth place understandably gave Bob a terrific sense of accomplishment although, comfortingly for the rest of the country, the British team still beat the students 119 points to 59.

With the memory of his triumph over Peter Cullen fresh in his memory, Bob toyed seriously with the idea of giving up cricket in favour of athletics but his father discouraged him.

My father encouraged me all my life. He was a great supporter of me playing cricket. When I said I might be giving up cricket to concentrate on athletics, it was the one time I saw my father break down in front of me and say "You mustn't do it". I think he thought I would come to regret it. He was an athlete himself. He ran against the great Eric Liddell when the Scotsman came to Manchester.

Exams were still a problem for Bob as he moved into his final term at Cambridge. He managed a few games before the demands of Finals overwhelmed him early in May but the first two games were as usual against strong Surrey and Yorkshire sides and were comfortably lost, Bob being caught at short leg off Alec Bedser in both innings. Fred Trueman collected seven cheap wickets in the first innings of the Yorkshire match and although two Cambridge men scored a century apiece in the match against Essex, neither of them was scored by Bob Barber. Against Lancashire in the last week of May, Cambridge fielded a considerably weakened eleven but survived, principally due to an outstanding innings of 185 by Ted Dexter.

Bob graduated from Cambridge with what was known at the time as a "Gentleman's Third", which he found satisfactory. He had lost some enthusiasm for the work after he had been compelled to take up Natural Sciences and his sporting activities excluded him from some work which a good degree would have demanded.

I didn't take lab work seriously because it took place in the afternoons when I was training at Fenner's, so I had to get high marks in Organic Chemistry to compensate for inevitable failures elsewhere.

Lab work was still a problem as he approached the end of his academic career at Cambridge and, in the circumstances, a Third was probably the best result he could have expected.

When it came to my Finals, I couldn't find the Cavendish Lab to go to. I turned up half way through the practical. I was given things to identify and all I could do was to take them around and sniff them. I couldn't go up to Aran at Easter to do field work because I was throwing the javelin at White City. I found mineralogy interesting and I did a half subject on the history and philosophy of science. I might have got a II(ii) but it was a degree and all I wanted to do was to pass and then do other things. Not knowingly, I got the ability to think at Cambridge.

Unlike the first two captains of England he played under, who had both attended university and left without acquiring the degree that was widely believed to be the logical end product of a higher education, Bob graduated with a highly respectable result, the limits of which had been set by his dedication to his sports. Sixty years ago, even thirty years ago, there were very few Firsts, a decent sprinkling of II (i)s but the largest class was always II (ii) with about three or four times the number of Thirds that are awarded today. Grade inflation has wrought havoc in subsequent years, and Firsts appear to be handed out now with the liberality of England football caps. In Bob Barber's day, the purpose of a university was a degree, the class of which did not greatly concern either future employers or the graduates themselves. Firsts and high Upper Seconds were the province solely of potential academics.

Freed from the anxiety of exams, Bob found form on the tour of counties that preceded the Varsity match in the first week of July. The highlight without question was Cambridge's victory by an innings against a shocked Lancashire at Aigburth. Nobody could have imagined after three quick wickets fell and Cambridge were left on 209-8, that the ninth wicket would put on 200 against a second string but decent attack of Colin Hilton, Alan Wharton, Brian Booth and Jack Dyson with Colin Smith hitting a spectacular 89. Eventually bowled out for over 400, Cambridge could afford to maintain attacking fields and Lancashire only reached 222 thanks to two dogged innings from Jack Bond and Geoff Pullar.

On a wicket increasingly receptive to spin, Bob Barber took four gleeful wickets for 41 runs against his county side, returning his best first class analysis to date. Lancashire were forced to follow on, but could only manage 166 second time round and they lost in the extra half hour of the second day. It was a humiliation and it did Geoff Edrich's chances of succeeding Cyril Washbrook as captain no good at all though, as we shall see, this match was not the reason he never assumed the captaincy. Bob had made a stodgy 19 at the start of the Cambridge innings, in partnership with the Australian Ian McLachlan who had pummelled a more adventurous 89, but whether it was Bob's batting or his destructive wrist spin or the humiliation Cambridge had inflicted on Lancashire, Jack Bond clearly remembered hearing Cyril Washbrook say, "There is no way, as long as I have anything to do with it, that Bob Barber will ever captain Lancashire."

In a way, this match can be seen in retrospect as an unfortunate precursor to the troubles that were to overwhelm the county in the early 1960s. The team that took the field that day seemed to have enough experience in Wharton, Edrich and Grieves to guide the youngsters who made up the rest of the team to victory. Geoff Edrich was greatly liked by his fellow professionals and the youngsters who were making their way through the second XI. In Bond, Pullar, Brian Booth and Alan Bolton, they had four talented young players of whom much was expected. The batting however collapsed, the bowling wilted and the result was a significant under-achievement. There were some good days to come before the rot set in during the early part of the next decade, but this match seems to be a harbinger of things to come.

The build up to his last Varsity match continued with a trip to play Hampshire in Portsmouth and here Bob passed the milestone which he had always scorned (and still does) but which he recognises is important for everyone else, even though he feels strongly that this is not the way you judge a cricketer. Nevertheless, in a high scoring match and against a Hampshire attack shorn of Derek Shackleton, Bob Barber passed his previous highest first class score of 91 made the previous season against Middlesex and added a further fifteen runs, at which point he was deemed to have become a better player. Had the total for which batsmen are usually praised been 107 it might be possible to have deemed the innings a failure but at 106 he was accounted more of a success than he had been when he had gone out to open the innings with an hour of the first day left to play. At the end of the Cambridge season though, even with the addition of this 106 against Hampshire, Bob Barber's average was a distinctly average 25.31.

Still, all the Cambridge boys would be judged not by their averages but by the result of the Varsity match. The Cambridge team in 1957, its batting led by Barber and Dexter, its bowling particularly strong with Colin Smith and Ossie Wheatley opening and Goonesena, Barber and Dexter to add their contributions, were hot favourites to win the Varsity match. Rather like the F.A. Cup Finals in the days when the competition mattered, Varsity matches frequently disappointed, the nervous tension of the occasion dominating the best intentions of the undergraduates.

The first day's play followed the usual pattern. Oxford lacking any star names (only A.C. Walton went on to enjoy a significant county career) batted below expectations. After an hour they were 16-4 and at lunch 44-8. Ossie Wheatley took 5-15 as Oxford, after a brief recovery, were bowled out for 92 in mid-afternoon. Bob Barber and the Australian Ian MacLachlan, opening for Cambridge, perhaps buoyed by the match situation, batted without nerves but both they and Ted Dexter were out with the score only on 67. By the close of play Cambridge had struggled into a lead of sixteen runs but had already lost five wickets. If Oxford began strongly on Monday morning, and with Cambridge having to bat last on a wearing pitch, it was possible that the Varsity match might yet produce a close and exciting finish.

In the event, they removed Colin Smith promptly but never took another wicket. Gamini Goonesena, the leg spinner who was a much under-rated batsman, made 211, Geoff Cook, the off spinner, made 111 and Goonesena declared before the close of the second day with a first innings lead of nearly 300. If the weather held on the third day, the result was a foregone conclusion. The weather held and Cambridge romped home to win by an innings and 186 runs. It was a joyful end to a Cambridge career that had, to be honest, stuttered at times.

Bob seemed to come into his own in the summer of 1957. Before his first match, which was scheduled to be the county championship game against Essex at Old Trafford at the end of July, a small article in the *Sunday Pictorial* speculated on what might happen when Cyril Washbrook eventually retired. It was written in a way that a reader might suspect that the journalist had been briefed by someone in the know, although of course, no source was quoted.

I would not be surprised to learn that Lancashire skipper and England stalwart Cyril Washbrook will decide to retire at the end of 1959 [he did]. In that season, Cyril receives a further testimonial to supplement the fabulous £14,000 benefit in 1948.

I'm also prepared to forecast that, if he seizes his chance, young Bob Barber may well succeed Cyril as Lancashire's captain.

Barber, who has now finished his Cambridge studies…has two years to learn the intricacies of county captaincy under Washbrook.

It's up to you, Bob.

It was the sort of tabloid gossip that would not necessarily have been well received by the likes of Alan Wharton, Geoff Edrich or Ken Grieves but it was hardly Bob's fault. The determination of the Lancashire committee to return to an amateur captaincy after the somewhat forced experiment of the professional Washbrook was clear for some time before controversy descended on Bob.

It was unfortunate that his finger was broken in the nets by a ball from Jack Dyson that lifted spitefully from a length just before the start of play in the match against Essex which would have been his first match for Lancashire in 1957. A paragraph in the *Manchester Evening News* sympathised with his predicament and called him a "popular amateur player" as if the term were an oxymoron. He did not return to fitness until the last week of August, which left him only four championship matches and the final match against the West Indies tourists to make his mark.

He now began a fruitful opening partnership with Alan Wharton, with Geoff Pullar taking Geoff Edrich's place at number three. Just looking at the scorecards, it is possible to tell that Barber now felt at home on the county circuit. He never failed twice in a match and he was clearly revelling in opening the innings. Against Worcestershire at Blackpool, he made a delightful fifty in a rapid opening partnership of 102 with Wharton. There was now no suggestion of Barber being the junior partner who had to be protected. The *Birmingham Evening Post & Gazette* sent its cricket writer to Blackpool and he reported back on

a glorious 105 minutes batting from the Cambridge Blue R.W. Barber. It has been suggested, that Barber having given up the idea of going into medicine is being groomed for the Lancashire captaincy as a future successor to Washbrook.… If there is any permanence in Barber's present form, he will be a worthy successor.

It was sheer delight to watch his footwork on Saturday, apart altogether from the precise timing which contributed so much to his ten 4s. That was perhaps why his 50 made a greater appeal than the more technically correct 70 of Wharton.

In the last match of the season against the touring West Indies, the *Manchester Guardian* also gave its approval to the now firmly established opening partnership of Wharton and Barber, as they made similarly successful progress.

Neither batsman had taken the hint of a risk. Better still, Barber had looked an extremely cool and composed player. His judgment and his footwork were good, so that he left himself time and room for every gracious and fluent shot he made.

On the last day Lancashire's second innings was curtailed by rain but

For Lancastrians…there was an hour in which to relish all the rich promise of young Barber.

Although he was restricted to a mere seven innings for his county, he finished the 1957 season top of the Lancashire averages for a change – which would only have increased his dismissive attitude towards them. Still it must have been nice to see his name on the top with an average of 49.50, ahead of his new partner Alan Wharton, who had made over 1400 runs, but at the realistic average on uncovered wickets of 34.65. Nobody else even got into the thirties. After finishing second to Surrey in 1956, a mere twenty points behind the champions, Lancashire slipped to sixth position in 1957, a discouraging 160 points behind the re-crowned champions. During the 1950s, Lancashire were a decent if underachieving team that failed to mount a significant challenge for the county championship but the seven-times champions Surrey had, during that decade under Stuart Surridge and Peter May, arguably the best county team in the history of the championship. And, in Bert Lock, some might have unkindly added, the most co-operative groundsman.

It was not a situation to which certain Lancashire supporters took kindly. The big crowds which had watched the revival of post war cricket ten years before were long gone and what remained appeared to be intensely critical of the slightest of failings exhibited by their players. These spectators were disinclined to leaf through *Wisden* whilst munching on their sandwiches and chatting amicably with their neighbours. Instead they greeted batsmen returning to the pavilion after dismissal with shouted comments of a distinctly hostile and aggressive nature. The players did not welcome such vocal criticism but the situation continued to deteriorate and indeed formed a topic for discussion at the 1957 Annual General Meeting.

Although it abated a little during the following seasons, as soon as Lancashire's performances started to slip it started up again, as unwelcome as ever and did nothing to foster dressing room harmony.

At the end of the 1957 season, Bob had a decision to make as to how he was going to earn his living. He had an active brain and a good degree from a well known university. Was he going to be able to reconcile his need to make money and his desire to build a business career with his love of cricket and a future of summers unclouded by the prospect of examinations? He was twenty-one years old and the world was his oyster.

One option, of course, was to become a full time professional cricketer but it was given scant consideration. This was still the 1950s, a decade of amateurism and social conformity. When Lancashire played at Lord's or The Oval the team was invited by a group of Lancashire MPs to dine at the House of Commons. Formal dress was compulsory. Lancashire had an abundance of competent wicket keepers in the mid-1950s – Alan "Ranji" Wilson, Jack Jordan, Bill Heys and Frank Parr.

Parr gained a permanent place in the Lancashire side towards the end of the 1952 season and played almost every match in 1953. He was a free spirit, a jazz enthusiast and no lover of the social stratifications and class distinctions that marked British society in the fifteen years after the end of the Second World War. When Lancashire played Middlesex at Lord's in August 1953, he decided to go to the dinner at the Mother of Parliaments in a black shirt and, in a possible later embroidering of the story, a pair of jeans. It is important to remember, when we learn of the consequences that followed his failure to conform to the accepted dress code, that this took place in an era of political paranoia when there was a deep-seated fear of what Communists or Communist sympathisers stood for. It wasn't a clearly thought out ideology so much as a deep rooted suspicion of others.

It was also a time when British cities were first experiencing waves of black immigration. Blacks, it was popularly believed, brought foreign smells into the country and they lowered house prices when they moved into white areas. Jazz was the music most closely associated with these people. White men who played jazz therefore, almost by definition, held an unhealthily high regard for black people. Although Parr had no interest in politics, certainly compared with the avowedly Socialist Alan Wharton, his love of jazz was enough to indicate that he was socially unfit to play cricket for Lancashire during the years of Cyril Washbrook's captaincy. As soon as Washbrook took over from Nigel Howard, Parr was dropped. He regained his place for a few matches in July 1954 but, after half a dozen desultory matches in the Minor Counties Championship of 1955, he left Lancashire at the end of Washbrook's second season in charge and disappeared from first-class cricket.

The fate of Frank Parr was a salutary reminder of the social order which determined the lives of professional cricketers in the 1950s. As a young amateur, Bob Barber always had an escape route into the world of industry and business which he found so interesting. It wasn't just Frank Parr's fate that made him conscious that, choosing to be paid for playing the game he loved and the game at which he was so proficient, was going to typecast him in an unwelcome manner.

You have to think about amateur status as it was at the time. Tell me anybody who had been to Oxford or Cambridge and turned pro besides Paul Gibb and he was regarded as a failure because he had to do that. He lost his membership of the MCC, left Yorkshire and spent some years out of the game before returning to play for Essex. Then he became an umpire and lived in a caravan that he towed round the country.

Bob just wanted cricket to provide him with some pleasure and some happy memories so that cricket was a part of his broader education. He wasn't an amateur in the sense that the Honourable Lionel Tennyson and Lord Hawke were amateurs. He had no private income or landed estate to provide for him but everyone automatically assumed that in the socially divisive world of English cricket in the 1950s, R.W. Barber of Ruthin School and Magdalene College Cambridge was obviously an amateur. It certainly did not by itself ingratiate him with the powers at Lord's.

I suppose I'd have been happy to have fifty quid stuck in my boots but it never happened. I suppose if Bill Edrich wanted to be captain of Middlesex or Wally Hammond wanted to be captain of England and the only way they could do it was to stick on a hat marked "amateur" then they would do it and just get on with it. When I was asked to go on tour or represent the Gents in the Gents versus Players match, I would get a letter from Ronnie Aird at Lord's that started "Dear Barber, Are you available…"etc until I finally wrote back and said "Dear Aird, yes I am available…."

There were by now constant rumblings about the status of amateur cricketers in the game. Many amateurs at the top of the game felt that overseas tours were becoming too expensive for them. MCC tried desperately to keep them in the game by stretching the rules governing amateur status to breaking point. A sub-committee set up at Lord's in 1957 decided that amateurs were important for the good health of the game and that everything should be done to ensure they continued as an integral part of the English game.

So well were amateurs compensated that, before the tour of Australia in 1958, Jim Laker, who had of course won the Ashes in 1956 almost single handed taking a record 46 wickets in five Tests, went to see Gubby Allen with an unusual but quite logical request. Could he possibly, he wondered, be considered as an amateur on the winter tour Down Under and then revert to his professional status at the start of the 1959 English domestic season? Allen was at first puzzled by the request and then, when he understood the logic of it, he was outraged. Jim Laker's opinion of Southern amateurs and MCC bureaucrats was on a par with the feelings held for them by F.S. Trueman. The level of suspicion was mutual. Gubby Allen's feelings about uppity professionals in 1958 would have been shared by Lord Harris in the nineteenth century.

The problems caused by the selection of amateurs happened when amateur captains or committees chose amateurs for social reasons. Bob Barber never had that problem because his talent was spectacularly visible from a very early age.

I think we're all talented in some way and we have a responsibility to develop and use that talent. That's why I played cricket. It was never an option as a career. I had a talent to score runs and get people out and that's why I played. If you are picked for a team just because you are an amateur that is clearly wrong and it should never happen. In the 1950s and 1960s, cricket was more county-centric and Lancashire supporters would have expected to have had the best team of available Lancastrians on the field. Professionals knew they would be playing with amateurs but that does not justify being picked because you were a good chap and you went to the right school and you were free in the holidays.

Laker and Lock, forever enshrined together in cricketing mythology, were in reality as different as chalk from cheese. Laker, on the surface a plain outspoken Yorkshireman was underneath a quiet but extremely sensitive man, quick to take offence. He considered the relative positions of amateurs and professionals in cricket to be a social anachronism, a division of favours deeply unfair to the latter. He let it all hang out in his notorious ghost-written autobiography *Over To Me* in which he tells of endless slights, in particular those committed by Peter May, who demanded that he bowl when his spinning finger was raw, like the ruthless Douglas Jardine making Larwood bowl almost on one leg to Bradman in the last Test in Australia in 1933 with the Ashes already won. May, "wrote" Laker, reported him to the Surrey committee for "not trying", a charge that incensed the bowler. Bob was well aware of Laker's feelings.

I know Jim Laker had a problem but Jim had a bee in his bonnet about amateurs. Surrey you see had a big dressing room for the amateurs which Lancashire didn't have. We had a captain's room but Surrey had this big room left over from pre-war days, effectively just for Peter and Stuart Surridge. I never gave a damn whether someone was an amateur or a professional. I am surprised that Peter went to the committee with that story. I can't see him doing it unless he was very, very hurt. I can see a committee man asking May why he didn't bowl Jim and Peter telling him what happened. There was a thought on the circuit that these things happened to Jim when he wasn't bowling sides out.

There were plenty of "amateurs" whom the counties were desperate to retain on their staff, some of whom became the Secretary of their clubs. Trevor Bailey and Wilf Wooller were certainly paid accordingly but Bob had set his sights higher than cricket administration. As soon as he left Cambridge, he set about climbing a parallel ladder in the world of industry and business.

CHAPTER FOUR

LIKE MANY YOUNG graduates, Bob Barber left university and returned to live with his parents without any very clear idea of what he was going to do, other than play cricket in the summer for a few years and hope to find a job that would start a career in business. For that he knew he needed a qualification for business life, which a degree in Natural Sciences did not provide. His parents were, as usual, supportive but made no attempt to interfere.

My mother never talked to me about my future. My father expected that with a Cambridge degree, I would get a decent job in industry or commerce. I had thought about switching to Economics when I left Medicine, so now the choice was between Chartered Accountant and Chartered Secretary. I went for the latter because I thought I could do it by correspondence, whilst I was playing cricket. I wasn't clear in my mind what job I would go for after I'd got that qualification. I think, for most people, things come across the horizon and you take them.

Lancashire certainly wanted Bob to play for the whole of the 1958 season but the club was aware of his off-field ambitions and introduced him to Tom Atherton, who ran a company in Salford called Dorman Smith which manufactured switchgear. It was only a small public company but the Atherton family had a major shareholding. In turn, Tom Atherton introduced Bob to his son Geoffrey who was also a director of the company, had studied at Cambridge, had been out to work in the United States as an electrical engineer and had returned to Salford. On Geoffrey's advice, the firm brought one of the first circuit breakers into the UK.

They asked me if I would like to become their first management trainee at £625 pa. I said yes as they were happy enough for me at that stage to go off and play cricket. I worked for them for four years, gaining experience in every department. I started off with the time & motion chaps which was fascinating. There would be women on drills in a lot of noise and dirt and they could perform their really quite precise jobs and never stop talking to their neighbours about their husbands or boyfriends for a minute. They took pity on me I expect because, in theory, I was the management enemy. Later, we had someone in from Associated Industrial Consultants, who at the time were one of the top three consulting firms. I became the leg man for Keith Glasby. He'd tell me to give him a report on how they were putting silver plate on components. Now you didn't want to be wasting this material because it was expensive. It was fascinating seeing how to improve the technology. It gave me very valuable experience. But I also worked in sales and, combined with my chartered secretary qualification, it gave me a legal as well as business background.

Bob's public school and Cambridge background had already marked him out as different from the other players in the Lancashire dressing room who left Old Trafford in September each year for a variety of different jobs, many of them not terribly inspiring. Tommy Greenhough was working for a wholesale newsagent when he had a disastrous fall which shortened his career. Ken Grieves worked for a brewery when he gave up football, Malcolm Hilton was a painter and decorator during the off season and Alan Wharton returned to teaching each winter. Bob, meanwhile, was a management trainee at Dorman Smith – different from the old-style amateurs as well as the professionals. It would be hard to see Gubby Allen or Plum Warner working for a switchgear manufacturer in Salford. As an amateur cricketer, he was a man of the rapidly disappearing past; as a management trainee at Dorman Smith he was in the vanguard of the future of technological progress.

There was one particular compensation for Bob in 1958. It was provided by Ted Greenhalgh, the Lancashire Second XI wicket keeper, whom he had known since 1952 when they had both played at Lord's for The Rest against Southern Schools. Ted was then seventeen and Bob sixteen and he had no idea that Ted had a very attractive sister.

Ted was a very good keeper. I remember him standing up to the quick bowlers at the start of an innings and he stumped the opener of the Southern Schools in the trial match, after which they would select the Public Schools side that would play Combined Services. He kept for Lancs Second XI and would certainly have played for the first team but his father was a serious minded man and thought his son shouldn't be wasting his time playing games. He was a good all-round sportsman though and played hockey for Warrington. When Dorman Smith moved their factory to Preston, I had digs both in Preston and in Blackpool where three of us persuaded the landlord to give us rooms over The Talbot pub. To go from Blackpool back to Chester at weekends, I used to have to change trains at Warrington. Ted lived in Warrington and we started playing the odd game of squash together on a Friday night and then go back to his place to watch Tony Hancock and have something to eat. I didn't even know he had a sister for some time, but once he invited me to a party. I was having great fun trying to open the tap on a keg of beer and the first time I saw Anne, I was lying on the floor underneath this thing.

Anne Greenhalgh, herself an excellent tennis player, and Bob Barber soon became an item. Bob was building a life for himself in business that was designed partly to ensure he could continue to play the game of cricket which he loved purely for the sake of enjoyment. The life of a professional cricketer was very different.

Most of them like Jack Bond, in and out of the side for most of his career until he was made captain in 1968, desperately needed their contracts to be renewed at the end of each season, otherwise life would be insupportable. Just after he returned to Lancashire, having completed his first summer of cricket at Cambridge, Bob was in the dressing room when Malcolm Hilton brought in the *Manchester Evening News* which announced that Winston Place had been sacked.

There was such an upset atmosphere round the place. Winston was a fine player and a lovely, popular man. The way things like that were handled was just awful.

Had he but known it, the incident was to prove a portent of what was to lie ahead for him. It made him think hard about cricket as a profession as against cricket as a game to be enjoyed. Of course, it was easy for him in the sense that he was prodigiously talented so that, in the unlikely case that Lancashire no longer required his services, he would be reasonably sure another county would. Also, he never wanted cricket to become his sole source of an income. In his final year at Magdalene, Bob might not have been certain of exactly what he would do after graduation, but he was absolutely sure that he would not be playing cricket after the age of 28 or 29. He didn't fear the sealed envelope that came round every August informing professionals if they were to be re-engaged for the following season. This annual ritual of fear must have impacted on the performances of the professionals who knew that, in the end, their livelihood corresponded precisely to the number of runs they made and the number of wickets they took. It was why Johnny Wardle gave Ken Taylor canny advice when the youngster tried to run out the opposition's number nine batsman. "You don't run out numbers 9, 10, Jack" he was bluntly informed. They were "free" wickets for needy professional bowlers.

The effect was that professionals did whatever was necessary for their own survival. As far as they were concerned, the prosperity of the team was important only to the extent that it prospered because of their own performances. Bob was too young when he first appeared for Lancashire to notice whether or not the professionals were playing for their averages. It was only when he became captain that such selfishness became apparent.

First, however, there were the summers of 1958 and 1959 to get through. 1958 was as cold, wet and miserable as 1959 turned out fortunately to be hot and welcome. Cold and wet are not conditions in which batsmen and wrist spinners thrive on seamer-friendly pitches. For a left handed batsman, such conditions pose special problems because the follow-through of bowlers, bad enough when pitches are hard, were particularly difficult when footmarks were embedded deep in the turf on the line of the left hander's off stump.

Ironically, the first match of the 1958 season took Bob back to Fenner's, where once again he was playing for Lancashire against a side containing many of his team mates from the previous season. It turned out to be Ted Dexter's match, even though Bob started it with a bright and breezy top score of 74 in Lancashire's first innings of 321, Ossie Wheatley claiming seven wickets. Dexter and the wicket keeper, Henry Blofeld, put on the only partnership of note in a disappointing university first innings but, following on, Cambridge batted out the last day for a draw with Dexter, coming in with the university side tottering on 68-5, adding a century to his first innings score of 92.

Clearly, the opening partnership of Barber and Wharton was becoming Lancashire's preferred combination at the top of the order. Bob liked batting with Wharton very much, though slightly resentful that the perception was growing that Barber was the dawdler and Wharton was the dasher. "There were plenty of times," he pointed out "when I outscored him". Neither made many runs in the Whitsuntide Roses match at Headingley, but the game was an acclaimed red rose triumph all the same.

On a helpful pitch, Brian Statham ripped out the vaunted Yorkshire batting, taking 6-16 in fourteen overs, before Yorkshire declared at 66 for 9 after only 27 overs, in a desperate attempt to get Lancashire into trouble before close of play. The tactic didn't work as Barber and Wharton, with difficulty, saw off the opening attack of Trueman and Pickles. At the start of play on Whit Monday, Johnny Wardle opened the bowling and removed both batsmen in a couple of overs. Only Cyril Washbrook and Ken Grieves reached double figures but it was enough to give Lancashire an invaluable first innings lead. Yorkshire fared slightly better in their second innings, but left Lancashire only 72 to win on the last afternoon, which they managed for the loss of two wickets, Barber remaining unbeaten as he and his captain knocked off the winning runs. It was a hugely satisfying victory, as all such Roses matches were, and Bob Barber was now an integral part of what was potentially an extremely good county side. Surrey still had one last championship left in them, but the Roses victory on foreign soil gave Lancashire supporters enormous hope for the future.

However, on their return to Old Trafford from the trans-Pennine expedition, it was Surrey that Lancashire found waiting for them in what had been earmarked as Alan Wharton's benefit match. This turned out to be an occasion that Bob recalled with clarity some fifty-five years later, because it contained a duel between Brian Statham and Peter May that showed both players at their magnificent best.

Peter May was post-war, up to the time I finished playing, the best English batsman – I count Denis Compton and Len Hutton as pre-war. I can't think of anyone to compare with him. He was a wonderful player. He retired pretty young and he was a very self-effacing fellow. Colin Cowdrey might be the first batsman to come to mind from those days but I would say that Peter was at least 25% the better player. Colin was a fine player of course, but he was inferior to Peter. In that match at Old Trafford, there was a battle that went on between Peter and Brian. Brian bowled beautifully to him. [Statham 6-78]. Peter got a big hundred; [174] Kenny Barrington had the advantage of batting with Peter and he got a score [74] but hardly anyone else got double figures. The battle went on for such a long time. They had huge respect for each other and it was a joy to be on the field and watch them.

May and Barrington were responsible for Surrey reaching 314 and, though Barber and Wharton put on 85 for the first wicket, Lancashire folded to the all-conquering Surrey attack, conceding a first innings lead of 120. Clearly the pitch must have started to deteriorate rapidly because Surrey declared at 83 for 4 (May 42*), leaving Lancashire 200 to win. They didn't quite manage to get there. In fact, it turned out to be one of the two Lancashire matches that season when the total number of overs bowled in an innings (32) exceeded the total number of runs scored in it (27). With a tail starting at number 7 when Malcolm Hilton went in, to be followed by Statham, Higgs, Wilson and Tattersall, it was obvious that the lower order was never going to contribute significantly, but when Hilton went in it was 16-5 and the result was a foregone conclusion.

Barber can, with justification, wax lyrical about the talent of Peter May. Oddly, May's reputation as a great batsman has not prospered, which perhaps owes something to his undistinguished tenure as Chairman of Selectors in the 1980s, but those who played with and against him and those who watched him at the height of his powers in the late 1950s will never forget the magnificence of May.

When he played at Lord's for the Gents v Players in 1961, Fred had been left out of the Test team and he and Jack Flavell were both steaming in and trying to show how fast they were. It was dark and they kept hitting the ridge. I'd gone out to open and I wasn't good enough to get an edge. Edward Craig and Ted Dexter had both gone early to Fred and Peter walks out. He'd hardly played any cricket that whole season up to that point [19th July]. He looks at the trees at the nursery end and at the pavilion where there's no sightscreen at all and he says, "This is a bit dark, isn't it?" The ball was whistling all over the place and I thought, "Thank God, he's going to appeal against the light." He stood there and I think he hit the first four balls for four. Two back foot and two front foot off Fred and I thought, "Strewth, I thought he was going appeal against the light!"

I remember we were playing Surrey and Tommy Greenhough was now a Test bowler and he was bowling to Peter and we had four players in a line on the off side. I was at extra cover and I was moving in as Tommy ran up, so I was cutting down the angle and Peter just pierced the field at will, hitting it precisely where the fielders couldn't get to it. He looked so beautifully upright at the crease. As a selector, he spoke to you politely, respectfully, as though you could play the game. He was a tremendous player. Think of the difference between Peter and Kipper. What happened when they died? There was a major memorial service for Colin with all the VIPs there. Peter, as I understood it, expressly said there will be no memorial service. That tells you something of Peter. I would never have described Peter as aloof. He was just a very nice man.

The novelist Simon Raven was a contemporary of May at Charterhouse, where his prodigious batting talents were so widely recognised that he became a figure of awe to schoolmasters and boys alike. Raven, who revelled in his promiscuous homosexuality, joyfully recalled in his autobiography that, when discovered *in flagrante delicto* with another boy in the cricket pavilion, he was dragged in front of the Headmaster whose admonishment concluded with the words, "Just think what might have happened if Peter May had seen you!"

May was a very professional and very successful amateur captain of Surrey and England in 1958. No doubt the Lancashire committee hoped that R.W. Barber of Ruthin School and Cambridge University would turn into a Lancastrian version of Peter May. Although there was controversy to come when Washbrook was eventually replaced as captain, in the summer of 1958, Lancashire decided to give Bob at the age of 22 a chance to show what he could do with the responsibility. He skippered the team in the match against the touring New Zealanders and again a few weeks later when Lancashire played Combined Services.

The first match saw only one completed innings, a frequent event in that soggy summer, but Lancashire won comfortably against a Services side containing Peter Parfitt, Tony Lewis, Graham Atkinson and Barry Knight. Certainly, Lancashire used the chance to test out not just Barber's captaincy credentials but the possibility of Peter Whiteley from Rochdale taking over from Malcolm Hilton as the orthodox slow left armer and Noel Cooke from Liverpool as an all-rounder in the Jack Dyson mould. Sadly, neither made the grade but although the bowling attack also contained Fred Moore and Colin Hilton, it was already clear that Ken Higgs,was going to be Brian Statham's long-sought for new ball partner for many years. Higgs had joined the Lancashire staff at the start of the season and had begun with 7-36 against Hampshire to help Lancashire to a welcome 7 wicket victory,

Geoff Edrich by now had been made captain of the 2ndXI and though he was making a big success of it, the fact remained that he would never succeed Cyril Washbrook as captain of Lancashire if the latter had any influence over the matter – and he did. The same could be said to apply to Alan Wharton, the perfect senior professional, an articulate school teacher who would have been equally acceptable to the other professionals. Not, however to Washbrook who reserved his venom for anyone who stood up to him and neither Edrich nor Wharton, having served in the war (in Edrich's case including three and a half traumatic years as a prisoner of the Japanese) was inclined to tolerate the petty tyrannies of a cricket captain. Although the succession was far from certain, Barber was clearly the coming man.

In August 1958, he was permitted to captain the side in a championship match against Glamorgan at Cardiff Arms Park. Washbrook wasn't playing but he decided to travel with the team to South Wales and spent much of the journey telling his temporary replacement to stand up to Wilf Wooller and, on principle, do the opposite of whatever it was Wooller wanted. It turned out to be shrewd advice.

Under scudding heavy grey clouds, Lancashire batted well on the Wednesday after Glamorgan had won the toss and elected to field (as they used to say). The wicket held fewer terrors than the opposing captain had imagined and Marner and Pullar put on 132 runs in 128 minutes. Although wickets tumbled thereafter, as Lancashire chased quick runs, they reached 351 and still had half an hour to bowl at the opposition, in which time Statham and Tattersall reduced them to 5-3. When Bob drew back the curtains in his hotel room the following morning the sky was still a thick grey but now the rain that had arrived in the night looked as though it had already set in for the day. However, prompted by Washbrook, he went along to the ground to have a word with the umpires and the opposing captain who was working in the office. Wooller, like Trevor Bailey at Essex, still retained his amateur status because the club was paying him a salary for a job that "had nothing to do with cricket".

Bob's polite enquiry as to the irascible Glamorgan captain's whereabouts was met with a brief shout of disagreement from the next room. "There'll be no play today. Go back to the hotel, young man" was the gist of it. With Washbrook's words echoing in his ear, the young stand-in captain said that he would hang around if that was all right, because it might clear up later in the day. Since there were no satellite weather forecasts to be consulted in 1958, this prognostication was greeted with another volley of abuse from the intemperate Wooller but Bob, encouraged by the start the Lancashire bowlers had made, refused to be intimidated and succeeded in inviting Wooller to join Washbrook and himself for lunch.

When we'd finished, it was still raining and there were pools of water lying all over the outfield. I said again that we had to take a decision about when we resume play and he hit the roof again. Once the captains disagree it reverts back to the umpires and they're looking at Wilf and they're looking at Cyril and they are just as frightened of him. They agree to look again at tea time. Meanwhile the lads had gone off to the cinema but at 3.30 it stops raining, the wind gets up, the sun comes out and the tide turns or whatever and we got out again at 5.30.

Statham then proceeded to bowl the next four Glamorgan batsmen and Tattersall took the last three wickets so that, before the close of the drastically curtailed second day's play, Glamorgan had been dismissed for a total of 26 runs made in 31 overs. That the total reached the giddy heights of 26, after the home side were reduced to 15-9, was only thanks to a last wicket stand of 11 between Wooller and Gatehouse, the left arm opening bowler, who edged Statham twice through the slips before being caught by Malcolm Hilton. Wooller stamped back to the dressing room in his pads and so furious was he with the pathetic attempts of his batsmen that he went back out again to open the second innings, Glamorgan now following on nearly 330 runs behind. There was time for Statham and Tattersall to bowl only three overs, all of which were wicketless maidens, before the players retired at the end of an incident-packed day.

Sadly, the story does not have a neat and happy ending for the following day, Friday August 8th, dawned just as grey, cold and wet as Thursday August 7th had started but this time the rain clouds stayed in place over Cardiff and the match ended in a draw. Still, Bob had done his captaincy credentials no harm, even if the success of his tactics, such as they were, owed nearly everything to Washbrook's sheer bloody-mindedness and the rest to the irresistible bowling of Brian Statham and Roy Tattersall.

Meanwhile, Bob's batting continued to mature, his class and talent visible to everyone. Although he failed to achieve the benchmark thousand runs for the season, he made an outstanding hundred against Warwickshire on another miserable dank day this time in partnership with Geoff Pullar who was on 157 when Washbrook declared at 350 for 2. Bob has fond memories of the left hander from Swinton who was born the same year that he was and joined the Lancashire playing staff at much the same time that Bob was being hustled into the first team. Now, along with Peter Marner, these three were forming the spine of a batting line up that had recently lost Winston Place, Geoff Edrich and Jack Ikin. Pullar, in his early days, batted in the middle order and was a good-looking free flowing batsman.

Geoffrey Pullar, when he was 18, was the most beautiful looking left-handed batsman I knew. It was later that he started all that nudging and nurdling, turning the ball round the corner.

It was probably the responsibility of opening for England that changed Pullar's style. Certainly, the memories most Lancashire supporters have of Pullar is of the nudger and nurdler, so it is good to be reminded of what a fine looking batsman he had once been.

One reason Barber never reached a thousand runs in his first full season in county cricket was that he had been involved in a car accident on the way to the return match against Surrey at The Oval. He and Noel Cooke were in a car that was hit by a lorry in Barnet and both were taken to Barnet General Hospital. Cooke had been rendered temporarily unconscious in the collision and Bob was kept in for a second night under observation. Jack Bond was put on the midnight train from Manchester, not exactly perfect preparation for facing Lock and Laker. Washbrook moved back up the order to open the batting with Brian Booth, though it did nothing to change what had been the regular result of this fixture for many years. Booth made a pair, Bond a duck in the second innings and Lancashire lost to the champions by eight wickets before lunch on the third day.

The days of Surrey's domination of the county championship might have been coming to an end, but they still managed to win the 1958 title, finishing twenty-six points clear of Hampshire in second place and a full seventy points ahead of Lancashire, who ended a disappointing seventh. One bright spot for the Red Rose was that Yorkshire fared even worse in 1958, finishing twelfth amid the sound of dressing room rebellion.

It was just before the second Roses match of the season at the start of August, when the festering resentment of Johnny Wardle became publicly visible. Chafing under the ignominy of taking orders from Ronnie Burnet, a 39 year-old engineer with no history of first-class cricket, Wardle's regular sarcasm increased in intensity when Burnet began to sort out a "difficult" dressing room. Wardle was the first victim of this new order. Summoned to the committee room in the middle of the match against Somerset at Bramall Lane, Wardle was unceremoniously sacked. He then put his name to a series of articles in the *Daily Mail* in which he claimed to have been dismissed for refusing "to accept the authority of the quite hopeless old man appointed captain". His invitation to tour Australia that winter was withdrawn by the MCC – much to the frustration of Peter May, the England captain, but Wardle's first-class career was over.

It was in this atmosphere that the Roses match began at Old Trafford. Lancashire gained a first innings lead but yet again the weather ruined any possibility of a result other than a draw. In fact the entire 1958 season was something of a washout. England hammered a weak New Zealand touring team, winning four of the five Tests by large margins and failing to win the last match at The Oval only because rain washed out two complete days. Thereafter the Kiwis were never permitted the compliment of being the only tourists in an English summer.

For Bob Barber, the 1958 season was one of decent consolidation. He fell just fourteen runs short of passing a thousand runs for the first time, at an average of just over 25. It doesn't sound particularly impressive, but only twenty or so batsmen in the country averaged higher than thirty, only one of whom was a Lancastrian (Peter Marner). The quality of bowling in the late 1950s was probably as high as it had ever been in county cricket. Even if every county didn't have express pace, pretty much every county had bowlers who took stacks of wickets year after year. At Hampshire, Derek Shackleton bowled at medium pace but took his 100 wickets every season. Don Shepherd at Glamorgan bowled his off cutters with similar results. Terry Spencer at struggling Leicestershire was still a handful for most good batsmen as was Ian Thomson at Hove particularly when the sea fret was helping him. Les Jackson at Derbyshire played only two Test matches in a long career but was a prolific wicket taker, causing good batsmen constant problems. It took time and patience and application to learn how to play these excellent bowlers and Bob Barber was still learning.

Frank Tyson on the other hand never took the wickets in county cricket that he was expected to take after his devastating Ashes tour of 1954-5. By common consent (withheld though, one suspects, by F.S. Trueman), Tyson was the quickest bowler of the 1950s. On the hard fast wickets of Australia he had been almost unplayable in 1954-5. In 1958, even if that blistering pace had started to diminish, he was still formidable, particularly when the traditionally slow wickets at Northampton had been quickened up by rain. Generally at Wantage Road, conditions favoured the spinners George Tribe and Jack Manning but, when conditions were in his favour at the County Ground in Northampton, he could be devastating. Tyson's action had caused the brains at Old Trafford to assume that his career would be blighted by constant injury, so they had decided not to sign him as a teenager.

His action was such that he started with his right hand almost touching the ground, which means he must have had a very strong back to do that. The only fellow who I think bowled as fast was Michael Holding. If you look at the batter and see when he's picking the bat up and how high his backlift is before he has to bring it down again, you can form a judgement. I faced Frank at Northants on a pitch that had been spiced up by rain and the ball was flying all over the place. Alan Wharton got hit in the throat and we were just trying to survive the evening.

The pace was allied to the problem caused by the back foot no ball law which was in operation at the time. It was only after the infamous Ashes disaster of 1958-59, when England believed they had been thrown out by Ian Meckiff and the great dragger Gordon Rourke, that MCC was persuaded to consider changing the no ball law, from one in which the back foot had to be behind the line of the wickets in the delivery stride, to the law we recognise today, in which some part of the front foot must land on or behind the popping crease. The implication for batsmen of the back foot law was significant.

Frank was bowling at a time when bowlers were letting the ball go significantly closer to the batsman than they are today with no protection at all apart from a box. Eventually I started using a rolled up towel to protect the inside thigh because that was the painful bit if you got turned round, not the outside of the thigh. The back foot no ball law made a huge difference. There's a lovely photograph of Fred bowling, his front foot is still up in the air and his back foot is coming past the wicket and his front foot is clearly going to land eighteen inches or more beyond the batting crease. Fred wanted to get close to the wicket to bowl so you work out where his right foot is going to end up – on a length right outside the left hander's off stump. Colin Smith was a very fine cricketer and in my opinion would have played for England if he'd wanted to pursue cricket as a career. I saw Colin at Fenners practising the drag. He'd been watching Fred and he knew how close he got before releasing the ball. He had an even bigger steel toe cap than Fred and there he was practising by himself in the nets, trying to get ever closer to the batsman before letting it go. You can't let the ball go until your weight is transferred to the front foot.

By the end of the 1958 season Bob was a capped player and Lancashire's regular opener in partnership with Alan Wharton; he was clearly marked out as Washbrook's logical successor as captain whenever the veteran was prepared reluctantly to let go of the reins, and, if his batting was steady rather than spectacular, the brilliance of his fielding and throwing was invariably commented upon.

His bowling was a different proposition. It wasn't just that he hadn't taken the wickets he was expected to have taken by good judges of leg spin bowling. In 1958, he took only nine wickets at an average of 25, although only the incomparable George Tribe with 120 wickets thrived in that damp summer. Indeed, that season was so unforgiving of leg spin bowling that Tommy Greenhough had been to see Washbrook and told him he was thinking of giving up the game. Washbrook encouraged him to hang on, as the following season was to see more covering of the pitches, and both were rewarded when, in 1959, the long hot summer saw Greenhough not only claim a regular place in the Lancashire first XI but make his debut for England.

Bob Barber never received from his captain that sort of encouragement for his bowling.

Cyril clearly didn't see me as a bowling all rounder because he never put me on. We had a very good spin attack of course and wet wickets aren't conducive to leg spin. I was not happy that Cyril would frequently ask me to bowl the last over before lunch. I don't think he was trying to protect me by bringing me on for the over when batsmen would be least likely to play their big shots. You've got to give your spinner at least three overs to get warmed up. I saw myself as a batter who could bowl. Dry or dusty wickets were a different proposition. I felt I could spin it from the wrist on any wicket whereas, fine bowlers though they were, Roy [Tattersall] and even Malcolm [Hilton] couldn't spin the ball on hard wickets. You wanted hard wickets because you wanted the ball to bounce from my height and then an edge to carry to the close fielders.

It is a matter of regret for the purist that there have been so few English wrist spinners. At Test level, they have been nearly invisible. During the luncheon interval, on the second day of the first Test match against India in the summer of 2014, a highly serious discussion broke out on *Test Match Special*, prompted by an interview with Peter Such, one of the spin coaches at the Loughborough training centre. Vic Marks concluded that, "the only decent leg spinner we've had since the days of Eric Hollies was a chap called Bob Barber who used to open the batting with Geoffrey Boycott". Clearly, as this book has attempted to illustrate, there was considerably more to Bob Barber's career than his Test partnership with Boycott, but it is in a way comforting that, when the discussion turns to Test class leg spinners, Bob Barber's name is still there.

One reason for the problems which beset wrist spinners rather than finger spinners is of course prevailing wet conditions but it is clear from Bob's recollection of his handling by all his captains, not only Washbrook but also Cowdrey, Dexter and even his good friend Mike Smith, that English captains have a hard time trusting the vagaries of the leg spinner. If you had a choice of throwing the ball to either Brian Statham or Bob Barber or later to Tom Cartwright or Bob Barber, there is no doubt which bowler Lancashire and Warwickshire captains trusted to take wickets and not give runs away. Bob might have seen himself as an all-rounder but, as the 1958 season ended, it was clear to most observers that not many others did.

He turned twenty-three that September and the fact that he had not yet made his Test debut might have been considered in some quarters to be a surprise. Of course, the England team was still reasonably settled and successful but the Old Trafford Test match against New Zealand had marked the Test debut of Ted Dexter, Bob's contemporary, who had lost two years to National Service. Dexter, fresh from captaining Cambridge to victory in the Varsity Match, had made a powerful 52 against New Zealand's limited attack, hinting of a significant career at international level. During the winter he was to be flown out to Australia as a replacement when injuries began to decimate an England side already wounded by the raw, if not necessarily legal, pace of Ian Meckiff and Gordon Rourke.

Lancashire found themselves with a new star batsman in 1959, one who would indeed make a successful Test debut, but his name wasn't R.W Barber; it was G. Pullar. They would also lend the services of their star leg spinner to England but that wasn't Bob Barber either. It was the man who twelve months earlier had thought seriously of retiring from the first class game. The new Lancashire and England leg break and googly bowler was Tommy Greenhough. Was Bob Barber ever going to fulfil that prodigious talent that had blazed so brightly during his schooldays?

CHAPTER FIVE

THE SUMMER OF 1959 would be Cyril Washbrook's last season as a Lancashire player. He was 45 years-old; he had made his debut in 1933, the year of Franklin D. Roosevelt's first New Deal, the year Hitler was appointed Chancellor of Germany, the year before Lancashire had last won the county championship outright. He had served Lancashire well for over a quarter of a century, but by the time he had finally decided to retire, Washbrook cut an isolated figure in the dressing room. He was nearly ten years older than Alan Wharton, his senior professional, and he was the only man on the staff to have played for the county before the war. The men of the future, Barber, Pullar, Marner, Higgs, Dyson, Clayton were over twenty years younger. Washbrook had learned his cricket under men like Ernest Tyldesley who had played for Lancashire in the Golden Age before the outbreak of the First World War. It had been a different time and had required different manners.

Washbrook himself knew he'd been playing on borrowed time for the past few seasons, since his legendary 98 at Headingley against the Australians in 1956 had been followed a succession of single figure scores. The match against Middlesex at Aigburth in June confirmed that 1959 would have to be his last season, when he was bowled for 19 in the first innings and 3 in the second. John Murray who was behind the stumps for Middlesex in that game recalls

Washbrook always made a big thing about "good players don't get bowled out". They get caught or they get their legs in the way. We played them at Aigburth and a boy called Ron Hooker bowled at very very medium pace, little seamers, and he did Washy in both innings. Apparently Washy told him, "When a piss awful bowler like you bowls me twice it's time I retired." John Warr got straight into him about good players never getting bowled out.

Washbrook had certainly been a very fine player but, as captain, he did not create a harmonious playing staff. Jack Bond, who was to become one of Lancashire's great captains, was nearly driven out of the game by Washbrook.

He ran me out several times and I didn't particularly like him. It happened three times on the trot and there's me trying to score enough runs to stay in the side and earn a decent living. The third time, we got half way down the pitch and I said, "It's all right, captain, I'll go" and I just turned walked off towards the pavilion. We never got on at all.

Ruthin School in 1950.

Lancashire debut at 18.

Lancashire opening batsman Bob Barber sweeps Hampshire pace bowler
Derek Shackleton through the leg trap for four runs.

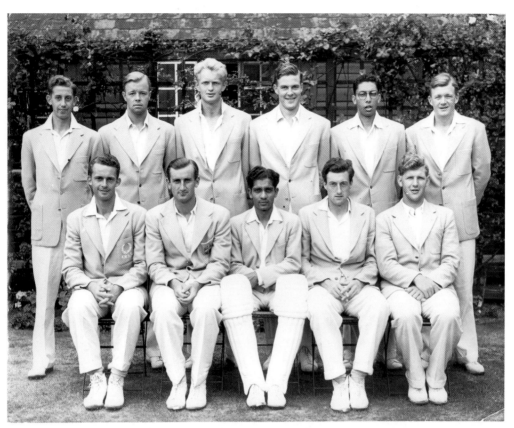

The Cambridge University team of 1956.

Barber succeeded Cyril Washbrook as
captain of Lancashire in 1960.

Bowling for Lancashire against Warwickshire in 1960.

With the MCC team in New Zealand 1960/61.
Back row: David Smith, Don Wilson, Roger Prideaux, David Sayer.
Middle row: John Murray, Jim Stewart, Eric Russell, AN Other.
Front row: David Allen, Jim Parks, Bill Watson, Bob Barber.

Exciting events at Buller Gorge.

E. W. SWANTON'S XI IN THE WEST INDIES 1961.

Chan's Photograp

BACK ROW:
Nawab of Pataudi, B. D. Wells, H. J. Rhodes, O. S. Wheatley, I. M. Mc Lachlan, R. A. Gale, A. C. Smith, A. A. Baig.

SITTING:
E. W. Swanton, R. W. Barber, E. Weekes, A. C. D. Ingleby-Mackenzie (Captain), R. R. Lindwall, P. M. Walker, J. S. O. Haslewood (Hon. Treasurer).

Lancashire CCC 1961.
Back Row: Jack Bond, Geoff Clayton, Ken Higgs, Colin Hilton,
Roy Collins, Alan Bolton, Peter Marner.
Front Row: Tommy Greenhough, Ken Grieves, Bob Barber (Capt.),
Brian Statham, Geoff Pullar.

Gentlemen v Players July 1961.

Warwickshire CCC 1963. The move to Edgbaston rejuvenated Barber's Test career.
Top row: Neal Abberley, Bill Blenkiron, Tom Cartwright, Rudi Webster,
Dennis Amiss, Terry Riley, Denis Oakes.
Middle row: Billy Ibadulla, Jim Stewart, Bryan Richardson, Ronnie Miller,
Basil Bridge, Michael Mence, John Jameson.
Front row: Norman Horner, Ray Hitchcock, AC Smith, MJK Smith,
Jack Bannister, Bob Barber.

Barber and Boycott became one of
England's most reliable and feared
opening partnerships.

Washbrook was a dominant figure and he attracted pronounced judgements. He never greatly trusted spin bowlers and handled Lancashire's two best spinners Malcolm Hilton and Roy Tattersall particularly badly. Jack Bond remembers that he was

> horrible to Roy Tattersall and a nicer fellow you couldn't wish to meet. Washy liked Malcolm Hilton who became one of his favourites and he helped him to drink himself out of the flaming game. He got away with murder as far as discipline was concerned – like other players Washy liked – while other players got hauled over the coals. He had no time for anyone he didn't think was going to be a world class player. He stayed at the same hotels but he took a bloke from Rochdale round with him because he provided Washy with cars. He socialised with this fellow not with the rest of the players. He liked Ken Grieves and Jack Dyson. He didn't like Geoff Edrich but then Geoff Edrich didn't like him.

The Middlesex wicket keeper, John Murray recalls a rain affected match at Old Trafford in July 1957, from which neither captain emerged in a good light.

> It rained for three days and we didn't start till the Tuesday, so we played for eight points or something. By the time it came to the toss on that Tuesday, W. J. Edrich had had rather a good weekend at the Mere Country Club – that was the only the reason he went up there – there were a few parties up there …anyway at the toss, WJ was the worse for wear – he was actually leaning on Cyril - and Cyril reported him to the MCC. Middlesex didn't think too much of that.

Jim Stewart of Warwickshire also had a distinctly negative view of Washbrook.

> He was not the nicest of men. I played against Lancs at Edgbaston when Washy was still captain and dear old Roy Tattersall was frightened to death of him. Washy had that swagger as he went from cover to cover keeping his back to Tattersall and when he got there he turned round and said to Tatt, "All right, you can bowl now." Roy Tattersall was a lovely man and a great bowler but Washbrook was an arrogant man.

During Washbrook's last season in charge, the form of both Tattersall and Hilton fell away badly. Tattersall played in only one match in 1959 in which he took five wickets but was never asked to turn out again for his county until Bob Barber replaced Cyril Washbrook as captain.

Bob's natural instinct is to defend Washbrook but he admits that

Washy was a martinet. Most of the time he was good to me. I got the feeling he was probably better to me than he was to most of the other fellows. I remember a game against Essex. Malcolm Hilton was bowling and Alan Wharton was standing at first slip. The batsman got an edge, Alan threw himself sideways, got it in the end of his fingers but as he hit the ground the ball came out. Washy exploded. To me it was a brilliant effort, not something to explode about. Then Dickie Dodds got after Malcolm who said, "Can I have a deep square leg, skipper?" and Washy said shortly, "If you can't bowl any better than that, you'd better give me the ball back."

There are two sides to every story and, to be fair, nobody would ever doubt Washbrook's commitment to the Lancashire cause or his deep-seated desire for Lancashire to do well. David Lloyd recalls that when he joined the Lancashire staff in 1964, when Washbrook was temporarily the manager of the team, he induced such respect that Bumble always called him "Mister Washbrook." Bob is careful to explain both sides of the Washbrook argument.

Cyril didn't welcome any input on the field, but he'd talk in the bar. On the field, he never asked anybody else's opinion – to my knowledge. There was always a lot of muttering about Cyril being a martinet – hence everyone enjoying watching him struggle against Doug Wright or George Tribe, but they did admire him because he was a very fine cricketer. He was…difficult. He became too powerful. If there had been dialogue, his life might have been better. He was an isolated figure. Geoff Edrich certainly felt that Cyril was playing the sergeant with them and they were still privates. It didn't make him popular, but he was devoted to Lancashire cricket. Yes, he wanted to be the captain of the side that won the championship but, above all, he wanted Lancashire to do well with or without him and he was certainly a superb batter. He had time. He picked it up early and his feet were always in position – like Cowdrey and Sobers - same thing.

Cyril Washbrook became Lancashire's first professional captain in 1954, following Nigel Howard's retirement, because there had not been an amateur of sufficient quality, or even an amateur of less than first class competence like Jack Fallows, who would be prepared to spare the time to play cricket for four months. To have ignored Washbrook's claim to the captaincy in 1954, would have taken greater courage than the Lancashire committee was wont to display. By the time he retired, there certainly was an amateur of quality, good enough as a cricketer to justify his presence in any team in the land. Bob Barber was, from a distance, the obvious man to succeed Cyril Washbrook as the captain of Lancashire CCC but what should have been a transition managed with ease and simplicity, ended by creating a dressing room that would be in turmoil for nearly a decade.

The 1959 season began as usual with two matches against the University sides. Washbrook did not play himself so Bob captained both games which were won easily, albeit with a full strength county team with the exception of the amateur Dick Bowman, a quick bowler and a decent batsman who might well have owed his place to Washbrook's (or the committee's) desire to make sure that Bob did not assume that the mantle of succession to the captaincy would fall on him as of right. When the first county championship match of the season started at Rushden in Northamptonshire, Washbrook was back in place of Bowman. Lancashire won impressively by eight wickets, with Geoff Pullar scoring heavily and Greenhough taking five wickets in the home side's second innings.

Lancashire's first visitors were Yorkshire, destined that year to end a thirteen year wait for the title. Lancashire despatched them convincingly, although with an hour to play Yorkshire, thanks to a resolute stand between Doug Padgett and Ray Illingworth, still had five wickets to fall. Higgs started the final collapse but the last wicket, Don Wilson caught at slip by Grieves off Jack Dyson, did not fall until five minutes from the end of the match. That presumably justified Washbrook's decision to declare Lancashire's second innings closed with Bob Barber on 95 not out in a Roses match. Earlier, he and Geoff Pullar had taken the score from 1-1 to 159 for 2, Pullar departing for a sparkling 105. Washbrook's feelings were clearly that if Barber couldn't score his century fast enough it was his own fault if his captain declared on him. Bob never complained, partly because he never set any great store by the acquisition of three figures but he doubted that he would have acted that way as captain himself.

Four matches played, four matches won. The Lancashire side seemed to have everything – youth, experience, fine seam bowling, excellent slow bowling. The batsmen were equally at home defending their wickets or tearing into the opposition bowling. In Greenhough, Dyson and Barber they had wrist spin and finger spin. Waiting in the wings were still the veterans Tattersall and Hilton. Perhaps the only negative was that the batting ended abruptly with Jack Dyson at number seven. The time when the tail enders would be expected to get into line and fend off hostile short pitched fast bowling was still some years distant. Neither of the two regular stumpers, Jack Jordan and Alan Wilson, could bat and with Statham, Higgs and Greenhough as nine, ten, jack that meant the tail was alarmingly long. Wilson, a fine glove man, was nicknamed Ranji, with a certain amount of sarcasm.

He was so called because he would play this immaculate cover drive and the ball would trickle out on the off side and just about reach silly mid off.

Fortunately the 1959 season saw the emergence of a bright new talent in the shape of Geoff Clayton. He crouched behind the wickets in a somewhat unorthodox style and quickly became known as "Chimp" because of it. His batting, however, was in a different class from that of the wicket keepers who had preceded him.

Hampshire came to Manchester after the successful Roses match and they too went the same way – bowled out by Greenhough, Statham and Dyson on the last afternoon to give Lancashire another victory that set them proudly on top of the table. It was still May, far too early to talk of championship victories but still, five matches played, five matches won…….. The possibilities of the remainder of the season seemed limitless.

Leicestershire, for many years one of the worst teams in the championship, were the next victims expected to prostrate themselves before the all-conquering maestros from Old Trafford – except that Leicestershire beat Lancashire by three wickets. The trauma of this defeat was so all-pervading that, with one exception, Lancashire didn't win another match until August. The exception turned out to be Surrey, who had seemingly been playing Lancashire throughout their title-winning years with one hand metaphorically tied behind their back.

This time there was no Peter May or Ken Barrington, who were both playing for England against India at Lord's, but Lancashire had lost Statham and Greenhough for the same reason and the Surrey bowling attack still boasted both Bedsers, Loader, Laker and Lock, who had bowled them to seven consecutive championships. It was a sparkling innings of 121 from Bob Barber which set Lancashire on their way. Higgs took 6-34 in Surrey's first innings and Barber 4-48 when the champions followed on to leave Lancashire just four runs to win, which they did by ten wickets. It had been a very good couple of days for both Lancashire leg spinners, as Tommy Greenhough had taken 5-35 in the test match at Lord's, confusing Godfrey Evans as much as the Indian batsmen and causing the great Kent wicket keeper to be dropped for the third Test in favour of Surrey's rising star, Roy Swetman. Evans never regained his England place and in future years whenever he spotted Tommy Greenhough, he would call out, "There's the chap who finished my Test career!"

Lancashire's season spiralled rapidly downwards at the end of May before picking up again in August, but Bob Barber maintained an admirable consistency. Despite the fact that he did not play a full season of county cricket, he nevertheless passed 1000 runs for the first time (although 23 batsmen passed two thousand and MJK Smith 3,000) and he finished with a more than respectable average of 38, one place in the national averages below H.D. Bird of Yorkshire, whose average was significantly boosted over his twelve innings by one score of 181 not out, after which he was told by Brian Sellers, Yorkshire chairman of selectors that he had been dropped back to the second XI. It was a decision that Mr Sellers, his heirs and successors, would hear much about over the ensuing half a century.

Bob Barber's reward came when he was selected for the first time to play for the Gentlemen against the Players at Lord's in July. Although it wasn't to be his match with the bat (it was M.J.K. Smith's match as it was M.J. K. Smith's season with the bat) he did dismiss both of the Players' centurions, Close and Illingworth (Yorkshire batsmen seemed to have a structural weakness against wrist spin), taking the wickets in seven overs, conceding 27 runs. The match effectively concluded Bob's 1959 domestic season for, as Lancashire continued to toil at home, Bob was off on a tour of Canada, organised by the MCC in one of its flag waving gestures in the distant parts of the Dominions.

By current standards, it was an astonishing thing to do in the middle of the season. Bob joined the party led by his first Cambridge captain Dennis Silk and which was comprised almost entirely of Oxbridge Blues and were therefore amateurs, clearly the right sort of people to send out to let the colonials know they were not forgotten back in St John's Wood. The squad, if such a professional appellation can be applied to it, included Michael Bushby, who had captained Cambridge University in the summer of 1954, the term before Bob matriculated, John Pretlove of Kent, David Green (D.J. not D.M.) of Derbyshire, Jack Bailey of Essex and A.C. Smith who was eventually to become a colleague of Bob at Warwickshire, but who was then captain of Oxford University. Smith recalls being extremely impressed with Bob's ability to extract turn and bounce.

Bob was an attacking bowler. Eric Hollies bowled like a slow left armer, didn't turn it much but he was very accurate. Eric didn't bowl bad balls. Bob ripped it, and bounced it but Hollies didn't do that. Hollies could spin the ball but he didn't choose to. He'd turn one a big way every so often, just to get the batsman unsure of when the next one was coming along.

Shortly after his return, on 4th November 1959 it was formally announced by Lancashire County Cricket Club that, following the retirement of Cyril Washbrook, the club would be captained in 1960 by the 24-year-old amateur R.W. Barber. It should have been the ascent to a period of glorious triumphs. A side containing experience and youth, captained by one of the brightest cricketing talents in the country, freed from the insensitive stewardship of the martinet Washbrook might now, under its clever, enthusiastic young captain, go on to fulfil the triumphs fantasised about so long by both the Lancashire players and their supporters. In fact, the hardest, unhappiest years of Bob Barber's cricketing career, which had started in a blaze of glory, were now upon him.

CHAPTER SIX

IN JULY 1959, LANCASHIRE played a friendly match against Ireland. It was very friendly. Arguably too friendly for a horrified young captain.

Cyril wasn't captain but he wanted to come with us, though he didn't want to play. He and a committee man called George Cadman travelled with us on the boat and as soon as they got on board, the drinks started. I was the captain and I could see what was happening. Cyril was laughing away, so I went off to bed. To me, being captain meant controlling what happened on the field. The next morning, I got up early and as we dock I see Noel Cantwell on the quay. He said, to my surprise, "What's going on with your team?" I said I had no idea. He told me the ship's captain had told him that there had been a serious risk during the night that he [the captain] would turn the boat back because of the wild behaviour of the Lancashire team. I knew nothing of all this but, fortunately, it was raining because there was hardly a sober man left standing. Cyril was present but I don't know if he was complicit. Nothing eventuated. It was swept under the table, but when I was asked to captain the team I was extremely wary.

When the announcement of Bob's captaincy was eventually made, Washbrook was noticeable for his absence.

Cyril never said a word to me. He never came to the ground during the 1960 season. He never wrote to me. He never wished me luck or anything. I accepted that it was likely to come my way and I suppose I was fatalistic about it.

Infamously, Bob was told that, on away trips, he was not to stay in the same hotel as the other players. It seemed an odd decision to most Lancashire supporters at the time and it attracted much unfavourable comment but to John Kay in the *Manchester Evening News* it appeared to make perfect sense. In an article headlined LANCS NOT CRICKET SNOBS, he pontificated

All the fuss about Lancashire's decision to accommodate new captain Bob Barber in one hotel and their professional players in another when the side travel to this season's away fixtures simply makes me smile. I think it's a good idea.
    To some, this segregation of amateur and professional players may smack of the dark ages in cricket. To others it might seem downright snobbishness.

But I have little doubt that the cricketers, Barber included, are in favour.

Lancs say their decision will give the 24-year-old Barber more authority on the field. And that's certainly important to a pleasant young fellow who will lead a side including many seasoned veterans in county cricket.

They also feel the move is in the best interests of the team – and Barber. So do I.

Most cricketers like to relax and enjoy themselves in a moderate manner when the day's play is over. Barber is a fine cricketer but also has a reputation of being a disciplinarian when captaining a side and it's just as well that the professionals should be left to themselves off the field.

Lancs HAVE the talent to win the county championship. And if Barber can get from the players the type of backing this move shows the committee are willing to give, he can lead them to the title in his first season as captain.

This decision is always seized upon as evidence that the committee was mad and Barber a fool to agree to it. The committee wasn't mad, though it might well be thought to have been bad and dangerous to know. Bob didn't have much choice in the matter, since his opinion wasn't sought and anyway the committee was his employer; although, as an amateur, he could have stuck two fingers up and walked back to his management role at Dorman Smith. Instead, he explains quite rationally his thought processes at the time.

Colonel Green, one of the cricket committee men who really was respected, was an old world gentleman. He captained the team when they won three consecutive championships in the 1920s and, if he said to me I should stay in a different hotel, I listened. It was odd, almost like coming out of a different gate. It was an attempt to get the Senior Pro to control the professionals. I was the youngest captain for sixty years. I wasn't in a position to say no. In those days if someone told you not to walk on the grass, you didn't walk on the grass.

This system of management had worked for Leonard Green in the 1920s, but in 1960 it seemed absurdly anachronistic and predictably it drove a wedge between the team and the new and still relatively young captain. In his history of Lancashire cricket, John Kay paints a portrait of Bob Barber as "a sad and lonely young cricketer in his first year as captain". Kay believed that he seldom sought to untangle knotty cricketing problems with his senior professionals and when reprimands were needed they came from the committee.

This strikes Bob Barber as manifestly unfair and untrue. He had enormous respect for the talent of the professionals under his command and he consulted the Australian Ken Grieves frequently during long stints in the field. Grieves had stood at slip for eleven years and proved an excellent analyst of the pitch, the bowling and the batsmen. It would be foolish not to have consulted him and Bob Barber might have been idiosyncratic but he was never foolish. He might not have forged a friendship of a lasting nature with Grieves who was fond of a good time in a way that Bob did not always find congenial but his relationship with Alan Wharton for example was extremely good. He has always attributed his much less successful second season partly to the committee's unwarranted and self-defeating termination of Alan Wharton's contract at Lancashire. As we shall see towards the end of this chapter, reprimands from the committee never proved helpful to the prosperity of the team.

It is arguable that one of the consequences of the captain's sequestration in a separate hotel was that the drinking, which had always been one that had gained Lancashire an unwelcome reputation on the county circuit, was exacerbated. The Lancashire side of the 1950s and early 1960s was certainly composed of fine players but they had too much of a liking for a drink.

Drinking and sport do not automatically make incompatible bedfellows, even in the professional sphere, at least not in the time before the advent of the nutritionist and the ice bath. The all-conquering Yorkshire team of the 1930s would spend the hours after the close of play back in the bar of the team hotel, carefully nursing a single pint of bitter but talking cricket all the time. It was the best possible education for an impressionable, talented youngster eager to learn about the intricacies of the game. Lancashire's drinking in the 1950s on the other hand, appears to have been on an altogether different plane.

Not all players are affected by drink in the same way. The England football team's greatest captain, Bobby Moore, was notorious for being the last one out of the bar at night but the first one onto the training field in the morning, working at full pace with no apparent ill effects. Brian Statham also drank more than his performances suggested.

Brian could down half a dozen pints of lager without blinking. I never saw drink have any effect on him at all. Brian wouldn't have been a bad influence on anyone. In any case I have no problem with anyone drinking a couple of pints – I buy you one you buy me one. The problem comes when it's 8 or 10 pints. We used to say about Kenny Grieves that it didn't matter what he'd been doing the night before. When the first one flashed off the bat, he stuck his hand out and caught it. Not everyone could do that and that's where the problems came. In my family though, there was a strong nonconformist feeling against drink. My father used to tease my mother's sisters at Christmas with the offer of a sherry!

There are some players, however, particularly in the culture of those times, whose alcoholic intake was clearly detrimental to their performances. David Green, who played for the Lancashire second XI when he was still at Manchester Grammar School, was immensely talented. In Bob's opinion, there was a problem when he was fielding. Bob himself was a superb fielder, whether in the outfield where his javelin training meant he ran like an athlete and had a throw like a dart, or close to the wicket where he also excelled.

Most people didn't run very well – nothing like now. It was more noticeable in the field, especially if you were a bowler. People like David Green, you couldn't put at extra cover because the ball would be past him before he could move. He might as well go and sit in a deck chair. I remember his father at fifty years of age was quicker; he couldn't keep up with his dad over twenty-five yards. There were too many fielders like that. Kenny Grieves was always at slip or at leg slip when Tommy was bowling googlies. Alan was good and Peter Marner was a bit deeper but it was good as a bowler to know that if you got an edge the ball would be caught.

The principle of the captain staying alone (or with other amateurs) in a separate hotel was intended to establish the power of the Senior Professional to be responsible for the discipline of the team. In reality of course it didn't work out like that, even when this position was held by the widely admired Alan Wharton. It wasn't that Barber was too weak with the players. When things began to go wrong in 1961, he was categorised in the *Manchester Evening News* as "a disciplinarian".

I have a letter from Geoffrey Howard telling me that the reason Jack Dyson was sacked at the end of the 1960 season was for "insolence and insubordination to the captain on the field". I never knew what incident that referred to nor do I remember anyone on the committee ever asking me. Jack Dyson could be a pain like Peter Marner. That was the sort of aggravation you got. I couldn't imagine Jack being my bosom pal but thinking about what he might have done on the field, I keep thinking about it and I just have no idea. My problems were with the committee, not the players. It was more than likely that the committee wanted to get rid of Dyson and used a trumped up or exaggerated charge of insubordination to the captain to do it.

Certainly, Jack Dyson was a fairly introverted character nicknamed "Deep", either because of his philosophical silences or because he was part of the Manchester City "Revie plan", which involved Don Revie wearing the number nine on the back of his shirt but playing as a withdrawn centre forward, in the style of the Hungarian, Hidegkuti. Unlike Peter Marner, who could be aggressively "bolshie", Dyson's manner and body language never suggested the waving of a red flag and the leading of a revolution. He did, however, manage to get himself sacked twice in four years. After Bob left Lancashire for Warwickshire, Dyson returned, only to be dismissed in even more public fashion, when the club spectacularly imploded in 1964.

The captaincy of a cricket team is more significant than that of captaincy in any other sport in that he has more responsibility. In the era in which Bob Barber captained Lancashire, it meant more than it does in the era of the twenty-first century, when the captaincy tends to get handed down to whichever senior player wants, or more frequently can be persuaded, to take on the chores involved in the administration of a captain's duties. In the 1950s and 1960s, county cricket was far more important in the English game than it is in 2015, as a consequence of which, the captaincy assumed an importance that made the appointment extremely significant. To be appointed captain for the 1960 season was an enormous honour for Bob Barber. To be relieved of the captaincy at the end of the 1961 season was a humiliation, which was undoubtedly exacerbated by the incompetent manner in which the Lancashire committee handled it.

In 1960, Lancashire, like many other counties, was being forced, with evident reluctance, to come to terms with the gathering pace of social change that had permeated the country since the end of the Second World War. It is received wisdom that the 1960s was the decade of change, but the seismic shifts of that time would not have been possible without the changes that had taken place in the middle of the 1950s. Certainly the 1950s was a decade of social conformism, illustrated perfectly by the fate of the Wolfenden Report in 1957, which recommended significant liberalisation of the current legislation dealing with homosexuality. An outraged popular press called it a "Pink Charter" and the Conservative government, which had no doubt commissioned the report with the best of intentions, quickly buried it. It was to be another ten years before the country was thought to be ready for the reforms that appeared at the end of the 1960s.

However, there were plenty of indications that, while Lancashire were asking Bob Barber to stay in a different hotel from the rest of the team because he was an amateur and that still signified a superior social status, Britain as a country was embracing the start of the changes that would flower in the following decade. The economy that had been ravaged by war and had been dependent on Marshall Aid from a paranoid United States anxious to reinforce its allies in Western Europe against the spectre of International Communism, started to grow. Credit restrictions were eased, encouraged by a Conservative government that thought, quite rightly in 1959, that manufacturing a consumer boom was the quickest route to an electoral victory.

Despite Macmillan's own warnings of the dangers of inflation in his notorious speech at Bedford in July 1957, which was thereafter mistakenly referred to as the "You've Never Had It So Good" speech, the appetite for consumer goods seemed insatiable. Households that never thought such luxuries were possible now could buy on the hire purchase the cars, washing machines and television sets that were the symbols of the new prosperity. Hire purchase wasn't just an easier supply of credit than had ever been previously available to the working classes, it symbolised a change in the mores of the country.

This consumer boom was fuelled by the sudden growth in the power of advertising and advertising itself was empowered by the arrival in the mid-1950s of commercial television, a long awaited competitor to the monopoly previously held by the BBC. ITV started transmission in the London area in September 1955 and Granada Television went on air for the first time in the North West in May 1956. ITV imported far more programmes from the United States than the BBC had been wont to do and, to the horror of the middle classes who believed that they could control the licence fee payers, they discovered that the licence fee payers had an alternative philosophy. The alternative was that it was a better idea to give audiences what they wanted rather than what a small social elite had deemed was best for them. As a result, American detective series like *77 Sunset Strip* and cartoon series like *Huckleberry Hound* were unleashed upon a grateful public who devoured them in large numbers, even as the audiences for talks given by ladies wearing hats started to shrink. The BBC seemed powerless to know what to do in the wake of this cultural invasion, despite support from those commentators who believed that everything that came from America in the shape of music, fast food, juvenile delinquency and cartoons on television was to be deplored, as it was destroying Britain's own indigenous social traditions.

When John F Kennedy ran his successful presidential campaign in 1960, he utilised the burgeoning power of television far better than his opponent, Richard Nixon. When Harold Wilson led the Labour Party into the 1964 general election against the Conservative Party led by the Old Etonian, the fourteenth Earl of Home, he tried to copy the now lamented recently assassinated President as closely as he could. When England won the World Cup in 1966, Wilson did his best to tie it to the "success" of the Labour government. When Bobby Moore held aloft the Jules Rimet trophy, Harold Wilson knew very well that to be associated with Bobby Moore, or to recommend the MBE for The Beatles, was a vital part of the politician's ongoing campaign for public approval.

As London transformed itself into a swinging city in the 1960s so Manchester made an effort to find a provincial version. At the start of the decade, the *Manchester Guardian* moved its centre of printing operations from Cross Street in Manchester to Fleet Street in London. In 1959, when we were on holiday in Cornwall, my family had to wait two days before the "real" newspaper reached our hotel by post from Manchester. When we returned the following year we could buy *The Guardian* in any newsagent's shop in St. Ives the same day, but we could no longer be certain there would be a report on the Lancashire cricket match.

The success of this "repositioning" of Manchester was cultural rather than architectural because, although the slums were slowly being cleared, whether by the Luftwaffe or order of the local council, what was erected in their place was simply a new and equally disastrous mixture of tower blocks and sink estates, patterned after the brutalist realist architecture beloved of East German town planners. Even as *Coronation Street* anachronistically celebrated the folksy community of back-to-back terraced houses, inner city areas such as Hulme were being rebuilt as instant slums, harbouring the germs of the disease that twenty years later would produce gang and drug-related crime on a scale previously unimagined in Manchester.

Granada Television on the other hand, transmitting from its production base in Quay Street, was an almost instant success, drawing creative inspiration from its Manchester location. *Coronation Street* gave to the world not just a host of unforgettable characters in a soap opera still going strong fifty years later but a sense of the heightened reality of life in Manchester. By contrast, *Crossroads*, made by ATV in Birmingham, gave absolutely no sense of the place where it was made, which many Mancunians thought was perhaps as well.

As Granada TV's drama department started to gather and nurture the creative talents of Jack Rosenthal, Arthur Hopcraft, Michael Apted and Colin Welland amongst others, across town Michael Elliott and Braham Murray were beginning to build a national reputation for their newly founded University Theatre, the forerunner of what became the Royal Exchange. In the Sixties, Manchester was "in", Manchester was sexy, but, sadly, wherever you went in the world, to the vast majority of the population the city meant only Manchester United and Georgie Best, with a dash of Bobby Charlton and Denis Law on the side. Football continued to be the city's greatest ambassador.

Sixties celebrity was a potent mixture of pop music, television, fashion, advertising and a physical beauty which the camera lens could convey to an eager public. The old style of Hollywood beauty - the cut-glass voices and immaculate grooming of David Niven and Audrey Hepburn - was giving way to an appreciation of other ethnic styles - the black Sidney Poitier and the Jewish Barbra Streisand amongst others. It took time for the major film studios, which had ruled the roost for forty years, to accept that a new generation of young people wanted something different from what their parents had liked. The founding fathers of Hollywood, the old Jewish moguls, were dying in the late 1950s and those who survived could not understand why young people didn't go to the movies the way their parents did. The new, the young, the hip, the dispossessed, no longer waited meekly for the handouts of their elders but not necessarily their betters. They knew what they wanted and they wanted it now.

The elders and betters felt that "young people" – by which they meant anyone under 30 – had no respect for them. They were not necessarily wrong. Respect had to be earned, it was no longer granted as it had been in former times merely as the inevitable consequence of chronological seniority. Young professional cricketers and university students alike felt an instinctive repugnance for the bland patronising condescension of the Macmillan years. The post-war world that these young people had grown up in was starting to break down in the late 1950s. They wanted to drive bulldozers through the stifling dullness and greyness of the landscape of their inheritance.

Geoff Pullar and Peter Marner would never be mistaken for Jonathan Miller and Peter Cook but if they couldn't articulate their feelings like the talented performers of *Beyond the Fringe* or playwrights like John Osborne and Arnold Wesker, it doesn't mean they didn't experience the feelings that those blessed with the command of words could express so powerfully in their plays and sketches. The draconian sentences and martinet behaviour displayed towards the Lancashire players by a remote, insensitive and ossified Lancashire committee, merely played out at Old Trafford one manifestation of this social revolution. The committee seemed (and was) composed of old men with outdated ideas (if any ideas indeed existed beyond the maintenance of the *status quo*). Their idea of duty was to keep the lower orders, by which they meant the men who marched onto the pitch trying their hardest to score runs and take wickets for the Lancashire cause, in the place they had occupied since the game of cricket had been developed in the eighteenth century.

When we look at the workings of the committee that ran Lancashire County Cricket Club, at the time when Bob Barber was its captain, it is important to see those men in the context of the times in which they lived. They were different from the administrators at Lord's in that they were mostly self-made businessmen with a provincial view of the country, palpably unable to appreciate the changing nature of English society. They seem antediluvian in retrospect and their behaviour rude, peremptory and inexcusable. It probably was that way at the time but the era of deference did not die overnight. When Colonel Green told the new captain that it would be best if he stayed in a different hotel, the 24-year-old man did not think to argue or, if he did, he quickly suppressed the urge. Besides, he had already been confronted with a different manifestation of the same social problem at work.

At Dorman Smith, I was the first management trainee and they simply did not know if I should eat in the executive dining room or the works canteen. They didn't want me to go in the canteen because I was management, but they were not at all comfortable having me in their executive dining room. I ended up going to the pub down the road and having a sandwich. It was strictly segregated from years gone by and the war and officers and other ranks.

This was the England of *I'm All Right, Jack,* with the deep division in British industry personified by the battle between the caddish management representative played by Terry-Thomas and the inflexible Soviet-loving shop steward played by Peter Sellers. The victim caught between the two, played by Ian Carmichael, must have evinced a wince of recognition from Bob Barber.

As a player, Bob had not previously had much interaction with the committee, though he had noticed that Cyril Washbrook would sometimes leave the field around 3pm, when the team for the next match had to be selected. Until he himself became the captain who had to negotiate with the committee for the players he wanted under his command, he had not given it too much thought. When he was suddenly confronted with the reality of county cricket captaincy in Lancashire, it came as a rude shock.

Bob has always admitted that the professionals in the Lancashire side would have preferred Geoff Edrich to assume the burdens of office.

I think looking back, the professional players would have preferred Geoffrey Edrich as captain to take over from Washy and no doubt Geoffrey would have been a better captain than I was, but they had wanted to get rid of him for some time and I think Washy had a knife into Geoffrey. Geoffrey's attitude under Washy was "I haven't come back from three and a half traumatic years in a Japanese prisoner of war camp to be told that I have to be here at a certain time and that I can't have more than two pints of beer after a match."

If not Edrich, then certainly Alan Wharton would probably have done a good job. Ken Grieves too, had ten years of experience and to all the professionals, any one of those men would have been acceptable. However, as Bob points out, they weren't asked. Edrich had been sacked at the end of the 1959 season and was only four years younger than Washbrook. Alan Wharton proved a loyal Senior Professional but he was regarded by Washbrook, and probably the committee, as a barrack room lawyer and, what was worse, a Socialist to boot, so if the committee were to have its way, Barber rather than Wharton was the obvious choice. Ken Grieves would have to wait until 1963 before he got his turn and that appointment was to end with another of Lancashire's public sackings. There was also a less likely possibility that the committee would appoint Dick Bowman, which Bob recognised. He also knew that, thinking along the lines that eventually produced Joe Blackledge, the long-serving Cheshire captain, Freddie Millett, was also a possible alternative. However, Barber was young, talented and in the eyes of the committee "controllable". He was the preferred option.

His captaincy, however, was nearly derailed before the very first match. Just before the cricket season started, the authorities realised that the fit young man, who had escaped the clutches of National Service in 1954 because he was going up to Cambridge to read Medicine, was now available for selection again. The Royal Welsh had spotted him and probably fancied the prospect of winning every cricket and athletic trophy in the army for the next two years.

I had a medical for the Army in Liverpool. I was passed A1 but my memory tells me that I had two medicals just before they ended national service altogether. I had another medical in Wrexham, because they were talking about taking me into the Royal Welsh. I did the intelligence test they set, but quite frankly a reasonably able chimpanzee could have passed that test. The major behind the big desk seemed impressed and asked me what I wanted to do. It was April 1960 and I was due to start captaining Lancashire and I knew that it [National Service] was finishing in a few months so I said that on the whole I'd prefer not to get involved. He looked at me askance but in the end I was never called up. Maybe he was very kind to me. Noddy Pullar didn't go in either. I think he had flat feet – like Colin Cowdrey.

Bob Barber had two seasons in charge of Lancashire. 1960 was to be the best season the club had enjoyed since 1934. 1961, with fundamentally the same side, was to be a very different story. However, hopes were realistically high at the start of the 1960 season if only because 1959 had been such a good year. Although Lancashire had finished fifth, a mere three more points would have seen them beat Gloucestershire into second place behind Yorkshire. Surrey's stranglehold on the championship had been broken and with the disappearance or decline of many of the players who had made them arguably the greatest ever county cricket side, Lancashire fancied their chances. Man for man they thought themselves, with some justification, the equal of Yorkshire. Bob Barber, handicapped as he was off the field by an unhelpful committee, had a highly talented squad of players at his disposal. He thought he could be the first captain since Peter Eckersley in 1934 to bring Lancashire the championship pennant. He would have been astonished to learn that it would actually take more than half a century before that happy day arrived.

Sitting down to examine the squad at his disposal before the 1960 season started, the new captain decided to apply to the science of producing a successful cricket team, the principles he had been learning in his business career. He soon realised that

There was no way that I was going to be able to run a side professionally. I use "professionally" as "thorough". I was going to be the man who defines the object and does everything within the legal and moral code to achieve that end. Why are German football sides so good? Look at Bayern Munich and the German national team. I feel that way about cricket. I made notes on all the players before the start of the 1960 season. I've still got the paper. I gave everyone marks for batting, bowling, fielding and for attitudes towards the team.

1 Geoff Pullar 27 points
2 Alan Wharton 37
3 Me
4 Ken Grieves 36
5 Jackie Bond 30
6 Peter Marner 24
7 Geoff Clayton 22
8 Tommy Greenhough 29
9 Brian Statham 35
10 Roy Tatt 36
11 Ken Higgs 25

The score he awarded Ken Higgs surprised him in 2014.

Probably a bit ponderous in the field and no bat. I wanted us to be professional like this. Maybe I was a year or two or ahead of others but it eventually changed.

He even had a 1960 version of today's mission statement.

a) Play and win 32 matches
b) Public entertainers
c) Remember objective from first ball

d) Explore every avenue to win before saving game
e) You can all come to me – worries and queries

It's a remarkable document and a revealing testament to the methodology the new captain would use in an attempt to inspire his side. It was predictably somewhat cerebral for the dressing room on which he had to impose such views, but then Bob Barber was probably thirty years ahead of his time rather than a year or two.

Jack Bond, who was to become one of the county's finest ever captains, admired the way Bob went about his captaincy.

Bob was a very approachable captain. You could always sit down and talk to him. Apart from admiring his obviously undoubted talent, he was a very knowledgeable cricketer.....He was very fit and conscientious about his fitness. He set a fine example to younger players the way that he conducted himself. At the end of the day you were representing Lancashire and the red rose and I think that meant a lot to Bob. They weren't playing for themselves or for Bob, they had to take a pride in playing for the county of their birth.

During the winter, Geoff Pullar had continued his Test career with a successful tour of the West Indies, opening with Colin Cowdrey in a batting line up that included only one other professional batsman – Ken Barrington. May, Cowdrey, Subba Row and M.J.K. Smith took the other places – on merit. Tommy Greenhough had been displaced from the Test side by the off spinners David Allen and Ray Illingworth, despite the fact that the Yorkshireman had taken just four wickets at a cost of 95 runs each. Bob believed that his job as the county captain of Pullar and Greenhough was to give them the best possible chance of furthering their international careers. He dropped himself down to number three to enable Pullar to open for Lancashire as well as England, despite his personal preference for opening and the knowledge that he was breaking up the successful partnership with Alan Wharton. Similarly, he always offered Greenhough first choice of ends, and bowled himself only in what he considered was the best interests of the team. He was rewarded when Greenhough forced his way back into the England side for the final Test against South Africa at The Oval.

The season began perfectly. Instead of the usual journey south to play the universities, Lancashire began with a match against Hampshire at the County Ground in Southampton. Hampshire were an improving side under the adventurous Colin Ingleby-Mackenzie and were more widely talented than the usual concentration on the performances of Roy Marshall and Derek Shackleton would suggest. In 1961, they were to win the championship for the first time in their history but, in the first match of the 1960 season, they were trounced by a rampant Lancashire who won by 171 runs. After a low scoring first innings in which Lancashire gained first innings points, and despite an eight wicket haul by the off spinner Mervyn Burden, a fine 92 by Wharton in the second innings set Hampshire a daunting 320 to win. Tattersall with four wickets and Barber with three spun Lancashire to a convincing victory.

Unfortunately, the next match on this opening southern tour ended in defeat by an innings at Hesketh Park in Dartford as Fred Ridgway took twelve cheap wickets and Dave Halfyard eight on a pitch which made batting extremely difficult. The scale of the defeat caused Cyril Washbrook to criticise from the safety of his sports shop on Deansgate, with a bitterness that was unjustified considering it was only the second match of the season and played on a sub-standard pitch.

Nevertheless, if the Lancashire committee wanted an excuse to interfere, this match gave it to them. Bob had been aware that his predecessor had talked to the committee about selection but had no idea of the reality that awaited him until he walked into the committee room in his first month as captain.

I went into the room and there were at least thirty of them around that long table with the chairman at one end and Stan Worthington, the coach, at the other. I was asked to sit by Stan. Over the years as an amateur, I was used to having lunch with committee members but it never occurred to me to challenge the system. You got irritated with Albert Rhodes, who used to spit his gin and tonic down your ear if you were sitting next to him. They'd been on the g&ts since play began at 11.30 and they'd had plenty of wine at lunch and the brandy and port after lunch, so when you went into one of these meetings, a number of them were very well oiled and it was a shock to me. Seven or eight players would be instantly agreed, but the other four seemed to merit a discussion. Once, they started discussing Roy Collins. They began at the far end and they came round to me and I said that Roy had done everything that had been asked of him. He bowled tight if we needed to keep the runs down, he'd come in and crack thirty quick runs if we were looking to declare. Albert Rhodes started talking about how he had once scored 200 on a Saturday afternoon for Accrington and he started having a go at Roy. The chairman said, "Is there anything else you want to say, Barber?" – it was always "Barber" – even as an amateur you were always called by your surname. On that occasion I defended Roy vigorously and said "With all the knowledge round this table why did you ever sign Roy to begin with?" It went down like a big lead balloon. Any member of the committee could sit in on a selection committee meeting and I frequently had thirty of them waiting for me.

Fortunately, that defeat by Kent was the only one of the season until Somerset beat Lancashire at Taunton in a nail biter at the end of June. The unbeaten run, including another convincing triumph in the Roses match at Headingley, gave Bob considerable leeway in his dealings with the committee that was eventually to stitch him up like a kipper – not to mention Kipper who was the captain of England when Bob made his Test debut against South Africa at Trent Bridge in the first Test of the summer against South Africa.

At the end of May, Bob had been selected to play for MCC against the tourists in the annual match at Lord's, which acted as a useful guide for the England selectors. The MCC side was usually composed in equal measure of Test players and potential Test debutants and the 1960 selection followed this pattern. The side was captained by Cowdrey, because May had not recovered from the illness that had beset him in the West Indies during the previous winter. The other opener this time was the young Surrey batsman John Edrich, and he was joined by Peter Walker of Glamorgan and Doug Padgett of Yorkshire, whilst Lancashire provided Ken Higgs as well as Bob Barber. It was a weather-affected low scoring game, which ended in a draw but, on a pitch which helped seam and swing, Bob bowled nineteen overs in the South African first innings, taking 1 for 24 and in the second he took 3 for 33 in fifteen overs. Denis Compton, writing in the *Sunday Express*, thought Bob Barber was England's best leg spinner since Doug Wright and told the selectors in no uncertain terms that he had to be picked to play in the first Test match.

Jim Parks remembered vividly his first experience of keeping wicket to Bob Barber's wrist spin in this match.

I'd never kept to Bob before that MCC match against South Africa, not even in the nets and he bowled a magnificent googly. The first one he bowled, I was outside the off stump and it scooted away down the leg side for four byes. I thought I had better start learning how to read him from the hand. He was a big turner of the ball and he made it bounce because he was tall. Particularly in Australia.

If circumstances had been slightly different, Parks might not have been chosen for that match. Instead, his place could well have gone to the Lancashire wicket keeper Geoff Clayton, who had emerged with dazzling brilliance in 1959 to make the role of Lancashire wicket keeper his own and put an end to the competition between Jack Jordan and Alan Wilson. It was the time of Godfrey Evans's displacement from the Test team and Clayton's name was spoken of as a possible replacement, for all the fact that Keith Andrew was the best keeper in the country. Andrew was, unfortunately, no sort of batsman. Jim Parks had just started keeping wicket to add to his undoubted talents as a batsman and had forced his way into the final Test on the 1959-60 tour of the West Indies, so technically the Sussex keeper was the man in possession. For Geoff Clayton, the chance to impress the selectors at Lord's for the MCC against the Champion County at the start of the 1960 season could have been a life-changing opportunity.

Bob remembers clearly why it never happened.

Geoffrey Clayton was a sad, sad case. Before he went off to do his National Service, Geoffrey Clayton was a fine cricketer and a very nice young lad but he went from being a very nice young boy into a fellow who just wanted to keep on tipping drink down himself. It was so sad because he was such a talented young cricketer. I can remember him doing his national service near Chester, so we invited him to our home, but by the time he'd been in the services for two years and then got under the influence of the fellows in the Lancs dressing room, he had totally changed. It was such a shame. He could have and should have played for England.

In 1960, he and I got picked for the MCC before the first Test. I walked into the ground through the Grace Gates behind the pavilion on the first morning and I hear a "Psst! Bob!" It's Billy Griffith and he says, "What's all this about Geoff Clayton?" I said "What are you talking about?" He said, "What's happened?" I said I'd been at home in Chester for the last three days and hadn't seen anyone yet. Apparently, Geoffrey Clayton had been at Belle Vue dog track, as was his habit at this stage, been out dancing, taken a fancy to somebody's wife or girlfriend, got duffed up and his eye was closed. He came to the ground and we had a one-eyed wicket keeper. That was the end of his England career. If it hadn't been for that incident I am sure he would have gone on the A tour to New Zealand. John Murray came on the tour and Jim Parks but Jim had hardly started keeping then. The press was sure Geoffrey was going and I think it is so sad he got into the company he did. Shame.

Even with one eye, Clayton was sharp enough to take two catches off the bowling of Brian Langford and one each off Ken Higgs, Alan Moss and Bob Barber. Nevertheless, when the names were announced for the MCC v South Africa match a month later, Barber was one of them but Clayton had been replaced by Parks. Sure enough, when the twelve names for the first Test match at Edgbaston were announced, Geoff Clayton was not among them but Bob Barber was, David Allen being unavailable owing to a sore spinning finger. On the morning of Thursday 9th June 1960, Bob was awarded his England cap. It was six years since he had made his Lancashire debut as a gawky, immature 18-year-old. He had arrived.

The press had an influence on selections in those days and in Manchester, we had a significant press section. I had played for the MCC against the tourists and against the champion county so I knew I was in their minds. I heard on the radio with everyone else on that Sunday morning that I was in the 12 for the first Test at Edgbaston. The day before the match, I was told by Kipper that I was playing, to save me being nervous, though it wasn't announced to the press.

It is a mistake to assume that because Barrington and Barber had similar attributes as all-rounders, the former was left out of the final eleven in favour of the latter. It is certainly true that the distraught Barrington took the decision extremely badly, and it seems as though he returned to Surrey determined to give the selectors the runs they craved even at the expense of his own stylish performances. Bob sets the record straight quickly. Barrington was not left out on the morning of the Test match because of him but because the selectors thought the pitch would be more conducive to the all-rounder Walker's swing and seam. Walker also bowled orthodox slow left arm, so the selectors clearly thought he had more to offer on that Edgbaston pitch than Barrington. On the other hand, fortune did not favour Walker in the match. He induced a thick under edge from "Pom Pom" Fellows-Smith which Jim Parks caught at the wicket, close to the bat. The umpire inexplicably gave it not out and Fellows-Smith, in no mood to welcome the debutant with his wicket, did not walk. It would have been the Glamorgan all-rounder's first and only Test wicket.

Bob, understandably, is concerned that he should not be somehow seen as responsible for Barrington's change of technique.

A few years ago I was shown a first day scorecard of that match and Peter Walker's name was down at the bottom – effectively as twelfth man. I remember Kipper coming back into the dressing room after looking at the pitch with the chairman of selectors, Gubby Allen. He then spoke to Peter Walker and then to Kenny and my understanding has always been that, because Peter Walker bowled seam as well as spin, he got the last position instead of Kenny. Ray Illingworth and I were there as spinners and I'd bowled reasonably well for the MCC against South Africa and I knew that one or two of those fellows couldn't play leg spin.

Barrington's metamorphosis from a stroke-maker to a run-accumulator did not begin that morning at Edgbaston.

I know what Kenny said to me late at night once on the tour of India when I asked him why he didn't play his shots. He was a wonderful stroke maker. He told me that in his first full year of playing for Surrey he started out in the second XI, got picked for the first team and then for England and then got dropped because they said he played rash shots, so he went back to Surrey and he was left out of the first eleven before the end of the season. [Barrington's experiences in 1953, 1954 and 1955 have all been rather conflated in this account]. "I decided that winter that it was never going to happen to me again and if they wanted runs I'd give them runs." That's why he ground away.

Dropping Barrington for that match was certainly one of those decisions made by selectors that causes players and spectators alike to question their competence. Admittedly, he had recently suffered three ducks in a row, but he had been picked the previous Sunday and was almost top of the first class averages at the time, so telling him to return to Surrey and regain his form understandably devastated him. Barrington was a highly sensitive man, by common consent a worrier of such proportions that it might well have contributed to his heart attack and early death on the England tour of the West Indies in 1981. It is no wonder that Bob wants to set the record straight that Barrington was not dropped in favour of him; because they both batted and bowled leg spin, it is easy to understand how the misconception might have arisen.

Lancashire had long regarded Barber as a talented batsman who could bowl a bit but since they already had Tattersall, Hilton, Greenhough and Dyson the need for his wrist spin was limited. It was therefore encouraging to know that the England selectors rated his bowling highly enough to pick him for it, but it came at a price. When Colin Cowdrey and Gubby Allen finalised the batting order R.W. Barber was down to bat at number eight. He was not pleased then and he is even less pleased today at the memory of the humiliation.

I batted at 8! The biggest insult of my life was being asked to go in after Ray Illingworth!

As it transpired, Bob's early England career was abruptly terminated after that one match. South Africa were not the force in 1960 that they had been in England in 1955, nor the force they were to become a few years later, when they found themselves boasting the talents of Graeme Pollock, Barry Richards and Colin Bland. On the other hand, although deprived of his new ball partner Peter Heine, Neil Adcock had returned to play against England and his pace and hostility proved too much for Bob on his debut. Batting like a number eight, he was beaten for pace, edged a lucky four and was trapped leg before, having made only five. The second innings was less productive; he was caught at slip by Roy McLean off Hugh Tayfield for four. He bowled six overs for 26 in the South African first innings and took his first wicket in the second innings when he had Sid O'Linn lbw.

Bob was not exactly made to feel welcome by the behaviour of his captain, who certainly didn't demonstrate much of a belief in his ability. The slightly strained relationship between them was to have serious consequences later in the season.

> I'd bowled well for the MCC against the South Africans in the second innings but when Kipper brings me on and I walk up to the wicket from the boundary, by the time I've taken my cap off, Kipper's put six fielders on the edge of the boundary. I said, "You must think I'm an awful bowler." He said, "Stop moaning and get on with it." Every shot they could then block for a single. I should have been used as an attacking bowler and I knew that having bowled at them at Lord's previously. And they knew it too. Jackie McGlew said to me afterwards that they could never work out why I wasn't used more. "We considered you to be far more difficult to face than Richie Benaud ever was". If Cowdrey wanted to close it up, he had Peter Walker and Ray Illingworth and, if he wanted to bowl fast, he always had Fred and Brian. What he did to me was just foolish. It was the negativity that bothered me.

Still, England won the match by the comfortable margin of 100 runs and he retained his place when the twelve players were announced for the second Test. He was looking forward to the game with some relish because he had bowled well on his previous appearance that year at Lord's, which he believed favoured spin and he knew the South African batsmen couldn't deal with the sharply turning ball and didn't read his googly from the hand. Unfortunately, his view of the pitch was not shared by the selectors who chose Alan Moss on his own ground and left the spinning entirely to Illingworth, who bowled exactly one over in the whole match.

> I was surprised to be dropped for the second Test because why did they take me down to Lords in the first place if they weren't going to play me on the wicket that best suited leg spin? I could spin it quicker and make it bounce more than an off spinner there.

Bob tried to see the benefit in being left out of a Test match in London during Wimbledon fortnight. He made it clear that he and his girl friend Anne Greenhalgh, an excellent player, would be very happy to spend a couple of days watching the tennis in SW19. It did not go down well with the England hierarchy.

The tradition was that a ground staff lad would do twelfth man duties until they got another pro in from somewhere, a good fieldsman like Mickey Bear from Essex. However, Kipper and or Gubby had overheard my light hearted remark about Wimbledon and I was made to stay and do twelfth man duties. I might be the only amateur who did that.

He was not asked to play for England for the rest of that series.

The Lord's Test of 1960, of course, of which Bob had a closer view than he might have wished at one point, became notorious for the prosecution of the South African opening bowler, Geoff Griffin, by the English umpire, Syd Buller, who called him for throwing. The recent Ashes tour of Australia had been disfigured by the throwing controversy surrounding Ian Meckiff, whose lethal left arm fast bowling had destroyed England's batting as surely as Mitchell Johnson's was to do in 2013. The difference was that Meckiff threw and Johnson didn't. There was a concerted attempt by the authorities to deal with the problem of throwing and Griffin was their first victim in a game that veered wildly from tragedy to farce.

Everybody knew that Geoff Griffin was a chucker. They knew before the game. It was expected by us that, if Syd Buller was standing at square leg and Geoff Griffin was bowling, he would no-ball him – which he did. The next day after the end of the Lord's Test match, there was a request from the South Africans to MCC that Syd should not stand again. They were entitled to make that request. The Test panel of umpires in those days was selected by the county captains and they needed a quorum. There were two county captains in London on that day – Donald Carr and myself. We got called in through [MCC Secretary] Ronnie Aird's back gate to avoid the press. Jackie made the formal request and we had no choice but to accept it and then decide who was to take over. Syd had caused an upset with the South Africans, so Jackie was representing the views of his team and management.

As county captain, Bob now had a say in the appointment of umpires to stand in Test matches.

Each April the county captains would be called to a meeting at Lord's to discuss the umpires and there would be a list with all the marks of the captains – like Cyril marking down Eddie Phillipson for giving him out. [It wasn't personal. Phillipson was known on the circuit as "Wyatt Earp" because of the speed with which his index finger went up for an lbw shout. Jim Stewart said that, "Tommy Cartwright would bowl uphill into a gale if Eddie Phillipson was standing at his end" but, as we now know, umpires in the pre-DRS era were far too cautious in their decision-making. Phillipson certainly stood in marked contrast to his contemporaries.]

Syd was always on the top. Frank Lee would be up there too. Once, Robin Marlar said, "I think Frank Lee might be deaf in his right ear. Last season I carried out an experiment. I went round the wicket and appealed quietly and he didn't seem to notice, so I won't disagree with the decision to appoint him to stand in the series provided he wears a hearing aid". Eventually he was told to shut up.

Bob returned to Old Trafford, relatively sanguine about what had happened at Lord's. *In my arrogance I assumed I would play again but I was pleased they picked Tommy Greenhough for the last Test.* Events at Lancashire, however, kept him fully occupied.

The side had started to win again and the habit once acquired seemed to be hard to break. It began, ironically, when Bob was at Lord's, playing for MCC at the end of May. The match against Leicestershire at Grace Road began uncontroversially on the Saturday morning with Terry Spencer and Brian Boshier bowling Lancashire out for 136 by the middle of the afternoon session. Opening the batting for the home side, Dickie Bird retired hurt on 1 but none of his colleagues managed to reach double figures, as Leicestershire were dismissed for 37 in just nineteen overs, Brian Statham taking 7-17 and Colin Hilton, playing in place of Ken Higgs, who was with Bob at Lord's, the other two. Before the close of play on that first day, Lancashire had reached 90 for 5 in their second innings. Twenty four wickets had fallen in the day and with Lancashire already 200 ahead, the result of the match was a foregone conclusion.

Apart from the occasional benefit match, Sundays during away matches were often free days for cricketers and Saturday night was traditionally "party night". With the match at Grace Road likely to finish in Lancashire's favour on the Monday (it did; they won by 122 runs with Statham taking a further seven wickets in the second innings) Saturday night was clearly promising to be a special party night. Once the players returned to the hotel, things soon began to get out of hand.

They persuaded the hotel porter to let them have a crate of beer in someone's room and around 2 am in the corridors of the Grand Hotel in Leicester, Colin Hilton appeared, yelling, "Fire!!" I was told that some frightened old lady came running into the corridor, asking in panic where was the fire, to be told by Colin "It's all right, love, you can go back to your room now. I've pissed on it and put it out."

The committee's hankering for the days when the Senior Professional exercised severe discipline seemed even then to be wishful thinking, coated in rose-tinted nostalgia. Alan Wharton, the Senior Professional, who was captaining the side in Bob's absence at Lord's, escaped the formal notice of the committee's displeasure, but it was another indication to the new young captain that he was facing potential disruption every time a pint of beer was filled.

Jack Bond, the abstemious Methodist and good friend to the new captain, remembers that Leicester was not the only occasion on which things got out of hand.

As long as Bob was around there was some sanity but when they made him stay in a separate hotel, it meant the senior pros could let their hair down and run riot. We got thrown out of one flipping hotel in Northampton on the first night and late on in the evening we had to go looking for somewhere else to stay and we ended up at The Angel Hotel, half way down the main street. The press were only there to report on the cricket in those days, so this sort of stuff never got reported.

The only thing that would enable Bob to keep the reins in his hands was if the team were winning. As it has previously been noted "team spirit" is almost exclusively to be found in the dressing room of a team that is winning.

Fortunately for Bob, in June and July 1960, that is exactly what his Lancashire team did. Comfortable wins against Warwickshire and Worcestershire were followed by another Whitsuntide Roses triumph – this time, one in front of the outraged Yorkshire crowd at Leeds, who hadn't seen anything as humiliating since 1924, when Dick Tyldesley and Cecil Parkin had bowled out the champions for 33 after they had been set 58 to win in the last innings. After years of relying on Brian Statham, it was impressive that Lancashire had won the match on a dusty Headingley pitch with spin as the most potent form of their attack. Greenhough took eight of the wickets to fall, Dyson four and Barber three but in a match when the second highest score was Ken Taylor's 38, what gave Lancashire control of the game was Geoff Pullar's outstanding 121.

On the Saturday, a stunned Yorkshire crowd watched in almost complete silence as Barber and Greenhough mesmerised their batsmen to such an extent that they were all out ten minutes after lunch for under a hundred. The match finished at half past four on the second afternoon. Not for 27 years had a Roses match concluded so swiftly.

After victory in the Roses match on foreign soil, Lancashire stood proudly on top of the county championship table. Even the Lancashire committee had to concede that the new captain must be doing something right. After a decade in which Lancashire had threatened but failed to turn from a good side with excellent players into a ruthless championship-winning side like Surrey or Yorkshire, it appeared that under this mild-mannered but fiercely determined, cerebral but passionate, professionally-minded amateur recently graduated from Cambridge University, the Red Rose county was finally fulfilling its potential.

Even though he failed to regain his Test place, despite being added to the squad for the third Test, the season was a good one personally for the Lancashire captain. At Queens Park Chesterfield, Bob produced his best analysis so far when he took 7-35 as Derbyshire collapsed to 85 all out in a futile attempt to chase Lancashire's target of over 300. In the next match Middlesex were set 280 and had wilted to 45-5, before a sixth wicket century partnership between Don Bennett and Ray White enabled them to escape with a draw.

Lancashire were on a roll and Bob seemed to be enjoying himself, despite the sniping from the sidelines, which rarely abated. Hampshire were walloped at Aigburth and a hard fought win was achieved against Sussex at Hastings so that, despite two surprising home defeats in successive games against Derbyshire and Glamorgan, Lancashire's eyes were firmly on the prize when Yorkshire, who were second in the table and, realistically, the only county who could deprive them of the longed for championship pennant, returned to Old Trafford for the August Bank Holiday Roses match.

It is possible to see in the declining attendances throughout the 1950s overwhelming evidence that county cricket was in terminal decline. Crowds which had peaked in the glorious Compton and Edrich summer of 1947 at 2.3 million had dwindled by 1960 to less than one million. It is therefore remarkable to record that the three days of the Roses match in August 1960 attracted 74,000 spectators, the largest such attendance since the 1926 record - a fitting tribute to the joint beneficiaries, the long serving spinners, Malcolm Hilton and Roy Tattersall, whom the parsimonious Lancashire committee had slighted by refusing them richly deserved individual benefit seasons. There were no celebrity pro-am golf tournaments and gala dinners to help the beneficiaries in those days and the professionals were almost totally reliant on the gate receipts from the big match for their future livelihood.

That 1960 Roses match at Old Trafford was the most exciting county match I have ever seen. Statistically, you can argue that it was no more exciting than any other game in which victory is achieved off the last ball. I believe, however, that limited overs finishes, though unquestionably exciting, are somehow less worthy than those which culminate at the end of a three, four or five day two innings affair because the artificial format of the one day game facilitates, indeed positively encourages such a conclusion.

That 1960 Yorkshire match assumes a significance in my mind greater perhaps than its real importance in the destination of the Championship in that season, because it was one of very few county matches I have ever attended in which I felt linked to the tradition of Lancashire cricket as Neville Cardus had written about it. It instilled in me a belief, which I still hold, that the county cricket championship matters, whether or not there is 20 over, 40 over or 50 over cricket to be consumed alongside it.

It can be argued that Roses matches, perhaps up to the late 1960s when Lancashire developed into a very good one day side under Jack Bond, were the last county matches to preserve that tradition. Thereafter the crowds came out to watch county matches only for the one day game. In 2014 Lancashire's biggest attendance for the season was the T20 match against Yorkshire in which, contrary to popular expectation, Andrew Flintoff did not make his long anticipated comeback. The return match, sadly abandoned without a ball being bowled, was also sold out.

When Yorkshire came to Old Trafford over the 1960 August Bank Holiday weekend, Vic Wilson's side arrived grimly determined to extract revenge for the defeat at Headingley in May. They didn't make much of a fist of it on the Saturday. Barber and Wharton in yet another of their splendid partnerships carried Lancashire past the Yorkshire first innings score with only one wicket down but Trueman and Ryan restricted the eventual lead to 72. When Statham and Higgs removed half the Yorkshire side for 36 it seemed likely we would be celebrating a rare innings victory. Led by Philip Sharpe, Yorkshire recovered to reach a total of 149 but that still left Lancashire to score a mere 78 in over two hours after lunch on the Tuesday afternoon. In view of the manner in which Lancashire had calmly collected eleven wins in the season so far, this did not appear to be too onerous a task.

However, Lancashire wickets seemed to fall more regularly than runs were scored and after an hour and a half, Lancashire were marooned on 43 for six as Trueman and Ryan worked their way steadily through the worryingly fragile Lancashire batting.. As so often in the past, Ken Grieves marshalled the desperate Lancashire rearguard action and the score crept agonisingly upwards towards the target. At 60 for 6, Grieves miscued Trueman straight to Vic Wilson at deep mid off. Wilson was one of the safest catchers in England. Old Trafford groaned as the ball dropped into those massive hands of his - and out again to a triumphant roar. Trueman's grand tragic gesture of despair only increased the crowd's happiness. However, with only two overs left, Lancashire still needed 18 - laughable in the context of today's limited overs cricket, but a veritable mountain on that hot August day. Geoff Clayton fluked two edgy fours off Ryan but the cries of ecstasy were stilled as Grieves nicked one to Jimmy Binks and was caught. At the start of the final over by Trueman, six runs were needed, there were three wickets left and the Lancashire tail was notoriously long.

Clayton was left with the dilemma of either protecting the tail enders or taking every run on offer. Off the first ball, he pushed a single and opted to take it. Five runs were now needed off five balls. Off the second, Trueman uprooted Tommy Greenhough's leg stump. What an idiot Clayton was to have taken that single, screamed twelve thousand Lancastrians. Jack Dyson, batting unaccountably below Greenhough and Brian Statham, came in to join Clayton and scrambled two improbable leg byes off his first ball. Three to win, three balls to go, two wickets left.

Dyson just dug Trueman's fourth ball out of the blockhole, but when he looked up he found his partner galloping towards him screaming the same words as everybody else in the crowd. Dyson just made his ground at the bowler's end in a flurry of bodies, bats and broken stumps. Clayton drove a single off the penultimate ball which meant that Lancashire couldn't lose. That wasn't much comfort to the crowd, or the rest of the helpless Lancashire players in the dressing room, since, for all but the last two hours, Lancashire had been winning the match since 11.30 am on Saturday morning. A draw now would be desperately disappointing.

The fielders closed in. Trueman stamped back to his mark. Dyson looked round the field. It was hard to see where that run was going to come from. There seemed to be no gaps anywhere. Contracts with God were being rapidly made all round the ground, as Trueman steamed in for the last ball. Gathering pace, he launched himself at the popping crease, the ball aimed unerringly for another middle stump yorker. At the last moment, it started swinging to leg, Dyson got a thick inside edge and the ball shot away past backward short leg and over the boundary at deep fine leg. The crowd erupted and spilled onto the pitch. The Whitsuntide match had been greeted with a shocked, disbelieving silence. This last minute, thrilling victory was won amidst the cheering ranks of Tuscany. It was Lancashire's first double over Yorkshire since 1893.

It was to be Bob Barber's supreme moment as the captain of Lancashire CCC and it came a month before it should have done. Immediately after Dyson's fortunate thick inside edge, the Lancashire players were on the road to Bristol where they played Gloucestershire the following morning on a wicket that clearly favoured the seamers. Statham and Higgs took eighteen wickets between them to win a nervy, low-scoring game by 23 runs. They looked at the remaining fixtures for August. There were four away matches at Southend, Cardiff, Northampton and Lord's and four at home, two at Old Trafford, one at Southport and the two final games of the season including the second game against the tourists would be played at the end of August in Blackpool, before the families came home from the boarding houses and small hotels and prepared for school and the onset of autumn. Would Lancashire be the champions by then they all wondered?

By this time of the season, fatigue would be a major problem, aggravated as ever in the pre-motorway days (the first 60 miles section of the M1 had just opened stretching from south of Coventry to Watford) by the relentless schedule of three day cricket. Back from Bristol they came on the Friday night and prepared to face Kent on Saturday morning. Bob was out for a duck in the first over caught by Roger Prideaux off Dave Halfyard. Aided by fifties from Grieves and Marner, Lancashire struggled to 249 but got rid of Peter Richardson just before the close. On the Monday, Barber, Greenhough and Higgs took wickets at regular intervals to give the home side a first innings lead of 70, which they increased to more than 250 when Wharton and Pullar came off the field at the end of the day, with the Lancashire score on an imposing 187 for no wicket.

Barber declared the Lancashire innings closed after an hour of the final day, leaving Kent to score 330 in four and a half hours to win the match. The odds clearly favoured Lancashire but Pullar's sparkling 125 not out demonstrated that there were no terrors in the Old Trafford wicket and, had Cowdrey been so inclined, he could have made an attempt to score the runs and still been in a position to draw the game if Kent had lost five or six wickets along the way. Another fair crowd had gathered to watch Lancashire gain a third consecutive victory on their way to usurping Yorkshire's crown. It promised to be a thoroughly enjoyable afternoon's cricket. It wasn't.

The captains' dressing room was between the home and away dressing rooms, so Colin Cowdrey and I were sharing this room. Before Kent went out to bat, there was a knock on the dressing room door and Arthur Phebey and Peter Richardson, the openers, were there. They asked, "What are we doing, skip?" and I heard Colin say, "We're catching the 6 o'clock train". I knew then that he had no intention of claiming the extra half-hour. I didn't bowl Brian Statham. I opened with Higgs and Dyson, just to keep Kent in the game but they weren't interested. Noddy Pullar bowled a few overs. Everyone in the side bowled except Brian and Geoff Clayton. They weren't interested and the game ended in a draw.

There was much talk at the time of the need for Brighter Cricket to offset the rapid decline in attendances throughout the 1950s. Bob had taken his responsibility to keep the crowd entertained as seriously as he took his ambition to win the championship. Cowdrey was clearly determined to frustrate the latter and didn't care if he abused the former as he did so. He would no doubt have claimed that, since Lancashire were chasing the title, it was up to them to bowl Kent out. Kent were under no obligation to go for the runs in order to provide the Lancashire bowlers with easy wickets. It's a moot point but it sits oddly with an establishment figure like Cowdrey, when the plea for brighter cricket had emanated from Lord's, where Cowdrey was such a well-respected figure.

Either way, Cowdrey's attitude destroyed what might have been an entertaining climax. In the event, Kent ended on 189 for 2 from 83 overs, some of which were bowled very economically by Noddy Pullar. Peter Richardson finished 84 not out, Cowdrey 55 not out and, to his no doubt immense satisfaction, Kent caught the six o'clock train from London Road station to Euston. It wasn't just the failure to win that particular match that derailed Lancashire's title hopes. That Kent game finished off not only the championship challenge but Bob Barber's hopes of ever captaining a Lancashire side that did so, because the fall-out from the match was considerable.

At the end of the match, I went home because I lived in Chester but Kenny Grieves, Peter Marner and probably Geoffrey Clayton went into the bar in the pavilion, where there were some pressmen. Next day, I arrived knowing nothing of this. I got off at Warwick Road station and the first thing I saw was a huge newspaper placard – GRIEVES SLAMS COWDREY or words to that effect. I turn into the gate and I run straight into John Kay, the Manchester Evening News cricket correspondent, and he points at the placard and says, "What do you think of that?" I said, "I'm not surprised; he was quite right" or something like that. By lunchtime, it was on the BBC that I had attacked Colin Cowdrey. Geoffrey Howard said to me, "You'll have to make a public apology to Colin Cowdrey". Which I did. As far as Cowdrey was concerned, it was because he was then the captain of England.

At that point, the fissure which had always existed between the Lancashire committee and the Lancashire captain opened into a breach that would never be healed. They had persuaded Bob to take the job, which more logically should have gone to Edrich, Wharton or even Grieves and then failed to defend him when they should have done. Instead, the craven behaviour of the committee made them look spineless and utterly destroyed the authority of the captain. It was hard enough for him to keep a hard-drinking, fractious dressing room in order when they were united in the belief that they could win the championship. The Lancashire committee's pusillanimous actions effectively handed the county championship to their closest rivals.

Although Barber and Greenhough still managed to bowl Lancashire to victory in the next match against a weak Leicestershire side, the heart and spirit had departed. They lost four of the last six championship matches of the season by large margins and drew the other two. When the final table was displayed Yorkshire had won by over thirty points. The fact that Lancashire were themselves nearly thirty points clear of Middlesex, who finished third, was a meaningless statistic.

More than the high table finishes of the 1950s, this 1960 season felt to spectators and players alike to be the most crushing disappointment. Something snapped in everyone. The two seasons that followed were to be Bob Barber's personal nadir, but while football in Lancashire produced champions every year from 1963 to 1968, Lancashire cricket in those years went into a spectacularly precipitous decline. In just two years, Lancashire went from their position of second from the top to second from the bottom, lower than the county had ever been in its history.

Looking at the teams that finished first and second in 1960, Bob Barber has not changed his mind in over fifty years as to their relative merits.

I believed then and I believe now that Lancashire were, man for man, a better team than Yorkshire. I was always expecting to beat Yorkshire. I would always prefer to have Ken Higgs in my team than Mel Ryan. I believe that if the committee had come closer to me and therefore enabled me to come closer to them, we could have been the team of the 1960s. We could have had that run.

It may be that, had they won the championship in 1960, the Lancashire team could be said to have overachieved as the 2011 championship winning side certainly did. The heavy drinkers would still have been drinking, the alienation from the committee would still have been festering but the surge of confidence that might have emanated from winning the title could well have been enough to keep dressing room and committee room united. As it transpired, after the fiasco of the apology to Colin Cowdrey, Lancashire and their loyal supporters were forced to undergo seven years of misery and torment. It was enough material for a new book to be added to the Bible – probably in the Old Testament between the wailings of Jeremiah and the Destruction of the Temple.

"Give me my crown/Put on jewels/I have immortal longings in me" says Cleopatra when faced with the prospect of life under Octavius after the death of Antony. Certainly, Bob Barber, twenty-five years old at the end of the 1960 season and approaching his best years as a talented cricketer, far from proceeding to his due with royal ceremony, was instead destined to stand at the top of Masada, as the Roman legions in full battle armour marched inexorably across the desert towards him.

CHAPTER SEVEN

BEFORE THE DELUGE, there were plenty of bright intervals. In the autumn of 1960, Bob was chosen by the MCC to tour New Zealand. The party, under the command of Dennis Silk, was composed almost entirely of Test hopefuls, with the addition of Willie Watson who had moved from Yorkshire to Leicestershire to prolong his career. John Kay, writing in the *Manchester Evening News,* predicted with some confidence before the party was announced that it would include five Lancashire players – Barber, Pullar, Higgs, Greenhough and Clayton. They would almost certainly be joined by Brian Stott and Ken Taylor from Yorkshire and Harold Rhodes of Derbyshire. In the event, only Barber from Kay's list of predictions was on the plane that took the MCC to New Zealand.

It might have looked like an England B side, but the names suggest the selectors had been quite shrewd in their choices. David Allen and Jim Parks had both played in the final Test match in the West Indies the previous winter; from Oxford came the wicket keeper A.C. Smith and the Kent fast bowler David Sayer. David Larter, the lanky opening bowler from Northamptonshire, like Harold Rhodes of Derbyshire, was already being spoken about as the future of England's fast bowling attack, as time would inevitably take its toll on the quick bowlers who had toured Australia - Statham, Trueman, Tyson and Loader.

It was obvious that Bob was still being chosen as a leg spinner who batted a bit because, despite the fact he had opened or batted at no.3 for Lancashire for three seasons, MCC placed him in the middle or lower middle order, with the opening positions being taken by Eric Russell of Middlesex and Roger Prideaux, who had just graduated from Cambridge and was playing for Kent. In a sense their judgement was vindicated because Bob finished the tour with 45 victims, comfortably the leading wicket-taker.

John Murray, the young Middlesex wicketkeeper, got to know Bob on that tour and soon developed a respect for his bowling, if not to the same degree for his batting.

I always thought he was a no.6 batsman who never played any shots. The great tragedy was that he never wanted to bowl and he should have been a high class bowler. He spun it but he never wanted to bowl and bowlers have to want to bowl – especially slow bowlers. He was always reluctant when the captain turned to him. He didn't really want to do it. It was David Larter who came back from the tour of New Zealand as the big success. He didn't like the hard work though and he kept breaking down. Bob though did well on that tour. I could pick his googly OK because it came out of the back of the hand but he spun the ball a long way.

For Bob, it was a mostly happy party but the big bonus was the start of a lifelong friendship with Jim Stewart of Warwickshire.

I first met Bob on the tour of New Zealand in 1960. He came from a public school and Cambridge; I came from the back streets of Coventry and a local school, but we hit it off from the moment we shook hands. And we've been friends ever since.

What Bob remembers is that the first item Jim took out of his suitcase when they arrived in New Zealand was a pair of slippers.

Jim was notorious amongst the supporters of Lancashire cricket, most notably for his performance in the match at Blackpool at the end of July 1959, when Bob was on tour in Canada. In a high scoring game that was eventually drawn, Jim Stewart scored two blistering centuries, smiting, what was at the time, a world record seventeen sixes. In the second innings, Jack Dyson bowled twelve balls at Stewart who hit them for 34, conventional T20 stuff in 2015 but unheard of in 1959. Jim smiles as he remembers what happened thereafter.

Poor old Jack Dyson would be wetting himself if he had to come on and bowl at me. He just couldn't do it. I remember getting out caught behind to Statham, and Dyson couldn't wait to get to Brian to congratulate him. He was so happy I was out. I'd traumatised him. I used to say to him, "Come on, Jackie, pitch it up. It's either you or me!" He was a good cricketer but a bit gutless if I'm honest. He was a chicken in fairness. I fancied his bowling, like I fancied Brian Langford's bowling and Brian was an excellent bowler.

Jim's fearsome hitting got him into the team but at the same time it nearly cost him his place.

Gubby Allen was chairman of selectors in 1960 and Wilf Wooller, who was a fan of mine because I was Welsh, was on the panel with him. We were playing at Taunton and I got 38 maybe 50, no more than that. Wilf saw me make those runs and next day I hear that I'm in the party to tour New Zealand but he tells me there was a hell of a row because Gubby had never seen me play. He said I was just a slogger even though he'd never seen me. Wilf got up and said I was slogging them pretty well because I'd got over 2,100 runs. In other words I had no chance with Gubby, even though he'd never seen me bat. Actually, the one thing I could do was to play quick bowling because I was an opener so I wasn't just a slogger. You either got Gubby's tick or you didn't and I didn't. I got picked for the twelve to play South Africa in the last Test at The Oval in 1960. In that game Doug Padgett was ill, a sore throat or something and "Cock" [Walter] Robins said to me, "You'll be playing, Jim". Doug came to the ground and declared himself fit of course and I never really got another sniff, though I just scraped onto the New Zealand tour.

The fly in the ointment on the New Zealand tour for Bob was the captain. Bob had not really hit it off with Silk at Cambridge five years earlier and Jim Stewart remembers mistily

Bob wasn't a big fan of Dennis Silk. I had played against him at rugby a few times so I knew about him but I think Bob and Silk had a bit of a clash on tour. I forget what it was about, must have been cricket related but it was quite a falling out.

John Murray recalls, with a little more clarity, evidence of the falling out which took place in full view of the rest of the party.

We stopped on the way out in Singapore and had a game there and Bob and Dennis Silk got involved in some kind of scuffling and high jinks. It began in the pavilion, it looked like it was just a bit of fun; it was playful. There was a big glass table and the next thing I remember they were wrestling and they smashed this table. They were both strong men – Dennis was big – a rugby player - but Bob was strong and there was a streak in Bob that you wouldn't want to provoke.

Bob remembers that he was not only responsible for Dennis losing his balance just before they collapsed onto the table but that, at a later date, he threw the captain into a swimming pool as the two men engaged in a trial of strength. The future Warden of Radley College was clearly not a man to harbour grudges. Although Bob had been upset to miss his Blue in his freshman year, unjustly deprived of it he thought by Silk's prejudice, he received the first of a number of charming letters from Silk when he was selected to play in the 1956 University Match. Even if the relationship was still strained in 1960, it certainly improved over the years, such that when Bob had his spectacular seventieth birthday celebrations, it was Dennis Silk who gave one of the warmest and most appreciated speeches of the evening.

There was certainly no amateur/professional divide on this trip. Most nights, Bob and Jim Stewart played endless games of snooker against Doug Padgett and Don Wilson, with Jim playing as an honorary Lancastrian in the renewal of a new series of Roses matches. It was the days before the five star hotels and ancillary luxuries of modern day tours but the players, both amateurs and professionals, seem to have enjoyed it all immensely, despite the relatively basic conditions.

Bob had an extra task imposed on him that none of the other players were subjected to.

My agreement with Dorman Smith was that I could go on tour to New Zealand in the winter of 1960-1 if I met with all their agents over there. It turned out there were over thirty of them.

So everywhere I went, it was my education in the six o'clock swill. The licensing laws meant the pubs closed at 6.30 so men would come out of work, go straight to the pub and drink as much as they could for an hour. They would have a long bar and they'd put all these empty pint pots that would cover the surface and then the landlord would go along with a hose pipe and squirt till they were full. The beer sprayed everywhere. I had to keep going to these places looking smart, dressed in a suit and they would all say, "Come and have a drink", so I would finish up with my suit full of beer. Eventually, the government realised this wasn't a good idea and changed the laws.

Bob was a good popular tourist but still, to an extent, a man apart. What was going on in his head was rarely what was going on in the heads of the other players. Jim Stewart's recollections of Bob's behaviour in New Zealand in 1961 was eventually echoed by Mike Smith's memories of Bob as a tourist in South Africa and Australia and remind the modern reader of nothing so much as descriptions of Michael Atherton on tour with England, particularly in the early part of his career before he was beset with the cares of captaincy.

Bob loved touring and sightseeing. He loved to open the batting in his cavalier fashion, smash a quick fifty, seventy, a hundred, get out, put his shorts on and go into the stand out of the way in the sun and read a book. Before the match had even started, he'd have been up at the crack of dawn and away somewhere to see something of local interest. He loved all that. We all laughed at him for it and gave him some stick but Bob could look after himself.

Bob's behaviour in the dressing room generally not just on tour marked him out as a singular man. A.C. Smith recalls

In the dressing room during a county match, some of us would be doing the Telegraph crossword, others would be doing the Express crossword and Bob would be reading an economics textbook. Cricket for Bob was just a recreation and he was always going to run the family business. When he retired, it was the right time for him to do that and he made it into a very valuable property. He thinks through what he wants to do.

Bob makes no apology for his reading – and indeed why should he? - but he points out that it came at a price. The picture painted by Alan Smith, of all the players busily engaged on their intellectual pursuits of varying difficulty, is not one with which Bob necessarily concurs.

It took some courage to take out something in the dressing room that wasn't Titbits or start a conversation that wasn't about birds or booze.

Clearly, Bob had that courage. Nobody wants to stand out for the wrong reasons in a dressing room, where banter can slide easily into antagonism, to say nothing of phantom Twitter accounts, but Bob's talent, and perhaps also his physical presence, which so many of his colleagues have noted, helped to ensure that his reading of John Maynard Keynes rather than Desmond Hackett did not attract adverse comment.

John Murray toured with Bob not only on this New Zealand trip but with the England parties under M.J.K Smith which went to South Africa in 1964-5 and Australia the following winter. He accepts that Bob was different in some respects from most of the others but that didn't mean that he didn't mix perfectly well with the rest of the party.

The boys wouldn't mess with him. You know what a dressing room can be like, but everyone knew you didn't mess with Bob Barber. He was a good tourist though, not like a Boycott. Boycott only had one interest and that was batting and the moment he wasn't batting he went off and you never saw him again. Bob wasn't like that. He was good tourist and joined in whatever was going on.

The New Zealand cricket teams had, with few exceptions, played in the past as if in awe of the presence of cricketers from the Mother Land. In 1949, their strongest batting team had drawn all four Tests in England, which caused MCC to reconsider their decision to allocate only three days to a New Zealand Test but, as late as 1955, the fearsome English bowling attack of Tyson, Statham, Appleyard and Wardle, that had just won the Ashes in Australia, dismissed New Zealand for a humiliating 26 all out. If the MCC party of 1960-1 thought they were in for an easy ride, they were soon disabused.

The sides they played matched MCC blow for blow. Although they began brightly enough with three wins in the first four games, when they came up against a full strength New Zealand side in the first unofficial Test at Dunedin, the match ended with the tourists, chasing just over 200 to win, slumping from 121-1 to 166-7 and clinging on at the end for a face-saving draw. Barber and Allen had distinguished themselves in the second innings, taking nine wickets between them. In the second of such matches at the Basin Reserve in Wellington, New Zealand dismissed the tourists twice for less than 150 and won by the comfortable margin of 133 runs. The final match of the three in Christchurch was ruined by the weather, after New Zealand had taken a narrow first innings lead. Jim Stewart was less than impressed with the opposition's opening fast bowler, Gary Bartlett, who was genuinely quick.

When we played in the last match at Christchurch the New Zealanders were getting desperate because we'd been beating them and they got some guy to bowl at us who chucked it but he chucked it quick.

Bob too recalled the bowler but he thinks he knows why Bartlett made such an impression on Jim Stewart.

Jim's a very good judge of a cricketer and, though he might take me to pieces, he knows me. He says, "You were the bloke at the other end who stirred them up". He was referring to a time in New Zealand when they had a very quick bowler called Gary Bartlett, a chucker; Many years later, John Reid, the New Zealand captain, told Jim that he had emerged from some kind of institution to play the game. He said that I stirred this chap up and Jim got hit painfully on the elbow and had to retire. He accused me of doing the same thing to Charlie Griffith at Edgbaston.

It is true that Bartlett was recognised as an extremely pacey bowler, but he only played ten Tests for New Zealand and his career rather spluttered to a halt in a miasma of allegations as to the legality of his action. He was, however, never officially called for throwing in a Test match but, at the end of the 1950s and start of the 1960s, the cricket world was hyper-sensitive to any allegation of throwing for perfectly understandable reasons. Standing less than twenty-two yards away from a man who could throw a hard cricket ball without any of the protection that enables modern day players to hook with impunity, it was widely felt by batsmen at this time that the cricket authorities would only do something after someone had been killed. Charlie Griffith, who was to feature significantly in Bob's future career, did indeed nearly kill the Indian opener Nari Contractor the following year, when he hit him on the back of the head with a bouncer.

Perhaps the most jovial match of the New Zealand tour came towards the end at Eden Park in Auckland, where they played the Governor-General's XI, a side which contained not only the West Indies players Gerry Alexander and Cammie Smith but also Ray Lindwall and, remarkably, the Honourable Charles John Lyttleton, the 10th Viscount Cobham KC PC GCMG, the Governor-General himself, indeed, the very model of a modern Governor-General, who had been a decent player and the captain of Worcestershire from 1936 to 1939. In MCC's first innings of 227, the Viscount contented himself with bowling three overs which were treated with great respect.

When MCC had reduced the opposition to 189 for 8, in strode Lord Cobham to great applause from the 27,000 who had come to watch. The MCC captain asked both David Allen and Bob who were bowling at the time to toss the ball up to the distinguished batsman. The outraged Gloucestershire off spinner refused, so Silk threw the ball to Don Wilson. Lord Cobham was offered a ceremonial one off the mark, which he took to smiles and cheers all round, and then proceeded to trample all over protocol by smashing Don Wilson and Bob Barber to all parts of Auckland, much to the enjoyment of the crowd. A first innings lead was obtained, when the noble Lord battered Wilson back over his head for six. The next ball was a little slower and flighted a little higher; the Viscount Cobham fell for it as countless English professional batsmen had done and the ball went straight up in the air. Unfortunately, underneath the catch stood Dennis Silk, a future President of MCC and a born diplomat. Perhaps entirely coincidentally, the ball fell harmlessly to earth. After 44 runs in 25 minutes off 39 balls, Don Wilson got his wicket when the Governor-General was caught at mid off by Eric Russell. The second innings was not quite so spectacular. Lord Cobham was bowled by Barber for 13 and the Lancashire captain took 7- 89 in 29 overs, as MCC ran out winners by 25 runs. Order had been restored to the colonies.

It was an eye-opening tour, made in the days when players were used to experiencing the discomforts of travelling. When the New Zealand tour of 1960-1 is mentioned by those who took part in it, they all shudder when they talk about what happened at Buller Gorge - which bore no relation to the umpire of the same name. Bob recalled

Probably my most bizarre cricketing tour travel experience was a journey from Nelson in the north of South Island, New Zealand to Westport on the west coast. We travelled by coach. The west coast of New Zealand enjoys a notoriously heavy rainfall and we travelled in stormy weather. When we arrived at the bridge to cross over the Buller river, we found that it had been washed away by a torrential flood, so our driver continued on a road along the eastern side of the river. The road was flanked on one side by a steep mountainside and on the other by the river. In places, there was an almost sheer vertical drop into the river of up to 50 metres. In places too, rocks were falling onto the road and at one point the driver was forced to stop. There was a minor avalanche covering the road ahead of us and rocks were falling behind. At this point the drop into the raging river was some 50 metres. Then without warning, just as some of us were considering getting out of the bus, the driver started the engine and accelerated at a small gap between the side of the road and the drop into the river. We bounced dangerously over rocks but fortunately got through. We exploded at the driver who explained "I needed your ballast to save going over the edge!" Some distance after, the road levelled with the river. We were told to disembark and found a man with a rowing boat waiting to carry us two at a time across the river. The current carried each pair perhaps a hundred yards down the river to where a tractor, with a flat trailer behind, had backed into the water. Each pair had to crawl from the rowing boat on to the trailer and, lying and holding its front end, be dragged from the river. Both times we had barely survived death by drowning!

It is a shame that Kevin Pietersen and Andy Flower never shared this kind of team-bonding experience.

The New Zealand tour finished in the middle of March 1961. Bob flew straight from there to the West Indies to join a touring party organised by E.W. Swanton. His fiancée Anne would certainly have received a sense of what married life might be like with a much in demand cricketer as a husband. Swanton's party was a delightfully eclectic mixture of players ranging from Everton Weekes on home territory to Ray Lindwall, who had retired from Test cricket, but had clearly not lost his appetite for the game. Abbas Ali Baig and the Nawab of Pataudi from India were joined by Bob's old Cambridge partner Ian McLachlan from Australia. Amongst the English players, there was a nice mix of amateurs - A.C. Smith, Ossie Wheatley and the captain Colin Ingleby-Mackenzie -and professionals like Bomber Wells, Harold Rhodes and Peter Walker.

The fun Bob had experienced on the tour of New Zealand was repeated in the Caribbean, partly because of the eclectic nature of the personnel.

Bomber Wells was a bloody good cricketer, but he was treated as a joke because of his physical shape. He bowled bloody well on that tour. Nobody got a grip on Bomber Wells in the Caribbean, despite the wickets. He bowled really well. The player who found it most difficult was Ossie Wheatley. He had a long run and I remember Asgarali standing there watching Ossie marking out his run and he must have thought, "Christ, it's Wes Hall coming in"; the ball just floated at him and he stood there transfixed as it eventually arrived at the wicketkeeper. The next ball he hit straight back over Ossie's head and over the sightscreen.

Bob had a lot of time for his captain, who understood leg spinners, gave him plenty of bowling and set attacking fields for him which made him feel confident. As a consequence, the wickets soon arrived. The party played nine matches in the Caribbean in less than a month, returning to England days before the start of the 1961 cricket season. Swanton's tours always had a purpose beyond that of giving the doyen of cricket correspondents a nice holiday in the sun before ensconcing himself at Canterbury or Lord's for the summer. He wrote from Port of Spain to the *Daily Telegraph* in the middle of the tour

Education is the key note of this tour and we have both learned ourselves and perhaps conveyed a little practical instruction…From the English viewpoint the most interesting things at the moment are the form of Rhodes and Barber… [Barber] has not only bowled several dangerous spells of leg breaks but has batted with a freedom and punch which would astonish the patrons of Old Trafford.

It was Bob's bowling which won the match against a Trinidad side including Joey Carew and Deryck Murray. He took 4-50 in the first innings and a match-winning 5-44 in the second to add to his bright and breezy 51, batting at number 3. It was to be his last bowling stint for a while. The Caribbean trip was a glorious month of happy cricket in which he revelled. The report in *Wisden*, presumably written by Swanton, noted that

Individually, the tour was a great success for the Lancashire captain, R. W. Barber. He headed the batting averages in the four first class matches and also took 19 wickets with his leg breaks.

The tour, despite its brevity, must have seemed like a dream when he returned to England and a cold, wet, uninviting English spring. Almost immediately, he found he had inflamed tendons in the wrist that prevented him from bowling. It was a painful reminder that the fun and games of the two tours was over and what lay ahead was a difficult season at Lancashire.

Memories of the turbulent end to the previous season must still have been vivid, when Bob learned that Jack Dyson had been sacked for "a serious breach of discipline and an act of insolence and insubordination to the captain" which puzzled the said captain, who couldn't remember anything of the sort, despite receiving a letter from the Secretary, Geoffrey Howard, confirming it. The decision lost Lancashire some useful runs and wickets but by far the more devastating blow was the departure of Alan Wharton who, having rejected an offer to captain the second XI, possibly learning from Geoff Edrich's experience, was "allowed" to leave for Leicestershire. Nobody in those days was desperate to play at Grace Road. It was where players like Dickie Bird went because he wasn't good enough to stay in the Yorkshire first XI or players like Willie Watson went to extend their time in the game, when their own committee made it clear they were now surplus to requirements. The Lancashire committee had struck a dagger to the heart of Bob's ambitions and it was to be by no means the last of their attempts to sabotage their own team and captain.

Alan Wharton had played for Lancashire since the first match of the 1946 championship season. It was not only his runs and wickets that had been so useful to Bob and the team but his seniority and his influence with the players. He had, to Bob's knowledge, been supportive of the young amateur captain, whatever his feelings about whether he should have been offered the captaincy himself. Bob is still sensitive when the issue of Wharton's departure crops up.

During the winter of 1960-1, they got rid of Alan Wharton, our senior professional, one of our best players and a man who had been a great help to me during that first season in 1960. It was never discussed with me and I never knew about it. They got rid of him because Cyril thought he was an agitator. He was a bit left-wing but, as far I was concerned, he was a great fellow. He was a schoolmaster and not fond of bowing down to anyone. They wanted him out and it saddened me. He went off to Leicestershire and he must have thought that I knew something about it all but I didn't.

Wharton and Barber had struck up a fine opening partnership together and the loss of his chief assistant was brought home to him in the most blatant manner when the first match of the 1961 season brought Leicestershire to Old Trafford and clattering down the steps of the pavilion in the ranks of the opposition was Alan Wharton. If it was weird for the crowd and his former team mates, it was a source of agonising regret for Bob Barber.

In the popular imagination of the supporters, 1961 was a truly terrible season, the start of Lancashire's fall from grace. In the sense that the county slipped from second place to thirteenth, there is some justice in the description. However, Bob, as usual, has a rational cerebral approach to it. He asks me to compare the statistics of 1960 and 1961 in terms of matches won, lost and drawn. It's not a difficult calculation. In 1960 Lancashire won 13 matches of the 32 they played, lost eight and drew ten. There was one "no result" because the match at Cardiff, not for the first time, was devastated by the weather. The following season included another no result for similar reasons, but the rest of the 31 matches divided as nine victories, seven defeats and no fewer than 15 draws, in days when counties were awarded two points for a first innings lead and a further two if runs were scored at a rate that encouraged the much sought after Brighter Cricket. However, a defeat by one run in a hard fought battle for first innings points in a drawn game could bring a county team no points at all.

Lancashire also suffered from being a major county and certainly, after the relative success in 1960, no county was going to make life easier for Barber by looking to offer a sporting declaration.

Lancashire was not the same as Somerset or Hampshire in the sense that if Essex were playing either of those two they'd have a game where they would risk losing to get a result. That never happened when teams played Lancashire, so we had to learn to bowl sides out and we never managed to do that satisfactorily. That was what we had to do to be the side that won the championship and that was what I told the chairman of the cricket committee, Frank Sibbles.

Sadly, to little effect.

1961 saw the first Australian tour for five years and it took place immediately after the triumphal series down under, when West Indies, captained by Frank Worrell, had taken on Richie Benaud's Australians and played out the celebrated tie at Brisbane. So captivating was the cricket played by the two teams that the West Indians, on their departure, were given a ticker tape parade through the centre of Melbourne. Suddenly, there was hope that cricket could arrest the depressing trend of its dwindling audiences.

When the Australians came to Old Trafford in May, at the start of their tour, the hosts certainly played their part. **Saucy Barber Gives the Aussies Their Brighter Cricket** was the headline over Crawford White's report in the *Daily Express*.

No fewer than seven 6s rattled into the stands. The run rate rocketed along at over 60 runs an hour. Then Barber topped off the whole glorious mixture by declaring saucily on 310 for 7 by 5.30pm....And then the great-hearted Brian Statham and Tommy Greenhough supported Barber's audacity by having Australian openers, Simpson and McDonald, dismissed before the close.

Peter Marner had hit three of the sixes in a whirlwind 87, Jack Bond had struck another three and the last had been smitten by Geoff Clayton. Not everything, however, was rosy in the Old Trafford garden, as White went on to note.

I do suggest that the 388 runs hit yesterday was tremendous entertainment and the attendance of 2,228 was a disgrace to the Red Rose county.

There has been a perception that Bob Barber at Lancashire was a stodgy batsman and it was only when he left and arrived at Warwickshire that he began to hit the ball with anything approaching freedom. His innings against an Australian attack comprising Alan Davidson, Garth McKenzie, Lindsay Kline and Bobby Simpson amounted to only 31 runs but the manner in which he and Marner put on 74 in less than an hour was received rapturously by the watching press. Denys Rowbotham wrote in *The Guardian*

Barber, from his winter's activities altogether more assured, upright and behind the ball in defence and swifter in judgment and footwork in attack, provided Marner with a partner no less admirable. The two, indeed, produced such a succession of flowing drives, bludgeoned square cuts, hooks and forces, broad sweeps, neat rippling glances and discreetly placed turned shots and pushes that only balls pitched impeccably or wide escaped some measure of punishment.

What frustrated the Lancashire public, which is why they did not turn out in their numbers to support the team as they had in the past, was that there was no consistency to their performances and days like this one against the Australians were spread too thinly throughout the season. As we have seen, in 1961, Lancashire actually lost fewer matches than they did in the successful season of 1960 but the basic problem, as the statistics clearly reveal, was that Lancashire drew far too many matches for which they received no points. It would also be foolish not to assert that the side simply wasn't as good as it had been in1960 and certainly didn't play in the aggressive positive spirit that had prevailed until after the Kent fiasco.

Cricket pitches dictate the cricket. 1959 and 1960 were good summers and Tommy and Brian were always going to get wickets. I suspect Cyril had some influence on the pitches Bert Flack prepared at Old Trafford. In 1959 and 1960 Ken Higgs was getting a lot of wickets and they dried up in 1961. Tommy Greenhough had wonderful seasons also in 1959 and 1960 but played only eight championship matches in 1961 and none at all after the middle of June. At the start of 1961, I couldn't bowl either. I had tendonitis in the wrist, like tennis elbow. I'd bowled a lot in New Zealand and a lot in the Caribbean with Jim Swanton's side, but I had inflamed tendons and it was too painful to bowl.

It is hard to know what exactly the magic ingredient is that transforms a group of talented players into a successful team. It is possible to isolate certain factors from the performances of successful sides but it is not possible to extract from them a scientific formula that would then be capable of endless repetition. Good players don't become bad players overnight and, throughout 1961, Pullar, Grieves and Barber scored runs in sufficient quantities to pass the benchmark of a thousand runs. They were joined at that level by Jack Bond and young Brian Booth, another leg spinning batsman who could open the innings. These two proved decent replacements for Wharton and Dyson. Colin Hilton, third in the line of opening bowlers behind Brian Statham and Ken Higgs bowled well enough to claim sixty-five wickets, in addition to the forty wickets which Barber took when his injuries healed sufficiently to permit him to start bowling again.

Colin Hilton's problems were symptomatic of what was going wrong at Old Trafford. Colin Hilton had started to play for the first team in 1957, but he, too, never fulfilled the talent his captain saw in him, a fact he attributed to the "unhelpful" attitude around Old Trafford.

Take Colin Hilton. Underneath the bluffness Colin was very nervous. His hands would sweat. He might bowl a couple of beamers when he started but it was because his hands were damp with nervous tension.

1961 was Colin Hilton's most productive year. By 1964, at the age of twenty-seven, he was finished as an opening bowler for Lancashire.

Of all the players he captained, in many ways the most frustrating for Bob was Peter Marner, who was regarded by everybody he played with as a considerable talent. A big hitting batsman, a useful medium pace seamer and an outstanding catcher at slip, his talents flared only briefly because of his temperament. He was a prodigious striker of sixes in days when boundaries were longer than they are today and he is believed to have hit the biggest six ever seen at Old Trafford when he deposited the Leicestershire off spinner John Savage over wide long-on into what is now the Indoor School. Unsurprisingly, this big-hitting batsman was a favourite of the Lancashire crowd, welcomed to the crease by everyone who expected the Marner show to start shortly.

He was a working class lad from Oldham, ten years older than the 17 year old David Lloyd whom he greeted into the dressing room by standing on the youngster's new bat. He was not a fan of Bob Barber, even though in Jack Bond's opinion (and leaving out Brian Statham), Barber and Marner were the two players in that Lancashire dressing room who had more natural talent than anyone else. Bond echoes Barber's assessment.

Peter Marner was a problem but what a talent – he hit the ball harder than Botham or Ted Dexter. He was a good bowler and great catcher but he had had meningitis and he had a spring on his leg that was fastened to his boot. That's why he had a funny run up but he made 70 odd as a 16-year-old. If he got a hundred, you could guarantee he wouldn't make a run for the next few matches because he reckoned he was all right for selection for a bit so he wouldn't bother. That was his attitude- just to do enough to stay in the first team. He had no ambition to play Test cricket. There was me struggling with what little talent I had and trying desperately to make the best of it and he was just throwing it away.

It is symptomatic of Bob Barber that he never bore a grudge, certainly not against any of the players, no matter how badly they behaved, a respect probably taught him by his father and a character trait that makes him in 1961 nothing short of saintly.

When Peter Marner died, I wrote to his wife and said I thought Peter was one of the most talented batsmen I had ever played with. Having played against Ted Dexter and Peter when we were all 16-year-old schoolboys, I felt that Peter was a more talented hitter of a cricket ball than Ted. Ted had weaknesses which Peter didn't have. Peter Marner could play fast bowling extremely well. He was a tremendous hooker and he was also a very good player of slow bowlers. Ted struggled against them but Peter had played against some great spinners in the Lancashire League.

Looking at the 1961 scorecards, it is possible to discern that, in some measure, the shape of the side had changed from the previous year. Change can be a good thing for a team that can bring talented youngsters through to refresh its vigour and to keep the seasoned professionals on their toes. When West Indies and Australia consecutively ruled the cricket world from 1980 to 2007 this was something each country seemed to manage effortlessly. Although it was perfectly reasonable that youth be given its chance, and that the old stalwarts who now included Peter Marner as well Statham and Grieves be made aware there was talent waiting in the Second XI and that the club would renew itself with it, the fact was that Lancashire in 1961 was starting a downward spiral and the captain, for all his best intentions, could do nothing to arrest it. The team, as all losing teams do, looked to point the blame. The captain was the obvious target. The insubordination that Jack Dyson had been sacked for was starting to become more evident to the committee.

At the start of July, Lancashire were playing Kent on a blazing hot day at Folkestone. The chairman, Tommy Burrows, by all accounts a perfectly nice man although unlikely to be asked to join MENSA at any point, came down to pay a royal visit. He told the captain that he expected the boys to be wearing their blazers during the luncheon interval. They were representing their county and they had to look smart on parade. Peter Marner, who had been bowled by Alan Brown for four to leave him disgruntled and had then had to field in the hot sun whilst Wilson and Stuart Leary slowly compiled a century partnership for the Kent fourth wicket, had no intention of putting on a blazer with the temperature soaring into the eighties. In fact, most of the team objected, but it was Marner's refusal to obey orders that resulted in his being "sent home" after the match, like a schoolboy caught smoking on a form trip to Fountains Abbey. It was the chairman's brilliant idea but, of course, the captain was the one to issue the order of execution. *Barber Sends Marner Home* read the headline.

The captain, caught between the devil and the deep blue sea, did the only thing he could do. He made big runs. Lancashire had started their second innings with a deficit of 169. Losing partners at regular intervals along the way, Bob Barber batted like everyone knew he could but hadn't seen too much of in 1961, stroking his way to a superb 175. Exactly as he was to do later that month at Worksop, Barber's response to problems in the dressing room was to stride out to the middle and express himself as a cricketer, displaying that magnificent talent which had been so apparent since his early days at Ruthin School.

Peter Marner spent two weeks in exile back in Oldham before being summoned for Second XI duties. Malcolm Hilton had been recalled to play for the first XI at Old Trafford against Warwickshire, so a nervous Bob Bennett was appointed the temporary amateur captain of the Seconds to play in the reserve team match at Mitchell's and Butler's Ground in Birmingham. His nerves were not calmed when he discovered that the understandably revenge-fuelled Peter Marner had been given to him as Hilton's replacement. "Have you ever captained a team before?" asked Marner. An embarrassed Bennett shook his head. Marner thought for a moment. "Don't worry, son. I'll look after you", he affirmed. And, to everyone's surprise, he did. A reassured new captain went out and scored 75; Marner, exhibiting no sign of behaving towards this amateur captain as he had towards the first team's amateur captain, then belted a rapid 34 and took four wickets for 25 runs.

He returned to the first team ten days later at the end of July, in the middle of yet another crisis for the beleaguered Barber, who was still unable to plug the leaks caused by the loss of key players either through injury or form. The biggest of these losses were Greenhough and Higgs and to a lesser extent Tattersall who had left in 1960. Greenhough had sustained injuries to his fingers, shoulder and his feet which eventually led to his disappearance from the game. The miracle was that he had reached the heights he did in the first place because in January 1950, he had suffered an accident whilst working in the loading bay of a wholesale newsagents, in which he fell 40 feet and smashed bones in his feet so badly that they never really recovered. Lancashire only agreed to engage him in the first place on a week-by-week basis. By the mid-1960s, his action looked so painfully low that Ray Illingworth said to him, "I don't know if you realise, but you're bowling on your knees." From being hailed as England's wrist spinning hope for the future in 1959 and 1960, he faded out in the middle of June 1961 with a variety of injuries, having taken just 26 wickets in nine championship matches, compared with the haul of 121 the previous season.

Ken Higgs didn't fade out in anything like the same way, but in 1961 he wasn't the bowler he had been in his first three seasons at Old Trafford. He ended up with a respectable ninety-five wickets but they came at nearly thirty runs apiece. In 1960, he had claimed 132 at less than twenty runs per wicket. The figures of Greenhough and Higgs do much to explain why Lancashire could not convert draws into victories in 1961.

It was an Ashes summer and Old Trafford played host to one of the most memorable of Ashes Tests. It was a match that lingered in the memory of all who watched it unfold gloriously over five full days. Brian Statham was there and Geoff Pullar was there but Bob Barber wasn't. Peter May returned to claim, by right, the captaincy and one of the batting places, although Bob might very well have thought that the place that went to Brian Close could have been his in other circumstances. As it was, he was committed to another season of torture with Lancashire, who missed the contribution of their two Test players more than they had missed the contribution of the three of them in the previous year. This time Higgs and Greenhough failed to take up the slack.

There were two elements of his job as captain which Barber felt had improved his position. One of them was that his petition to stay with the rest of his team at the same hotel had been granted and the social anachronism, that was supposed to return Lancashire to the winning ways of the 1934 season, had been abandoned.

The other was the reduction of the Lancashire selection committee from 31 to three – himself, the coach, Stan Worthington, and the cricket committee chairman, Frank Sibbles, who had played for the club as an off spinner during the great years from the mid-1920s to the late 1930s.

On the face of it, that was great, but I hardly ever saw Frank Sibbles. I saw him at the start of the 1961 season, but he was in business with Cyril at Tyldesley & Holbrook, so you can imagine the conversations that went on there.

It was the end of July, when the new system turned out to be just as flawed as the old system. It was the day before the start of the Old Trafford Ashes Test, so in addition to the injured Greenhough and the suspended Peter Marner who was still kicking his heels in Oldham, Lancashire would be without Pullar and Statham for the next two matches. In fact, that Fourth Test of the summer of 1961 turned out to be a memorable game and the Lancashire captain would have been forgiven for wishing he was back in the England side at his home ground and being a part of the Test match atmosphere once more.

Instead, he was in Worksop, captaining Lancashire, who were due to play Nottinghamshire at the Town Ground. Bob was preparing to leave the hotel for the ground at the start of play, when the telephone rang. He picked up the receiver to discover the voice of Stan Worthington on the other end. What he heard, defied belief. Ken Higgs had been taking wickets regularly but not at the rate of the previous season, nor at the same economical cost. It was the opinion of the committee, the captain was informed, that Ken Higgs was tired and needed a rest. In fact, he needed a rest so badly that he was to be left out of the match that was starting in just over an hour.

Bob was appalled. He did not think Ken Higgs was tired. Nobody who watched the indefatigable Higgs bowl over after over for nearly twenty years could imagine that Ken Higgs ever felt tired. In any case, this was no way to select a cricket team and the timing could not have been worse. What possible authority would remain for a captain who went up to his main strike bowler half an hour before the start of play and told him that the committee in Manchester had decided he was too tired and he was being left out of the match?

The captain tried to convey some of these thoughts to the coach. The coach was completely uninterested in starting a discussion. He was simply conveying an order from the committee. Heart sinking rapidly, Bob told Stan Worthington that he would talk to the bowler and see what he thought. He rang off and went to find Ken Higgs, who was as mystified as his captain when told of the conversation with the coach. He accepted that he was not bowling as well as he had the previous season and when the captain asked why he thought that was the case, the bowler replied simply, "I haven't bowled enough, skip."

Bob went back to his room picked up the telephone and told Stan Worthington that Ken Higgs was far from tired; indeed he thrived on hard work and wanted more. Once more, Worthington instructed the captain that the decision to rest Higgs had been made by the committee. Bob responded with the observation that he thought selection had now been restricted to just the two of them and the almost invisible Frank Sibbles. Worthington knew that coaching jobs in first class cricket didn't grow on trees, that in fact there were only seventeen of them and currently he had one of them. He wasn't prepared to jeopardise it by disobeying committee instructions, so he reiterated the command down the phone.

The conversation was terminated because the captain had to leave in order to be present at the toss. Ken Higgs was not dropped but the captain lost whatever small amount of faith he had retained in the committee during his time in charge. "I could have walked away at that point. Maybe I should have walked away", he says today, looking back on an incident that was almost as wounding as the fiasco of the Cowdrey apology.

Barber refused to drop Higgs for the match against Nottinghamshire, thereby incurring the undying enmity of the committee. They might have thought, when they appointed him, that they could control this new young captain but they knew now, if they didn't know before, that the captain had a mind of his own. Unfortunately, it was to be a single victory in a war he would ultimately lose and he knew it as he put down the receiver. His time as Lancashire captain was effectively over at that point.

It was a terrible day. Barber won the toss and put Nottinghamshire into bat. The home side proceeded to run up 431 for 4 declared with Maurice Hill and Geoff Millman, the wicket keeper, both making centuries. Ken Higgs bowled 21 overs and took 1 for 73. In the twenty minutes of play left at the end of that first day Lancashire lost the brilliant young Cambridge philosopher and opening batsman, Edward Craig, bowled by John Cotton for 0 in his very first innings in the county championship. It was dismissals like that which might have made him a more profound philosopher. Craig thought that he had simply missed a straight ball but he was kindly assured by Millman at the close of play that he had been the unfortunate recipient of an extremely good ball which cheered him a little. Barber and Clayton, the night watchman, survived overnight, but the captain must have returned to the hotel feeling utterly wretched.

The next day was just as bad. Bob was out in the first over, caught behind off Andrew Corran and Lancashire crawled to a miserable total of 154 all out on a flat pitch but in grey and gloomy weather. Nottinghamshire were not able to enforce the follow on as, for that season, MCC had taken it into its head to abolish the concept, though it was soon restored when the brighter cricket, which it had been supposed might follow in its wake, did not materialise. Notts strode out to grind Lancashire into the dirt of the Worksop pitch and Norman Hill and Hugh Winfield raced to 94 for no wicket when the weather closed in and there was no play after tea. The agony had to finish the following day and it did when Notts declared at their overnight score, setting a demoralised Lancashire a notional 372 to win.

Led from the front by their captain, who scored a blistering 104, Lancashire won the match by six wickets. The first session was two and a half hours long, in order to make up some of the time lost on the previous afternoon. The allegedly poky Lancashire opening batsman was back in the pavilion by lunch, having blasted his way to an outstanding century. It was the second of the two centuries he scored that season, both of them made in the face of adversity. Every batsman contributed; after an opening partnership of 165, Edward Craig, initially relieved simply to avoid a pair, made a fluent 89, Ken Grieves a rapid 59 and Jack Bond stroked 65, as he brought his team home. Craig had barely passed fifty when Barber reached three figures. Nottinghamshire's two opening bowlers, who had so demoralised Lancashire on the Thursday, were soon blasted out of the attack by the Lancashire openers on the Friday and, though Bomber Wells wheeled away at one end, there was no stopping the runaway progress of Lancashire's batting.

Where that performance had come from, nobody knew. Even more frustrating was that it was never seen again for the rest of the season. Lancashire managed only one more win, losing some, drawing some, usually with one or two outstanding individual performances but no sense of the irresistible force that the team had engendered the previous season. Lancashire drove away from Worksop, delighted with their unexpected victory and pleased to have left the aggrieved Notts players, who could not understand how they had managed to lose a game of which they had had complete control. It was grand larceny.

When Lancashire took the field the following morning at the County Ground in Northampton, they did so with Peter Lever replacing the "tired" Ken Higgs. Miraculously, the Staffordshire born bowler was back for the following match against Essex at Blackpool. If the captain thought he had appeased the committee by resting Higgs for the game against Northamptonshire, he was mistaken. His card was marked and the end of his time as captain, possibly the end of his time as a Lancashire player, was now in sight. Quite frankly, he had ceased to care. The only person in that dressing room who could have interceded with the committee on Bob's behalf, believes John Murray, was Brian Statham, but Statham made a point of never becoming embroiled in the politics of Lancashire cricket. Bob was isolated.

The return of Peter Marner to the side for the match in Northampton was followed by something rather more sinister. At some point during the 1961 season, possibly before Tommy Burrows had been so outraged by the sight of the burly Marner in his shirt sleeves in Folkestone, Marner and Ken Grieves arranged to meet the chairman at Haydock Park races. The only item on the agenda was the captaincy of Bob Barber, who knew nothing about this meeting for two years after it had taken place. It was symptomatic of the atmosphere in the Lancashire dressing room in 1961, which was deteriorating by the day. For all his native talent, for all the success of the previous season, for all his studious, enthusiastic, committed approach to the captaincy, a gap was clearly opening between the players and their captain. In modern parlance, as applied to football managers, he had "lost the dressing room". He had tried so hard and he had cared so much, it must have been intensely dispiriting for him. In addition, although he had suffered lapses in form as all players do, Bob Barber's rise to Test status and the Lancashire captaincy had been the story of a meteoric if meritocratic ascent. In 1961, he appeared to have hit the buffers at Old Trafford and it must have been a shock to the system. Hard work allied to talent and desire had, mysteriously, not produced the expected result. The optimism with which the young captain had returned to Manchester, after happy tours to New Zealand and the Caribbean less than six months earlier, had entirely dissipated.

In the wake of the publication by Kevin Pietersen of his book detailing what he perceived as an unpleasant atmosphere in the England dressing room, even during the team's ascent to the exalted position of number one in world cricket, it is worthwhile examining what determines the dynamic of a team game. Cricket, uniquely, combines individual battles of bowler and batsman with the team game in which individual performances contribute to the team's success. Which was the true reflection of Andy Flower's England team – doing "The Sprinkler" at the conclusion of the 2010-11 Ashes tour or the mass urination on The Oval pitch after the 3-0 win in the summer of 2013? Edward Craig today remembers his own insecurities as an individual player, but was not aware of a particularly fractious dressing room. Indeed, he thought that the Lancashire players were very kind to him, despite the fact he had suddenly shown up at the end of the Cambridge University academic year and taken the place of a professional. Did Pietersen's intense dislike of Matt Prior and Andy Flower hinder his ability to contribute to the England cause? Was the awkward attitude of Lancashire's "heavy brigade" during the period of Bob Barber's captaincy the real reason that victories dried up for the county once they had lost their place at the top of the championship in mid-August 1960?

A look at the composition of those Lancashire teams in 1961 reveals more chopping and changing than is good for the health of a side with serious championship winning ambitions. There had been much more stability in team selection in 1960, despite the Test calls for Pullar, Greenhough and Statham. A number of players were tried and played maybe twenty or more games without ever establishing themselves in the side – Gerard Houlton from St. Helens, who batted at 6, Kevin Tebay from Bolton who batted at 3, Ken Howard, the off spinner, who tried to fill the hole left by Greenhough, Tattersall and Hilton. Edward Craig managed only six appearances. Alan Bolton was, according to Bob, an excellent player but, after forty matches, he hadn't made a permanent place for himself in the batting order and, after the infamous match against Notts at Worksop, he never played county cricket for the Lancashire first eleven again. Ken Higgs never gave less than his best, but his best was nowhere near as good as his best had been in 1960, whatever the number of overs he bowled.

The ghastly 1961 season ground on as it did in those days without any one day cricket or promotion and relegation issues to spice up the last month for sides not in contention for the county championship. The August bank holiday Roses match in Sheffield was effectively rained off – the Whitsuntide match at Old Trafford which had inevitably aroused strong memories of the now legendary match the previous August, had ended in a comprehensive defeat by ten wickets. At its conclusion, over the loudspeaker, Stan Worthington ordered the Lancashire players into the nets for an hour's intensive practice. Long before the term "Naughty Boy Nets" was coined in the 1980s to refer to the practice of sending losing second rate England teams into the nets after a Test match defeat in a show of public penance, Lancashire were doing the same brainless counter-productive nonsense.

Arthur Booth, the old Yorkshire left arm spinner, wrote in the *Manchester Evening News* five years later

> *Of all the stupid morale-sapping orders I have ever heard that was the limit. A ten wicket defeat is a blow but not a debacle. Practice before a game yes, but to subject senior and England players to the comments of irate members and humiliate a young captain was, I think, damnable.*

In the light of these setbacks it is remarkable that Lancashire managed to record as many victories as they did in 1961. There were wins against Sussex at home, against Worcestershire at New Road and Gloucestershire in Cheltenham and a number of players put in some decent performances, none more so than Roy Collins who scored a century and took nine wickets in the victory over Sussex. It was the sort of match-winning effort that was expected of the captain but he was becoming as disengaged from the job as Ted Dexter during the Open Golf Championship.

Bob Barber's future was not as grim as the day-to-day environment made him feel. In particular, he had two positive events to which he could look forward with some relish. As soon as the 1961 county season drew to its unlamented close, he was going to marry his fiancée, Anne Greenhalgh. Shortly after the ceremony, he was flying off to the Indian subcontinent, to spend the winter on tour with England in India and Pakistan, a part of the world he had never seen and was looking forward to exploring. He would be playing Test matches in Kanpur and Calcutta, Lahore and Karachi to say nothing of the match against Ceylon in Colombo on the way home. Whatever happened out there it would, thankfully, be a long way from the Town Ground in Worksop.

CHAPTER EIGHT

IN A LETTER from the Lancashire County and Manchester Cricket Club, the chairman wrote to Bob Barber as follows:

Dear Bob,

Many thanks for your letter, contents duly noted.

As I explained to you at Liverpool, the Cricket Committee were of the opinion that one of the contributory reasons for the sides [sic] failure this summer, is the fact that you have not bowled enough, (only 478 overs for the season). They appreciate you have made a sacrifice in the interests of Tommy Greenhough and Brian Booth, but feel this has not got the side or yourself anywhere.

I would think that your future objective in Cricket would be to get in the England side next summer, and if you are successful you are pretty certain to be invited to go to Australia in 1962-63. You say in your letter that you cannot concentrate on your batting as well as your bowling, if I may you give you some advice which is shared by the most knowledgeable people in Cricket both at Old Trafford and Lords, forget all about your batting and concentrate 100% on your bowling, this is your great potential, the Australians think you could be the best in the world, but you will never make it unless you get down to it seriously which means bowling a lot more than you have done, and as long as you are Captain of the side we feel that you will not bowl yourself enough.

In the interests of Lancashire Cricket and yourself, the Committee have decided to appoint a new captain for 1962 and it is our earnest wish that you will continue to play Cricket for Lancashire. I cannot at this stage tell you who your successor will be, as he will not be appointed until the Cricket Committee meets on October 4th and the appointment will have to be confirmed by the General Committee on October 25th 1961. I can tell you however that the new Captain will not be a member of our professional staff.

I would like to hear from you before you go to India and hope that you will continue to play for us next summer, and I offer you my sincere best wishes for a successful Tour.

Yours sincerely
T.E. Burrows

The letter is actually signed "T.E. Burrows". Not "Tommy Burrows" and certainly not "Tommy". Burrows's lack of belief in Barber's captaincy is mirrored in his lack of belief in full stops and indiscriminate use of capital letters. The letter is dated 18 September 1961, but it was not received, and certainly not opened, by the intended recipient until after he returned from the tour of India, Pakistan and Ceylon in March. The news of the assassination was instead given to him in a hot and sticky hotel room by the Tour Manager, T.N. Pearce, whose brusque lack of sensitivity was reflected in the telegram he read out to Bob, which he remembers, was something brief and to the point like TELL BARBER HE'S SACKED. Even Kevin Pietersen got better treatment. Bob Barber's Lancashire captaincy ended, as it had started, in yet another piece of inept mismanagement by the committee, which pretty much summed up the whole sorry saga.

It is odd in 2015 to read of a bowler who "only" bowled 478 overs as being underused. It is also odd to realise that the chairman had no idea that the low number of overs was also partially due to Bob's return to a cold April coinciding with inflamed tendons that prevented him bowling at all in the early part of the season.

The tour of Pakistan started in early October 1961, shortly after the solemnisation of the union of Robert William Barber of Chester and Anne Greenhalgh of Appleton at Daresbury Parish Church, just outside Warrington, at the end of September. The engagement had been announced in May 1960 and the marriage followed at a respectable distance, although the actual moment when the news was relayed to their respective parents provided sharply contrasting reactions.

I went to her house to ask for her parents' blessing on our plans. Her mother was in bed, she had a heart condition, and when she heard Anne was going to marry me she burst into tears. My parents, however, were very happy about it. When I got back from India, we moved into our first house, a little bungalow in Upton near Chester. My brother Tony who was an estate agent and a chartered surveyor oversaw the deal while I was in India. Anne and her mother kitted it out. I was in clover.

Although it was accepted on all sides that the wedding ceremony would take place conventionally in a church, the Barber family were, says the bridegroom still smiling at the memory of it, "all heathens". Bob himself has wavered between belief and agnosticism but all the Barbers were perfectly happy to conform to the social niceties of the day and to the wishes of the bride's family.

What is clear from talking to Bob's playing colleagues was that he did not take them into his confidence regarding the deteriorating nature of his relationship with the Lancashire committee. Instead, he repressed his feelings in a way that would not be to the benefit of his emotional health. It hardly makes him unique. In 1961, that pretty much was how everyone dealt with their problems. The idea of talking to a psychiatrist or a sports psychologist would have been greeted with scorn. The solution to one's problems was to "get over it", "stop feeling sorry for yourself" and understand that "worse things happen at sea" and so on. This belief in self-help was probably even more pronounced in the north of England than elsewhere. It was the prevailing culture and it would take a very brave man to row a boat against that current, borne back ceaselessly into the past.

Fortunately, he could talk to Anne who was a sympathetic listener and, as someone who had played sport to a decent level herself and whose brother had been around Old Trafford long enough to breathe the polluted atmosphere, Anne was uniquely placed to provide a receptive ear. She supported his decision to remain with Lancashire for the 1962 season but was greatly relieved when he left Old Trafford and moved to Warwickshire. In October 1961, however, as a newly wedded wife she found that her husband was flying out to the Indian subcontinent and wouldn't be back until the spring of the following year. The substitute for the absent husband was the house in Upton and the opportunity to furnish it as she wished.

In the 1950s and 1960s, many senior England players did not feel the need to tour India and Pakistan. If fit, May and Cowdrey, Trueman and Statham would always reclaim their places in the England side for the first Test the following summer. In this respect, they were rather like Hollywood actresses who will do anything to advance their careers at the start but, having achieved a certain fame and respectability, can afford to tell clamouring producers that they won't do nude scenes any longer. A body double is therefore summoned.

On the 1961-2 tour of India and Pakistan the body doubles included, besides Bob Barber, Barry Knight of Essex, Butch White of Hampshire, Alan Brown of Kent, Geoff Millman of Notts and Peter Parfitt of Middlesex.

Dorman Smith had generously given Bob time off work to tour New Zealand and West Indies in the winter of 1960-1 so it was with some trepidation that Bob went back to see the Managing Director, Geoffrey Atherton, to discuss whether he could also tour in the winter of 1961-2.

He said that Dorman Smith had trained me sufficiently and they were ready to offer me a full-time job in charge of an enclosed switchgear system. I think they wanted to use my name, but to me, work and play were different things and I wanted people to respect me for my work and respect me for my play but not respect me at my work because of my playing cricket. Frankly, I wasn't sure that I was competent enough to do what they were asking. I went to the electrical engineers exhibition the previous winter and I was on a stand looking after a piece of equipment that was boxed in. In those days a lot of electrical switchgear used to be on open busbars and there was always a risk of dirt getting in and therefore creating short circuits and other problems. At the exhibition, there was a spy hole at the end so any engineer who came up could look in and see what was inside. I was regarded as the fellow who knew what all this was about, which I really didn't because I wasn't an electrical engineer. A fellow came up and looked through the spy hole and I said to him, "Can I help you, sir?" He looked me up and down and said, "I don't think so" and he turned out to be the Chief Electrical Engineer for British Thomson-Houston. I knew very well that whatever I knew, he knew a hundred times more. Dorman Smith wanted me to go around selling their equipment and I didn't want to be a travelling salesman.

Nevertheless, Dorman Smith had given Bob an invaluable training in business and management but it was time to look elsewhere to expand that experience and the obvious place was on his doorstep – to work alongside his father in the series of small businesses that Jack Barber had collected.

I was with Dorman Smith for about four years but I was then working with my father all the way through to 1970. Sanoda was one of those companies which was part of the group that my father was involved with. His company pre-war had been called something like Cambrian Holdings. It was a small public company that was trying to develop fuels. They got involved in gas works and water works and were nationalised in 1950 so they had a pot of money and, unless they were to be taxed as if they were an investment company, they had to buy something. After nationalisation, Cambrian was reformed as a small private company called North Cambrian Holdings Ltd. They bought at least eight small companies – one was bricks, Sanoda was another; there was the company in Blackburn that made industrial leather gloves, a company in Bury that used to clean out boilers… so there was a variety of different things. I was not involved in the boilers or the gloves. I wasn't there in 1950. The idea was that if they were lucky, they would have a couple of the eight that would turn out to be profitable and worth developing and if they were very lucky there would be three. By the time my father died, they also had a brick works up in Lytham on the Fylde and one in Tattenhall in Cheshire. In addition to Sanoda, there was a company that made tinplate serial numbers for tyre identification. They would be put in moulds. For a car it would be a batch, for an aeroplane it was a one-off. If there was an accident, they could identify which mould had caused it.

In theory, working for his father released the anxiety attendant on going to Dorman Smith and asking for time off. In practice, it probably increased the anxiety, because if Dorman Smith were happy to give Bob permission to tour, it meant he could pack his cricket bag with a clear conscience. It was inconceivable that his father would ever stand in his way if he wanted to tour during the winter or play county cricket during the summer, but the moral responsibility of possibly causing his father more trouble by appearing and disappearing at the behest of MCC or his county when it wasn't convenient weighed heavily on Bob. After all, the reason he had changed from Medicine to Natural Sciences in Cambridge in 1954 was precisely to avoid burdening his father, whose health he knew was not robust. Now he was off to India and Pakistan from early October 1961 until at least late February 1962.

Fascinating as he might find the culture of the Indian subcontinent, Bob was also aware that it would be a hard tour physically and some of the cricket would be played in an atmosphere unknown in Harrogate or Horsham. Geoffrey Howard, the Lancashire Secretary, had been the manager of the previous MCC tour to the subcontinent in 1955/6 when the umpiring had been so awful, the England players had doused Idris Begh, the main umpire responsible for the worst decisions, with a bucket of water, thereby creating the biggest international incident since Bodyline over twenty years earlier.

Jim Parks was on the receiving end of a terrible injustice in Lahore.

The cheating was unbelievable. I was given out in Lahore, in one of the unofficial Tests. I got a thick under edge, the ball bounced two yards in front of the keeper who threw it up and I was given out. Fred Titmus was at the other end and he went spare. Neither of us had ever seen such blatant cheating. Fred went storming over to the square leg umpire, "Did you see that?" After we doused the umpire and got reprimanded, we formed an Idris Begh Club and I was made Chairman because he'd done me so often.

Lahore was to be the location for the first Test match in which Bob Barber would represent his country since the aborted start at Edgbaston eighteen months previously. He took six wickets and made a fine fluent 39 in the second innings in an unbroken partnership of over a hundred with the captain Ted Dexter. They were still at the crease when England won the match by five wickets. As they came off the field, Bob was delighted to be greeted by a familiar face.

My friend Ifi Bokhari and his friends were at the side to say well done and I stayed talking to them. Ted went into the dressing room and the other lads had changed and gone ahead to a shoe store in Bata, where the MCC players were due to be presented with a pair of shoes each.

A taxi was arranged to take him to the shoe shop, but when he got there he discovered that the players had already left for the airport. However, diplomatic niceties still had to be observed so it was only after the tea ceremony that he could get back in the taxi to drive to the airport. He then discovered that the taxi driver, who spoke no English, had no idea where the airport was.

We start to leave the lights of civilisation behind and then we turn into a small field surrounded by Nissen huts out of which emerge some menacing looking tribesmen and I think, "I'm being held hostage". I have my hand on the door handle because I reckoned I was pretty fit and could outrun them but, it transpired that these were men who knew where the airport was, which was more than the taxi driver did. The field had previously been an RAF station and the driver had managed to mistake it for the commercial airport in Lahore. Anyway, half an hour later we drive into the real airport and I get out. I ask the girl at the reception desk where the MCC party is and she says that they all flew off half an hour ago without leaving me a ticket, my passport or any message. The next flight to Bombay is of course full. There are no seats in the airport, just odd benches so I stretched out on one and waited. Forty-five minutes later Ifi Bokhari arrived with Shuja a left armer who played for Pakistan. Shuja is a 5 foot 1 inch colonel in the Pakistan army and, when they find out what has happened, he orders someone to be ejected from the next Bombay flight so I can get on.

Understandably, Bob was less than impressed by the organisational efficiency demonstrated by the manager. He was able to find his way to the team hotel in Bombay and knocked on the manager's door at what he considered the respectable time of 6 am. If he was expecting an apology from Tom Pearce, he was to be sadly disappointed.

His greeting was, "Where the hell have you been?" He gave no explanation as to why he had flown off with my ticket, passport, money and watch, left no message and made no following-on arrangement. I don't believe he even knew I wasn't on the plane and I wonder when he learned I wasn't there. I doubt he checked. He was incompetent and wasn't fit to be a manager. I don't think he could have organised 'something' in a brewery! I am confident I will have expressed myself strongly but I do not remember the exact words.

It isn't too difficult to supply the words that were probably used.

Relations between the two men deteriorated from that point, much as the results of the cricket they played did not add greatly to the gaiety of the party.

Nobody in the team had played in Pakistan previously, but they had all heard the stories. In the Lahore test match, Mike Smith, the vice captain, was given run out on 99 and Ken Barrington, who made 139, went the same way. If the England players had their suspicions the successful outcome must have enabled them to allay them for the time being. Bob was never entirely convinced by Dexter's captaincy credentials but, such was the nature of the sub-continental pitches, it was obvious he was going to get a great deal of opportunity to display his talents as a wrist spinner on them. Given his reluctance to bowl himself at Lancashire, when it might deny chances to Tommy Greenhough and Brian Booth, this must have been welcome.

In the Brabourne Stadium in Bombay, England made 500, India 400, and, when England set India to make 300 to win off 75 overs in the final innings, the Indians settled for the security of 180 for 5. In the second Test at Kanpur, Bob, batting at number six, made an outstanding unbeaten 69 in a disappointing England response to a big first innings total by India. However, the way Bob played, taking the attack to the opposition, demonstrated the way forward and although they followed on, England responded with big centuries from Pullar, Barrington and Dexter, as the match meandered its way slowly to another draw. It looked as if the entire series was going to be played out in that fashion but the Indians won the last two Tests to take the rubber 2-0, although, when England returned to Pakistan in January 1962, to play two further Tests, both matches ended in a draw which meant they had at least won that series 1-0.

We lost the last Test in Madras in early 1962 quite heavily but we'd lost heart by then. We'd been on top at the beginning of the series but by the time we got to Calcutta, the lads were tired and they all felt they got chopped off by the umpires. I had gone for a walk with someone outside the ground and a lot of wickets went down in half an hour because I was nearly not back in time to go in and get rolled over.

One way of dealing with the sense of embattled isolation that afflicts touring teams away from home for a long time, even in an age of five star hotels and instant internet communication, is to draw tighter together as a squad of men sharing the same sense of persecution. In 1961-2, it wasn't surprising to see that the England party looked forward to their Saturday Night Clubs. With no play on

Sundays, England cricketers had always been used to Saturday night being party night and India and Pakistan was to be no different. Before the tour started, all the players had signed a form confessing that they were alcoholics to a man so that beer could be imported into a dry country. In the event, they saw no beer at all, even though Tom Pearce was a director of Watneys ,but everyone noticed that the manager always had a bottle of whisky to hand.

The Middlesex wicket keeper, John Murray, remembers one particular Saturday Night Club which came to an abrupt end.

The management liked the idea that we were all together for that one session instead of splitting up and wandering off. We had a room and that was where we settled all the fines that people had accumulated during the week. Two or three guys were appointed to be barmen and their job was to keep the lads filled with drink for an hour. We let our hair down, which was very necessary on a tour like India where there was nothing to do. On this particular occasion, the barmen were Butch White, Alan Brown and Geoff Millman, the Notts keeper. They had set up jugs of water at places hidden round the room at various points. There was going to be a given moment when they …well this was typical of fast bowlers, wasn't it? The water was going to go flying and it did. Bob wasn't going to have any of that and I can see his face now. Poor old Geoff Millman came through a door with one of the jugs of water and Bob kicked him straight in the knackers. You didn't mess with Bob. That was the end of the party though.

Bob believes that he attempted to kick the water jug out of Millman's hands but admits he might have missed the moving target and made contact in quite the wrong place.

It is not difficult to see another side to this anecdote. This was the winter of 1961, at the end of a particularly disappointing season, and the behaviour of the Lancashire players, especially when stimulated by alcohol, had done damage to the morale of the squad and to the captain's fervent hopes for their future glory. His philosophy of "You buy me a pint, I buy you a pint and we sit and drink them and chat about the game" had been violently rejected by the players who preferred evenings of wild revelry. Somehow, this particular Saturday Night Club must have awakened all those feelings of anger, despair and helplessness. The hapless Geoff Millman was hardly to know the detail of Bob's life at Old Trafford. Particularly, since he had been on the receiving end of the fourth innings thumping at Worksop, he might well have assumed that Barber had complete control of a well oiled Lancashire match-winning machine.

Bob was not alone in his negative feelings about Tom Pearce. John Murray confirms that the entire squad thought Tom Pearce was, at least on that tour, an idiot.

Tom Pearce was a bit of a joke. Typical of those times when the manager of a tour was always the chairman of a club. Pearce was as bad a manager as Cowdrey and Dexter put together. He was hopeless. Six and a half months in India with no decent hotels, it was very difficult. He couldn't organise anything. We lost Butch White and Alan Brown for four or five days. They buggered off. Brown was never going to be picked for the Tests and, now this is typical Dexter, he decided that Butch was never going to be able to bowl well on those pitches, so he bowled Barry Knight and David Smith, two medium pacers, for half a dozen overs each and then it was David Allen and Locky. Tom Pearce would walk into the changing room and a typical remark would be, "Where are my two so-called fast bowlers?" That's Butch and Brown. He deserved to be treated with contempt. I can certainly see Bob getting a black mark with him.

Pearce contrasts badly with Donald Carr and Billy Griffith, who were to be the managers of Bob's next two England tours, but the manner in which he had given the news of Lancashire's telegram shows how inept Pearce was to be in charge of a thinking player like Bob Barber. Bob is quick to concede that his relationship with Tom Pearce was not good and, if he had been a professional, he would undoubtedly have been denied his Good Conduct Bonus. However, R.W. Barber was a gentleman and an amateur so T.N. Pearce had to find a different way to demonstrate his disapprobation.

I think I got blackballed after that tour. Before they picked the party for Australia in 1962-3, there was an article written by a respected journalist suggesting that Graham Atkinson and I were being considered by MCC as the openers, rather than Noddy. Noddy was being considered in the middle order. We thought the Press was briefed with titbits of information to put out before the announcement of the Test team on the Sunday. The Gents v Players was a trial match for the touring party and I bowled pretty well at Lord's, although I only took a couple of wickets. I remember I tied Tom Graveney down for a long time and he was a great batsman. That night Bill [Willie] Watson asked me to go and have dinner with him. He was a selector at the time and he was a lovely fellow. He said I bowled well and I said thank you. "We're not allowed to consider you for the trip to Aussie, so when you hear the news that you've not been picked, I don't want you to get discouraged." I think it must have been Tom Pearce who would have done it because we did not get on well during that 1961-2 tour of India and Pakistan. It was a strange thing to say but Tom Pearce must have written a report – it was on the basis of those reports that the professionals got their good conduct bonuses but whether they wrote reports on amateurs I don't know. [No such report can be found in the MCC's archives.] It might have been just word of mouth but something clearly happened. I never talked with Ted about it. To be honest, I never talked with Ted about anything much when we were playing. We never communicated.

The England party returned home with some relief. There had been no international incident to rival the Idris Begh affair in 1955/6 and there had even been time to enjoy some off field activities. One of Bob's friends at Cambridge, who had played occasionally for the university cricket team, had been Aizaz Fakir, one of the sons of a distinguished military man who had been a Colonel in the Indian Army. When the MCC plane landed in Pakistan, the first two locals waiting on the tarmac to greet the party were Aizaz and his cousin Ifi. In January 1962, Aizaz was selected for a Combined XI to play the MCC at the Bahawal Stadium in Bahawalpur. The match was unmemorable, having been ruined by rain, but Bob was invited to meet the Colonel at dinner in the family home in Karachi. Aizaz was in a state of acute anxiety, begging Bob not to reveal what he had got up to in Cambridge and particularly not to explain the vagaries of the Cambridge University examination system.

Aizaz had done almost no work in his time at Cambridge, a not unknown phenomenon, especially for sporting undergraduates who were not destined for a career in a cut-throat world, and came down with what was known as a "special", a form of degree that was so mediocre it was one slight rank above expulsion. He would not be allowed to use the abbreviation (Hons.) after his B.A. since he didn't have any honours. On informing his father that he had been awarded a special degree from Cambridge University, the Colonel cabled his congratulations and an instruction that Aizaz should go out immediately and buy himself a Mercedes. Which Aizaz did, with all speed.

There were plenty of other misdemeanours that Aizaz also felt his father should not be troubled with. "For God's sake don't tell my father", he begged. On arriving at the house the father solemnly proclaimed the enormous gift the ex-Lancashire captain had brought simply by honouring the house with his presence. He led Bob into his study for "a talk". He asked if Bob wanted a drink. Bob, surprised to be offered alcohol in this strictly Muslim household, gladly assented and the Colonel reached under the pillow of the day bed for a carefully hidden bottle of whisky. He poured out a generous measure for Bob and an equal one for himself. They clinked glasses. "For God's sake", said the Colonel anxiously, "Don't tell Aizaz."

If you ask Bob Barber where he had the best meal in his life, he will reply immediately, "Frankfurt Airport". The plane that returned the exhausted MCC party from Colombo to London stopped at Frankfurt. The England players, who had existed on the most meagre of diets for months, raced to the very ordinary café in the airport and devoured food they could recognise as familiar once more. The connecting flight was about to leave so they only had time for bread rolls and a carafe of red wine but they tasted like nectar. Even the return to England at the end of a cold damp winter was to be welcomed and of course Bob had the additional bonus of a delightful new wife on hand to make the welcome complete. The only fly in the ointment was that he now opened the letter from Tommy Burrows which confirmed the information so abruptly conveyed by Tom Pearce that he was no longer the captain of Lancashire.

Although Burrows's letter had stated that he was not then in a position to reveal the name of Barber's successor, by the time he was back in England, Bob knew that the Lancashire captain for 1962 was to be Joe Blackledge – to which everyone in Lancashire apart from regular spectators of Chorley in the Northern League said, "Who?" Blackledge had appeared for Lancashire Second XI between 1950 and 1953 in the Minor Counties Championship but had played most of his cricket as a batsman for Chorley. How he could possibly be regarded as a better choice than a man who had just returned from a successful tour as an England Test match all-rounder was a mystery at the time and remains one to this day. The committee's vain hope was that he might turn out to be Lancashire's answer to Yorkshire's successful appointment of Ronnie Burnet.

The appointment of Blackledge turned out to be as disastrous as everyone, including Blackledge but excluding the Lancashire committee, had always known it was going to be. In Blackledge's defence, the players all liked him and knew he had been handed an almost impossible task, although Ken Grieves, by then the senior professional, who had been a Lancashire stalwart since 1949, must have had reasonable expectations that he was the fit and proper choice to assume the mantle of captaincy. When he learned of the committee's decision he demonstrated his disapproval by collecting his cards and going into business, whilst turning out occasionally for Rawtenstall.

It was to be the final season of the amateur cricketer and in their decision to appoint Joe Blackledge as their captain, the Lancashire committee had demonstrated to the world exactly why the anomaly of the amateur had to be abolished. Ironically, after this last attempt at maintaining the ideal of the amateur captain had failed, the Lancashire committee had no choice but to return to Ken Grieves and offer him the captaincy. It was removed in high dudgeon just over a year later when he was publicly sacked, as feelings about what had happened to Lancashire ran extremely high. Even more ironically, fourteen years later, in another era entirely, Ken Grieves was invited onto the committee where he served happily for a dozen or more years.

Bob could have walked out after the game at Worksop in July 1961 but it was not in his nature to let down the rest of the team and similar considerations were at work again at the start of the 1962 season, when he decided he would remain with Lancashire until the end of the season, before retiring from the game in order to concentrate on his business career.

I didn't walk out because I didn't want to be accused of sulking and besides Joe was a nice fellow. Joe said to me, "They won't want me for more than a season" so we bought a copy of the **Good Wine Guide** *and we had a different bottle every night as we travelled around. Poor Joe struggled against anybody who bowled short and quick at him. I think the pros in the dressing room regarded Joe as the nice man that he was.*

The Lancashire crowd, who had not taken kindly to being pipped at the post by Yorkshire at the anti-climax of the 1960 season, and who were outraged by the team's decline to thirteenth in 1961 were in a veritable rage throughout the 1962 season. Results were appalling; only two matches were won and the team finished second to bottom of the county championship, the lowest placing ever in its history. During August they were dismissed for under 100 five times, four of them coming in two matches, away against Gloucestershire and at home to Somerset. Young players were brought into a losing team, taking the places of angry and insecure professionals, which exacerbated the tension and ill feeling in the dressing room. Their failures meant that the team was not being rejuvenated from below and the crowd was constantly on the backs of the players which, of course, did not create an atmosphere in which they could flourish, which they needed to do if they were ever to turn the ship around.

I had an unhappy time at Old Trafford and I didn't want to finish my career feeling as bitter as I did when I left Lancs. There was so much moaning from the members. They expected Lancashire to be always at the top of the table, to be making a hundred every time you went out to bat and taking ten wickets when you came on to bowl. And they wanted to play on hard wickets and not do what Surrey did and rough the damn things up. The atmosphere in Birmingham was very different. It was friendly and welcoming. They said "bad luck" if you got out, not "What did you go and play a bloody stupid shot like that for?" which was what you got at Old Trafford.

Walking out to bat down the steps of the pavilion, or, more relevantly, returning to the pavilion after another cheap dismissal, it was impossible to be unaware of the opinions of the crowd because they had no compunction about letting the player know the strength of their feelings. By 1962, the section of the crowd in and around the pavilion became known to the players as the Pit of Hate. Bob passed 1,000 runs for the season but at the unremarkable average of 28. His bowling declined, as he sent down fifty fewer overs than he had in 1961 taking only 32 wickets at a cost of 38 runs each. Statham just about claimed his hundred wickets, but at an average of more than 21 runs per wicket, as opposed to his usual sixteen or seventeen. Ken Higgs took only 66 and Tommy Greenhough 55.

The season started poorly, with a defeat by six wickets by Glamorgan in Cardiff and it deteriorated from there. Yorkshire won the Whitsuntide Roses match at Headingley by seven wickets and were in a strong position to complete the double at Old Trafford in August when Lancashire were saved by the rain. The end couldn't come soon enough and, by the middle of August, it had arrived.

On Saturday 18th August, shortly after the mysterious death of Marilyn Monroe in which President John F Kennedy and Attorney General Robert F Kennedy were implicated but not, oddly enough, Tommy Burrows and his committee, Lancashire arrived to play Essex at the County Ground in Leyton. Joe Blackledge was injured so the captaincy for the last time reverted to R.W. Barber of Cambridge University, Lancashire and England. He made 25 batting in the middle order but only Peter Marner, with a typically belligerent 93, dragged Lancashire up to the heights of 153 all out.

It proved to be enough for a first innings lead of 19, as Essex succumbed to Tommy Greenhough, showing a flash of his 1960 form, as he took 5-21 from 21 overs. In their second innings on the Monday morning, Lancashire collapsed in the face of good bowling by Brian Edmeades and Ken Preston, who finished with twelve wickets in the game. Their miserable total of 80 left Essex just 100 to win, which the home side did for the loss of a single wicket.

Well before the close of play on the second day, Lancashire were leaving the field a thoroughly beaten, not to say abject, side. In his last innings for the red rose county whom he had joined eight years before with such hopes and dreams, Bob Barber was out for 1, caught at the wicket by "Tonker" Taylor off Ken Preston. For the final four county championship games of 1962, Bob's place in the batting order was taken by the 5'3" nineteen year-old Harry Pilling. Three of those four matches also ended in defeat.

It must have been a horrible way to finish and yet, at the same time, the circumstances in which the domestic seasons of 1961 and 1962 had been played out must also have given Bob Barber a sense of profound relief that the agony was at last at an end. He assumed that his future lay in his business career, which indeed it did, but before then, and it would have come as a big surprise to the captain who trudged his way back to the pavilion at Leyton for the last time as a Lancashire player, his greatest moments as a cricketer were still to come.

CHAPTER NINE

LANCASHIRE MADE NO attempt to plead with Bob Barber to return for 1963, or to make life difficult for him by retaining his registration. Instead, he was permitted to play for Warwickshire under the terms of a Special Registration. Two years before Bob moved to Warwickshire, Tom Graveney had left Gloucestershire after a dozen years of distinguished service, when his committee removed the captaincy from him and handed it to an amateur called Tom Pugh. Graveney wanted to go to Worcestershire but Gloucestershire made Graveney, still a Test class batsman, miss a year of his professional life while he obeyed the rules and qualified to be allowed to play for his new county.

Lancashire certainly didn't behave like that but then again, R.W. Barber was a gentleman and Graveney T.W. wasn't. Also, Lancashire presumably did not think they were losing a player who could have helped their cause, though why they thought that it is hard to fathom. Their experiment with Joe Blackledge was abandoned after the one disastrous season of 1962, as everyone, with the exception of the Lancashire committee, knew that it would have to be. The winter tour to Australia by the MCC ended in a 1-1 draw, with Australia retaining the Ashes they had won in 1959 and retained in England in 1961. Bob knew he hadn't been considered for it and, having closed his account with Lancashire, he assumed that his cricket career was to all intents and purposes finished at the age of 27. He had always imagined that he would probably retire at 28, so the loss of another year didn't greatly trouble him. It was time to put away childish things and apply himself to the serious purposes of life – work and family.

The pages of the large files in which the press reports of his cricket career are stored with impressive organisation can be turned so that his public life appeared to move seamlessly from the published first class averages of 1962 to a photograph of Bob Barber and Alan Smith reporting for the first day of training for Warwickshire in the spring of 1963. It is appropriate in that it was Alan Smith who played a key role in Bob's move to Warwickshire.

I first got to know Bob on the Canada tour of 1959 and, though I was picked for the 1960 tour of New Zealand during that winter, it overlapped with the new term at Oxford and my college wouldn't let me go. We were then both on Jim Swanton's tour of the West Indies in March 1961. I went away with MCC in September 1962 and Mike Smith rang me up in Australia and said, "Look you know him better than I do. Bob Barber wants to leave Lancashire and we think he wants to join us. What do you think?" I said, "You absolutely have to go for him." We were getting a lot of runs on flat pitches at Edgbaston and we had a good seam attack but we didn't have any spinners, so I said to Mike, "You must get him. He's a very good bowler and he'll make a big difference to us with the ball." I thought he was very high class, big spinner, good, high action, a bit like Benaud and as you know Bob is a very strong man. He made the ball bounce so much it sometimes became difficult to keep to. He had a googly which I read and it turned. Keepers read wrist spinners better than batsmen because you see so much of them. He didn't have a flipper as I recall but I don't know how much Bob actually enjoyed bowling. I was conscious that Bob thought Mike wasn't getting it right with him but at the time Bob was the only spinner we had. We had an off spinner called Bridge who lost it. If Mike wanted a variation he turned to Bob. It might not have been ideal for Bob but Mike would have seen Bob as having a particular job to do.

Bob's move to Warwickshire for the start of the 1963 seems, in retrospect, a natural stage in the advancement of a career that was shortly to flower so spectacularly, but the files, with their well-ordered sequence of photographs and match reports, give no indication of how he made the transition, nor of the social revolution that overtook cricket in the six months between the end of one season and the start of the next.

There is a well-advanced theory in British social history, that the disastrous invasion of Suez in 1956 prompted seven years of cultural turmoil which culminated in the extraordinary events of 1963, the year that effectively divides the twentieth century. In those seven years, so the theory goes, Britain shuffled off the constricting attitudes of a class-ridden society and embraced the new social order that scorned the conventional notion of social deference.

In 1963, The Beatles emerged in their full mop-top glory, most of the public took the side of the audacious Great Train Robbers against the police who were trying to capture a gang of armed robbers and revelled in the scandals revealed by the Profumo Affair. 1963 was the year that the much reviled and out of touch Harold Macmillan, though forced to leave office by illness, appeared to have resigned in the face of a satirical broadside issued by *Beyond The Fringe, Private Eye*, The Establishment Club and ultimately the most powerful weapon of all, *That Was The Week That Was*. He resigned in favour of yet another Old Etonian, who still sat in the House of Lords, but in accordance with fashionable theory agreed to renounce his peerage. This change was symbolised politically the following year when plain Mr. Harold Wilson from Huddersfield, with his stated predilection for H.P. Sauce and St Bruno pipe tobacco, led the Labour party to an electoral victory which replaced Sir Alec Douglas Home and his cabinet full of Old Etonians.

In amidst this social revolution, cricket produced one of its own. Cricket is frequently, and sometimes quite rightly, *pace* the Lancashire committee, seen as a game administered by blinkered reactionaries. However, to put it in perspective, cricket made two significant innovations in the early 1960s which the Lawn Tennis Association, the Royal & Ancient, the Amateur Athletic Association, the Rugby Football Union and even the Football Association would have regarded as revolutionary. On 26th November 1962, to the surprise of nearly everyone and certainly that of the Duke of Norfolk and Ted Dexter, manager and captain respectively of the MCC party then on tour Down Under, the Advisory County Cricket Committee passed by 12 votes to 7 a proposal by Glamorgan that the status of the amateur cricketer be abolished entirely. Given the fact that only four years previously the committee, which MCC had set up to examine the threatened status of the amateur cricketer, had returned a verdict that the preservation of the *status quo* was vital to the good health of the game, this rapid reversal reveals how far changes in British society had gone that even MCC was obliged to take note of them. From the start of the 1963 season, there would be no amateurs and no professionals in the old sense of the word. All the players would simply be cricketers and the absurd anomalies of amateurism were thankfully consigned to the grave.

There was another, perhaps even more significant change to the structure of county cricket. It was decided to experiment with a new knock-out one innings competition that would last one day only. Each side would receive 65 overs and the result, weather permitting, would mean that anyone who came to watch and stayed till the end of play for the day would see the result. The seventeen counties did not quite divide evenly and a preliminary match between the sides finishing sixteenth and seventeenth would take place before the full first round draw was made.

Lancashire, having finished sixteenth in 1962 were thus at home to Leicestershire who had finished bottom. Lancashire scored over 300 in their 65 overs, thanks to a brutal innings of 121 by Peter Marner, who claimed 3-49 and the very first Man of the Match award, although Brian Statham's 5-28 must have made it a close call. Leicestershire, despite a century from Maurice Hallam, lost by 101 runs. Alan Wharton made 0. Lancashire were to progress to the semi-final of this inaugural year's competition, giving a hint of one day triumphs to come. There were to be many more years of championship failure but, for Lancashire, the advent of one day cricket indicated light at the end of the tunnel.

Although he doesn't embrace the notion, Bob Barber's game was also built for one day cricket in the sense that he was an attacking batsman and one day cricket was devised to encourage those qualities in the game. Of course, it quickly developed into a contest between batsmen edging towards the last ten overs with wickets in hand against bowlers with defensive fields, whose intention was to dry up potential runs rather than take wickets.

I did well in the one day game for the first few years but I still preferred first class cricket against a top Test or county side because the one day format takes some of the skill out of the game. As a batter you can get away with things you couldn't in a normal game. You didn't have a conventional attacking field so you could nick it and get away with it. They also didn't have much truck with spinners, though Yorkshire did with Illy and Don [Wilson]. There were a lot of phantom medium pace fellows.

More significant for Bob, was the change at the end of the 1962 season in the Laws of Cricket relating to no-balls. For years, he had despaired of tall fast bowlers dragging through the crease and delivering the ball from nearer than twenty-two yards, as well as those who did so from close to the stumps, thereby leaving holes in the pitch on the line of the left hander's off stump. In 1963, the front foot law, which still applies, came into existence. The back foot position became irrelevant because the bowler in his delivery stride now had to have some part of his front foot behind the popping crease. This automatically abolished the danger caused by "dragging". If it was a legitimate delivery it would be delivered from just short of twenty-two yards and not just over nineteen.

His new captain at Warwickshire Mike Smith recalls

I always thought when Bob came to us and changed his religion from the nudger and nurdler he'd been at Lancashire to giving it a whack, it coincided with the introduction of limited overs cricket. Bob however says no, it had nothing to do with the Gillette Cup; it was to do with the change in the back foot no ball law in 1962.

Certainly, at the back of Bob's mind, there had long been the desire to play one innings exactly as he had always believed the game should be played and, being Bob, this innings would have to be played in Test cricket because he was only really motivated by the prospect of matching his talents against the best in the world. In order to play Test cricket again, however, he was going to have to play for a county other than Lancashire. Warwickshire ticked most of the boxes but he went principally because of his friendship with and respect for Mike Smith.

If it hadn't been for Mike Smith I wouldn't have gone to Warwickshire. In fact I wouldn't have played for anyone. I'd had enough but Warwickshire was a happy club. Mike Smith said, come down and talk to the chairman. I never signed anything for Warwickshire because I was so deeply sceptical about the way people were in cricket. I agreed to play a certain number of games and I said if I didn't enjoy it, I'd be off. I also talked to Leicestershire but to be honest Leicestershire wasn't somewhere you'd want to go for your holidays.

If he were to play for Warwickshire, he would be playing for a good side who would be motivated by the fact that they hadn't really won the trophies their talented squad might have expected and, significantly, he would be playing for one of the best captains in county cricket, his friend Mike Smith.

I don't know if I was the one who persuaded Bob to come to Warwickshire, but it goes without saying that I thought he was a bloody good cricketer. We played on good batting wickets at Warwickshire and we had a good seam attack so the idea of having a good batter and a bloke who could take a fair number of wickets as well was very attractive. As far as the batting was concerned, you knew you'd get a job out of him. I didn't know he was going to play the way he did but as soon as he started scoring runs like that, I just let him get on with it. I looked upon him being an asset to the side. As far as who was going to make way for him, that was always going to happen. It happened when I got in the side. It's the same as anyone going into a new job at any company. Somebody's nose is going to be put out of joint.

However, it was one thing being slowly introduced into the Lancashire team as a shy, introverted and unprepossessing 18 year-old; it was entirely different to go straight into the Warwickshire side as a seasoned Test and county cricketer. It caused him some concern, because the one thing he did not want to do was to go from the frying pan of the Lancashire dressing room into the fire of the Warwickshire dressing room. He was only going to Warwickshire so that he could play cricket for enjoyment. If he was going to be the cause of unrest at Edgbaston, he wouldn't stay very long.

When I went to Warwickshire, I did say I did not want to be competing with Ray Hitchcock. He was also a left hander who bowled leggies. I knew he was a popular fellow, a nice bloke and I just didn't want to be in that position. Somehow, as Mike always does, he brushed it off and said, "You don't know what you're talking about." In the end it was fine. Ray was looking to get out of the game anyway. He was 35-years-old and had successful sports shops. He was a bright fellow.

Playing for Lancashire, Bob had lived in and around Chester but commuted easily enough to Old Trafford. Playing home matches in Birmingham, raised the problem of finding more accommodation in addition to the house they had bought when Bob was in India in the winter of 1961-2. The abolition of his amateur status at least meant that he would be earning something from his cricket.

I was probably on something between £1000 and £1200 and that was quite reasonable. In those days, if you were earning £2000 per annum you were doing quite well, plus for the first couple of years at Warwickshire, they found accommodation for us which the club paid for. The first year it was a place just opposite the BBC in Pebble Mill. It was a converted coach house and the deal was we had to be prepared to share the accommodation with Alan Smith. That was no problem. We had a bedroom at one end and Alan had a bedroom at the other. That worked fine until Sandy was born, when the arrangement was no longer appropriate. It wasn't fair to us or to him. We got on well with Alan but we had a baby so they found me accommodation at Ladbroke Hall in Tanworth-in-Arden. That was a beautiful village. Anne and I had the converted stables there.

By that time Alan Smith was also engaged to a woman called Anne, so although the converted coach house worked well enough in 1963, it was in both parties' best interests that they separated the following season. Initially, however, the domestic and playing situations seemed to have resolved themselves to Bob's satisfaction without any snags. It should have put him in the perfect frame of mind to start off the 1963 season with a bang, but professional sport simply does not work like that. In fact, in the first game for his new club against Hampshire on the now defunct Courtaulds Ground in Coventry, Bob Barber and Ray Hitchcock both played and Warwickshire won by four wickets without a contribution of any significance from either player. Mike Smith's century settled it and though Bob picked up the wicket of Colin Ingleby-Mackenzie, his own involvement as a batsman amounted to being run out for 2 in the first innings and caught at slip off Butch White for 0 in the second.

What was different from his experience of failure at Old Trafford was the reaction of crowd, players and above all, the committee.

I didn't express my opinions at Old Trafford at almost any point. Dirty looks and black marks and "This fellow's a troublemaker" was what you got. In no time at all, the Secretary at Warwickshire, Leslie Deakins, who had been there a long time and was a significant man in the game, wrote to me and signed his letters "Leslie". My first chairman in 1963 was Alec Hastilow and his deputy who became the next chairman was Edmund King. He would sign his letters "Edmund". I never got a friendly letter like that from anyone at Old Trafford. At the end of a day's play at Edgbaston often, Cyril Goodway, who became deputy to Edmund King, would come into the dressing room and say, "Good day, lads. Anyone want to come up to the committee room for a drink?" At Old Trafford you never even got invited for a cup of tea! The whole atmosphere was different. Everyone was on the same level. Any member of that Warwickshire side could go into the committee room for a drink.

Bob's experiences with the Lancashire committee were not unique to himself or to his position as captain. All the players felt alienated from the committee who effectively employed and had a duty of care towards them which they singularly failed to discharge adequately. Jack Bond, who had his own problems with the committee even in the glory days of the late 1960s and early 1970s, is in no doubt that

The major problem here was the committee. There were committee men who would call you by the wrong name. That happened all the time. They would come into the dressing room and when they left the lads would all go, "Who was he?" It was Us and Them and they were all on that side and we were all on this. We should have been a family club because we couldn't have had anyone better than Geoffrey Howard as Secretary. He was a genuine and honest man, even though there wasn't a lot of money about. As far as the committee was concerned, the cricket was just a part of their social life, being able to come down here and wine and dine.

The difference in the atmosphere at Warwickshire was one reason why results and Bob's form soon began to pick up. Gradually, the philosophy of cricket, which Bob had long espoused but been unable to demonstrate consistently, started to become visible at Warwickshire because he was no longer so anxious. Before moving into the Edgbaston flat with A.C. Smith, travelling seventy miles from Chester to Birmingham was a pleasure to be anticipated, whereas previously, the short train ride to Old Trafford had been a fearful affair.

My belief is that in the battle between batsman and bowler, one of them is going to dominate so I wanted it to be me from the first ball not from three overs in. But at Lancashire, there were plenty of occasions certainly in 1961 and 1962 when we might have been 23 for 3 and you simply can't play like that. I had also decided after I left Lancs that I never wanted to captain any side ever again. I was once asked to captain Warwickshire in a game against Scotland or someone and I said very firmly, "No, thank you". I wanted to play and have the chance to express myself in the way I felt the game ought to have been played, in terms of trying to win the match. The game needed to bring spectators in. I never liked the term "brighter cricket"; I preferred "positive cricket". I felt we were part of the entertainment business. When I went to Warwickshire, it was all different. Who could I open with? Norman Horner? Billy Ibadulla? Jim Stewart? Norman and Jim both had flashing blades and Billy used to get on with it too, scampering up and down. Jim was probably the most circumspect of the three, despite all those sixes. A wonderful judge of the line, and if you were playing against a good side he was a very good fellow to have up the other end because he was a fine player, even on difficult wickets. None of them was selfish. Ray Hitchcock was coming in at 7, and Alan Smith at no.8. It didn't matter if I holed out early on. At Lancashire with the ball I was probably relaxed but with the bat I was always extremely tense.

Despite the worst efforts of Tom Pearce, Bob clearly still featured in the minds of the England selectors because he was chosen to play for MCC against the touring West Indies in the early season match at Lord's which was regarded as a Test trial. Unfortunately, things did not go well for Bob.

I can remember playing at Lord's for MCC against the West Indies in 1963 and Rohan Kanhai hitting me into the Grandstand. There were a lot of West Indians in the crowd in those days and they were baying for blood, so when I came on to bowl leg spinners they were anticipating carnage. This made me a bit tense and I pulled the first ball down a bit short and Rohan hit me for four through square leg. The crowd loved it which made me even more tense. Next ball was even shorter – bang! Six. The crowd's in ecstasy. I don't know where to pitch it but I have an idea where it's going – bang! Straight onto the balcony of the old Grandstand. By the time the ball came back I had plenty of time to think about where the next one was going. I suspected it was going into the Finchley Road. But then, unaccountably, I started to relax. I shrugged my shoulders. This over can't get any worse and I started to bowl on a length because I didn't much care.

He took 0-91 off 23 overs in the West Indies first innings, did not bowl in the second and travelled back to Birmingham having made scores of 9 and 16 batting at number three in the first innings and number eight in the second. He was not called upon to resume his England career that summer, although oddly enough if there was one match in that summer of 1963 which demonstrated to all and sundry if not the "new" Bob Barber then at least the new version of the original Bob Barber, it was the match against the West Indies played at Edgbaston in early August.

The opening pair of Norman Horner and Billy Ibadulla had both gone early to Wes Hall and Charlie Griffith and Mike Smith had been dismissed without scoring so it was 26-3 when Bob joined an embattled Jim Stewart at the crease. Stewart had been on the receiving end of a barrage of bouncers from Griffith, whose action was to say the least suspicious. Lance Gibbs, who knew all his future team mates at Warwickshire, thought this was the perfect time to play one of his infamous practical jokes. Jim Stewart remembers ruefully,

Unbeknown to us, Lance had said to Charlie, "When the bald headed bloke [Stewart] comes in, he hates blacks, you chuck anyway so bowl from Buller's end." In my first over I got three balls that hit me in the throat. Second over, I got hit so badly that I was taken to hospital. I came back just after lunch and Bob had made a hundred and was out already! Charlie had only bowled about three overs before Bob had hit him out of the attack. I didn't play again for about four or five weeks.

You might be forgiven for thinking that the friendship between Jim Stewart and Lance Gibbs might start to wear a bit thin after that incident but Stewart just smiles jovially and demurs, saying, "Lance was a great guy. He was a great leg puller". Cricket was clearly a different country in 1963.

Although dropped three times during his explosive innings, Barber made 113 sparkling runs, before being caught by Solomon as he tried to deposit Lance Gibbs beyond a boundary. It was his first century for his new county and set the tone for what was to follow. Bob believes that people have made too much of the batsman he was at Warwickshire, compared to the way he had batted at Lancashire and, to an extent, this belief is corroborated by the review of Warwickshire's 1963 season in *Wisden* which noted approvingly

Barber reached 1,000 runs and....brought a touch of Northern dourness to the batting that proved beneficial to an order that was prone to brittleness.

However, there clearly was a change in Bob's batting style that was soon noticed on the county circuit. Jim Parks remembers Bob Barber at Old Trafford as *being a very stodgy batsman. Used to nudge it down to third man, that sort of thing. When he went to Warwickshire he played every shot in the book. When he was in the England side he was a magnificent striker of the ball.*

John Murray laughs when he recalls

Everything from Bob used to slide down to third man but it all changed when he went to Warwickshire, going in first, the start of limited overs cricket. That gave him licence to play as expansively as he wanted. He might have matched Alan Wharton shot for shot but old Alan, he wasn't a stroke player was he? He was a nudger just like Bob.

The affable Murray does Alan Wharton something of a disservice. Bob rates Wharton very highly indeed as a fast scorer and wishes fervently that he could indeed have matched him stroke for stroke. Jim Stewart remains grateful for the liberating influence that batting with the free-scoring Barber had on him, although he too recognised a change in the Bob Barber he had known playing for Lancashire.

I used to tell him at Lancashire he was just a squirter down to third man. "That's the only bloody shot you've got, Bob!" He got runs, yes but you knew where they were going at Lancashire. When he came to Warwickshire it was different.

You knew batting with Bob that if it was wide he would slash it and if it was pitched up he'd whack it. When he was in that mood I just gave him the strike and played in the V myself. He didn't run that much, he didn't need to but he was quite leisurely running between the wickets. However, he was a great fielder, an athlete. He was good to open with because you knew he was going to put them under pressure. I dare say one or two bowlers fancied him because he'd always give it a go. Once he got going, 15 or 20, hit three fours, there was no way he was going to stop.

E.J "Tiger" Smith, the stalwart Warwickshire wicketkeeper from the Golden Age before the First World War, was still around the club in 1963 when Bob arrived. He saw at once how Bob could be improved as a batsman.

As a player I believed in attacking the ball and I didn't change my mind when coaching. I remember helping Bob Barber change his style after he came down from Lancashire. He was a stodgy defensive player and I took him to the nets and told him, "You can no more play defensively than a schoolboy", made him play his shots and within a year he was in the England side and helping Warwickshire win the Gillette Cup.

It wasn't quite that simple of course, but Bob certainly acknowledges the advice Tiger Smith gave him.

He said I should just stand up and swing the bat. Certainly I did that, so he did have some effect and I do remember him.

The matches against Lancashire, home and away, were played consecutively in the middle of June 1963. Bob was now on a mission.

I have no idea if I got 4 or 44 but I used to stand outside my crease, which I did to Kenny Higgs and he saw me doing that so he bowled it wide outside the off stump and I managed to cut it for four on the half volley and his expression was priceless. Those are the sorts of things I remember. The result of the match is a mystery to me.

He tried the same approach to Brian Statham and smashed his first ball from the great bowler through the covers for four. He noticed Brian nodding briefly and smiling gently to himself. The next ball rose from just short of a length. It was wickedly straight and about to hit Bob in the throat when the batsman just managed to get the bat handle in the way. A shaken and grateful Barber saw the ball drop at his feet. He looked up to see Statham at the end of his action waiting for him. "Bob, don't do that to me again" said the great man gently and turned round to walk back to his mark. Bob retreated to stand inside his crease.

After the end of the first day's play in the Lancashire match, the opposing captain, Ken Grieves, invited Bob to join him and Statham for dinner. They had something to say to him. He wondered what it could possibly be that hadn't been said in the eight years he had been their team mate.

I knew there would be nothing negative from Brian, though I couldn't be sure what Kenny was about to say. Anyway I went off with them and over dinner they said, "We're very sorry. We'd like to apologise for the things that happened when you were captain."

It would appear that Ken Grieves was now experiencing at first hand what it was like trying to captain Lancashire, whilst beset by the committee that had done for many a captain before him. It seems as though they now understood for the first time what Bob had been through. If Bob had talked to them about his problems back in 1960… but he hadn't. Bob Barber never lacked physical or moral courage. His decision to remain silent appears very odd in today's tattle tale times, in which tabloid newspapers would pay good money to affect a prurient sympathy they could share with their readers. In the early 1960s, however, it wasn't the way we were as a country of generally repressed Englishmen and it certainly wasn't the way Jack Barber had raised his sons to behave.

By today's standards, it also seems remarkable that amongst the small number of men who played regular first class cricket, there was not one man to whom Bob felt he could unburden himself. His problems at Lancashire, he had always felt, were his to bear alone and even when he left to go to a county which behaved relatively normally, he couldn't tell anyone how awful it had been at Old Trafford. There was no doubt in his mind that it would have sounded like self-pitying whingeing and besides, it was behind him now and for that he was grateful. It would be over fifty years before he truly felt able to express the emotions that he had suppressed for so long. The idea now was simply to enjoy his time at Warwickshire, knowing that it was of a very limited duration and that his business career, for which he had been assiduously preparing for so long, would soon claim his permanent attention.

M.J.K. Smith felt similarly that Bob's career at Warwickshire was likely to be short but possibly very sweet and entirely understood Bob's mindset.

I read Geography at Oxford but I didn't have a clue what I was going to do with it, unlike Bob who always did. In the back of his mind I felt he always held the opinion that he'd had a good time playing sport at school and university but now it was time to get a job and get a career moving. Although he enjoyed his cricket, with perhaps the exception of those years at the end of his time at Lancashire, it was only putting off the time when he was going to get stuck into his career. He never seriously considered cricket as a career. Peter May was in insurance so his name and connections would have been very valuable in that sort of business. Doug Insole had a long career with Wimpeys and Trevor Bailey was employed by Essex but I can't think of anyone who created his own business as successfully as Bob.

Bob's cricket was benefitting from the situation he found himself in. He now had a wife and a baby girl, whom they called Sandy, he was developing his business career alongside his father who was, as ever, extremely supportive of his cricket and he now knew that he had joined a county club where he was immediately accepted, made friends quickly and was popular with the Warwickshire supporters. His cricket took off and didn't look back. It was fun and it was successful.

Entirely typical of his change of fortunes that went along with the change of county was his hat trick against Glamorgan in August 1963. The Welsh county was subsiding slowly to an innings defeat when Mike Smith tossed him the ball. In the space of five overs he took 4-14. The ball with which he completed the hat trick remains on his bookshelf in the flat in Switzerland, although he points it out with some embarrassment. He dismissed Don Shepherd, Ossie Wheatley and Jeff Jones with successive deliveries, but his reticence is based on the acknowledgement that they were three of the cheapest wickets he had ever taken.

In 1963, Warwickshire finished equal on points with Sussex in fourth position but, rather like Lancashire in 1960, with only a few matches to go they had Yorkshire and the championship in their sights. Unfortunately, in a wet summer, their last three matches were all badly affected by the weather, the match against Hampshire at Bournemouth being abandoned without a ball being bowled. The season fizzled out like a soggy squib but Bob had certainly contributed significantly to Warwickshire's spirited challenge. His bowling gave his new county's attack a different dimension and he finished third in the Warwickshire averages, behind Rudi Webster and Tom Cartwright, with 64 wickets at 21.

The following season they finished as runners up to Worcestershire though forty points behind their neighbours. Lancashire were also climbing the table at the same time though hardly to the same heights. Second from the bottom in 1962, under Ken Grieves they rose one place in 1963 to sixteenth and in 1964 they finished as high as fifteenth. They did, however, get to the semi-final of the Gillette Cup in both of the competition's first two years. In 1963, having defeated Leicestershire, Essex and Derbyshire, hopes of an appearance at Lord's in the first ever one day final were dashed when they were resoundingly defeated at Worcester, having been dismissed for just 59 in 31 miserable overs. Kenyon, Horton and Headley knocked off the runs in an embarrassing ten overs. In 1964, good wins over Kent and Glamorgan brought Warwickshire to Old Trafford for an eagerly anticipated semi-final. Warwickshire, by contrast, had lost to Northamptonshire in their only Gillette Cup match in 1963, but made up for it the following year when they returned to Northampton and walloped the home side by a massive 147 runs. Bob Barber took the Man of the Match award with a scintillating 114 and Alan Smith believes it was this innings that saw the start of the "new" Bob Barber.

Bob's change wasn't that noticeable in 1963. I think the Pauline conversion was the Gillette Cup match against Northants in 1964. He saw the shine off the ball and then proceeded to play a vast array of shots and got a hundred before lunch. He then said, "I will never bat any differently again" and he didn't. That innings was the turning point. He was a huge success and opponents were frightened of him because, if he stayed in for any length of time, he'd make big runs. As I remember, in 1963 Bob rarely opened - it was Horner and Ibadulla most of the time.

Despite the acclamation, one day triumphs produced a slightly muted response in him. For all Bob's reservations, however, the competition had proved an instant winner, crowds were large and growing as opposed to the dwindling attendance at championship matches. Lancashire supporters had had almost nothing to cheer since Bob's side had beaten Yorkshire in the Roses matches of 1960. The expectation at Old Trafford was enormous as Warwickshire arrived for the semi-final. Surely Lancashire had learned their lessons from the previous year and there would be no repeat of the capitulation at Worcester. The Gillette Cup was starting to give cricket something of the flavour which the FA Cup competition bestowed on football.

Bob loved the big occasion and this one was no different. He was in terrific form, his life on and off the field was enjoyable and successful. Whatever happened at Old Trafford he would get in his car afterwards and drive back to his flat in Tanworth-in-Arden. He would not be around to experience the reaction of the Lancashire crowd whatever happened, or so he thought.

Lancashire won the toss and decided to chase, but their bowling attack was confronted by a former Lancashire player who was determined to seize control from the first delivery. He did. Statham, Higgs, Ramadhin, Marner and Lever all suffered as Barber swung the bat with fearsome intent. The first wicket fell at 93 when Billy Ibadulla was run out after a mix up. He had made 17. Barber went on his way, cutting and driving until he had made 76. Mike Smith passed fifty and when the sixty overs were up, Warwickshire had made an imposing total of 294. The match was effectively won. In those days 180 off 60 overs was regarded as good going. Lancashire didn't have a prayer – which they knew.

In response though, David Green and Duncan Worsley, two graduates from Oxford University, set off like a train. Sixty-nine runs rattled up in the first twelve overs and M.J.K. Smith was getting nervous. The Warwickshire captain replaced his opening strike bowlers, Jack Bannister and Rudi Webster with Tom Cartwright and Billy Ibadulla, whom he instructed to bowl short of a length to a deeply defensive field, including no fewer than six men on the boundary. Off the next ten overs Lancashire managed only 24 and after thirty overs the score had only reached 110.

By now frustration had gripped both the batsmen and the large 21,000 crowd and inevitably the wickets started to fall. Nevertheless, when the wicket keeper Geoff Clayton strode to the middle with twenty overs remaining, Lancashire needed 134 with five wickets left. In today's one day cricket climate that might be considered a sporting bet but Clayton clearly was not of that opinion. It seems that with the approval if not the instigation of the captain, Ken Grieves, Lancashire had decided not to give Warwickshire the satisfaction of bowling them out, so Clayton made a paltry 19 in forty-five minutes, patting everything, including half volleys, back to the bowler. Ray Hitchcock bowled ten overs for twenty runs. To add to the joys of his day, Bob was thrown the ball and dismissed Peter Lever, bowling seam up. The crowd turned ugly and the slow handclap was replaced by something more menacing, which could have drifted down Warwick Road from the other Old Trafford. Jim Stewart recalls the Warwickshire players' reaction.

We just thought what a bloody idiot the Chimp was. You could understand the crowd going mad with him. They knew they weren't going to win but if he tried and made thirty it was better than what happened. It was one of the worst atmospheres I'd ever played cricket in.

As the boos started to reverberate round Old Trafford, one man ran onto the pitch to remonstrate with the Lancashire wicket keeper but without noticeable effect. After 60 overs Lancashire had reached 209 for 7 and had lost by 85 runs. Alan Smith echoes the feelings of the whole Warwickshire team.

Mike took the view - we've got 300, now you get them. It was particularly effective at Old Trafford because Lancashire just got cross and surrendered instead of saying, "We're going to have to push into the gaps and run lots of twos." They just got the hump. It was a big enough playing area. I was vice captain and if Mike hadn't been playing I'd have done the same thing. I didn't care why Chimp did that; I just said to myself, "Oh good! Lancashire have given up on the game and we've won." I was delighted. The crowd's reaction didn't bother me. If Lancashire wanted to give us the game - thank you very much.

The blame was laid entirely at the door of M.J.K. Smith who, fifty years later, is quite unapologetic about what happened.

I got man of the match, which I didn't deserve, and Jim Swanton wrote in his piece that he hoped it wasn't awarded for my captaincy. I put the field back but why didn't they just dob ones and twos? They batted very poorly. They're 60 for 0 off ten - you'd settle for that now. I had to tighten it up. I didn't have nine on the boundary as it's sometimes written. I had a bloke either side in front of square saving one. There were so many opportunities to take easy singles and twos, I don't know why they didn't.

He might also have pointed out with some justification that when Ted Dexter had to defend the Sussex total of 168 in the first Gillette Cup Final played at Lord's the previous September, he did so by successfully employing exactly those tactics to which Worcestershire did not have an answer. Smith had taken his cue from the newly crowned master of one-day cricket tactics, the cavalier Dexter, who had attracted no opprobrium.

All the pent up frustration of the crowd over the past few years seemed to spew forth at the conclusion of this match. Afterwards, Ken Grieves defended Clayton and his own tactics, much to the fury of Cyril Washbrook who had returned to Old Trafford that season as the Team Manager. The committee backed Washbrook's decision to discipline Clayton by dropping him for the Roses match against Yorkshire which followed immediately after the semi-final disaster. Lancashire lost by an innings and 131 runs after forty minutes play on the morning of the third day. The County Club was in crisis. Again.

They bumbled on for the last month of the season but on 31st August, in the middle of the MCC v Lancashire game at Old Trafford, arranged to celebrate the County's centenary, it was leaked to the local paper that Clayton, Grieves, Marner and, for the second time, Jack Dyson were all going to be sacked. In its typically inept way, the Club initially denied the rumour then confirmed it in an official statement a few days later. Clayton went to Somerset, Marner left to join Wharton at Leicestershire and Grieves and Dyson both retired.

Bob could look back up the M6 and see that the chickens which had hatched during his time were now coming home to roost.

I didn't feel any antagonism at Old Trafford, but I certainly didn't have people coming up to me saying we're sorry you left. I have no negative personal memories of that occasion but of course we did well and won and I enjoyed it. I was embarrassed by the way that Mike decided to win the match but that was his job. I felt a bit sorry for Geoff Clayton. He got a lot of stick. I didn't hang around after the game. I wanted to get away. He may have been doing what he was told to do by Ken Grieves and he might have taken his own attitude to what was happening. The crowd was certainly unhappy. They weren't thrilled the way Mike put the field back and maybe Geoff Clayton was picking up the crowd's feeling and siding with them. I remember Billy [Ibadulla] won the game with his double tops; he wasn't the easiest to get away. To me, that game was symptomatic of the malodours that came out of Old Trafford.

Shortly after the debacle in the Gillette Cup, the Lancashire committee commissioned Cyril Washbrook to write what Wisden called

a survey following complaints by other counties of the behaviour of some players
and of the manner in which Lancashire batted ...against Warwickshire.

What emerged was a report in which Washbrook fiercely defended his own conduct, whilst blaming everyone else. It was typed on a flamboyant blue ribbon and pasted ceremonially into the committee's minute book. It contained not just the recommendation to remove the four alleged villains of the piece but an observation that gambling on dogs and horses was taking place in the holy sanctum of the dressing room and, predictably, the discipline he had imposed during the Golden Years of his reign had dramatically declined since his retirement. It is hard to ignore echoes of Claude Rains as Captain Renault in *Casablanca*, desperate to find an excuse to comply with Major Strasser's demand that he close Rick's *Café Americain*. "I am shocked," he announces, "*shocked* to find gambling is going on here." "Your winnings, sir" says the croupier played by Marcel Dalio approaching with a fistful of banknotes. "Oh thank you very much" says Rains, stuffing the cash into his pocket.

Bob could contemplate the disaster that was Lancashire from a safe view point and apply his own analytical mind to it, secure in the knowledge he no longer had to deal with these people.

If it's any organisation, besides a county cricket club, you can't keep ignoring the
top management if things are going badly wrong on the field and it starts with
the chairman. We're not talking about the captain. It's not just the fellow at the
top but he should be setting the atmosphere and for many, many years that did not
happen at Old Trafford.

At the end of the season, at a tempestuous emergency public meeting at Houldsworth Hall on Deansgate, the committee was effectively ousted. The leader of the revolution was Cedric Rhoades, the vanguard of a new generation that would thankfully bring success back to Lancashire.

Meanwhile Bob's 1964 season simply got better and better. Warwickshire were at the top of the county championship table and, when the Australian touring team came to Edgbaston to play Warwickshire, they were greeted by one of Bob's special innings, which according to Wisden "dwarfed everything else in the match". Opening with Norman Horner, he scored a century before lunch as he clouted 138 with twenty-two 4s made in two and a quarter hours, moving the watching Keith Miller to acclaim in the *Daily Express*

Barber set off at such a pace that boundaries trickled from his bat over after over. It looked more like festival cricket than a match against the holders of the Ashes... Barber's fantastic innings was hailed by 20,000 spectators, who gave him one of the most rousing receptions ever heard at Edgbaston.

It wasn't the strongest Australian side. Having survived the marathon Test match at Old Trafford when Bobby Simpson made 311, Dexter 174, Barrington 256 and the first innings were not completed until the fifth day (The Test That Died of Shame was the headline that best summed it up), the Australians rested Simpson, Redpath, Hawke and Veivers. However, such was the dazzling nature of Bob's innings, so spectacular had been his form throughout the season, that it was impossible for the England selectors to ignore him any longer. The Australians had retained the Ashes and there was a party to be chosen for the winter in South Africa. Although Ted Dexter was still the captain when the England team arrived at The Oval, he had turned his mind from the Open Championship to the possibility of becoming Prime Minister.

To that end, he had been adopted as the Conservative candidate to fight the constituency of Cardiff South-East against the sitting Member of Parliament, James Callaghan, in the General Election due to be held in the autumn. If elected he would not be able to play in the first Test match in Durban, although Dexter, being Dexter, the thought must have crossed his mind that he could vote when the House divided at 10pm, get on his motor bike in Palace Yard, tootle out to an airfield west of London and fly his plane to South Africa, in time to go in at the fall of the first wicket the following morning. The England selectors, willing though they had always been to indulge Dexter, decided this time that it might be safer not to do so again. M.J.K. Smith was appointed to lead the MCC tour party to South Africa.

Once Mike Smith became the captain, Bob's recall to the England side was inevitable. His remarkable season of 1964 had earned it in any case, but he and Ted Dexter, who had known each other since their teenage years as schoolboy prodigies and then again at Cambridge and on the tour of India and Pakistan, had never been close friends. They could hardly fail to admire each other's talent but both men had in their time been accused of aloofness – ironically, in both cases it was a question of shyness and not social disdain. Barber remained unconvinced of Dexter's leadership credentials. He wasn't the only one of course. John Murray expressed similar reservations.

It was with some trepidation then that Bob drove to The Oval for the final Test match of the 1964 summer, which would turn out to be Ted Dexter's last Test as captain. He expected to be thrown the ball when the Australians were 235 for 2 and the captain had run out of options but at least he would be opening the batting this time and not going in after Ray Illingworth. This information, however, was not communicated to him until thirty minutes before the start of play. His partner was to be the young Yorkshire opener Geoffrey Boycott, who had risen rapidly through the ranks to the surprise of many to claim a Test place. In 1963, he hadn't been certain of being in the Yorkshire team. At the start of the 1964 Ashes series, he was opening for England in the first Test at Trent Bridge.

> *I don't think I played against Geoffrey before I opened the batting with him against the Aussies at The Oval. I knew who he was from the lads. The Warwickshire match against Yorkshire didn't take place till after that fifth Test and he was injured for the first match at Edgbaston… I remember talking to the Yorkshire lads and John Hampshire said to me, "This so and so will block or pad up for five balls and off the last ball he'll tuck it down to long leg for a single or he'll be running you out." I said to Geoffrey before that first Test together, "You can have half the bowling but I'm having the other half and if you think I'm going to stand there and watch you nudge the last ball for a single, you can forget because I won't run and I mean it."*

He certainly did mean it as Boycott would find out in the Durban Test in a few months time but, as they walked down the steps at The Oval together for the first time, Boycott was as unsure as to exactly what to expect from Barber as Barber was from Boycott. In fact, Bob was not even sure himself as to how he should be playing and clearly he didn't feel able to talk about it with the captain.

> *I was puzzled as to how I was expected to play. I got a hundred before lunch at Edgbaston and I was hitting it on the up but now I'd been recalled to the Test team, I did not know how I was expected to play. I'd been out of the team for a couple of years and the main openers had been Noddy and Peter Richardson on the subcontinent. I much preferred opening but I'm playing in a different way, going after the bowling. I wasn't sure if I should play as I did for Warwickshire or as a traditional opener. I didn't know I was opening the innings until half an hour before the match started. I think John Edrich might have been made twelfth man. Bill [Willie] Watson was one of the selectors so I asked him. He said I should hit the ball but I don't think I did in that match. I was still slightly inhibited. In South Africa it was different.*

It certainly was, but Bob's return to international cricket was, as he remembers, somewhat surprisingly muted. Dexter won the toss and chose to bat so Boycott and Barber went down the steps of the pavilion together for the first time. They put on a circumspect 44 in just under an hour before Neil Hawke bowled Bob. He did the same to Boycott shortly afterwards, finishing with 6-47 as England mustered a disappointing 182 all out. Sadly for Hawke, his contribution to the match is better remembered for his edging Trueman to Cowdrey at second slip and so giving "the finest fast bowler that ever drew breath" his three hundredth Test wicket.

Runs from Lawry, Booth and Veivers gave Australia a first innings lead of just under 200, but the last day of the match was washed out and an improved England batting performance in the second innings enabled the home side to avoid defeat with some comfort. Boycott and Barber this time put on 80 for the first wicket, but the Warwickshire opener seemed to retreat into his Lancashire style of playing and had only made 29 in over two hours of cautious batting when he was adjudged lbw to Garth McKenzie. It was disappointing for anyone in the crowd who had come to see the birth of a new England star. In fact, they did see one even if it wasn't the one they were expecting. Geoffrey Boycott, fighting for his place and fighting to save a Test match, was in his element. He batted for five hours in making his first Test century and gave the crowd a preview of many days to come over the next seventeen years.

Boycott and Barber met again the following week in the county match between Warwickshire and Yorkshire at St. George's Road in Harrogate. Both made runs but in more conventionally contrasting styles, though this is not the reason that Bob remembers the match so vividly.

A.C. Smith persuaded the club to buy an estate car so he could travel by car and carry the bags. We decided to go on the morning of the game and travel from Birmingham to Harrogate in time for an 11.30 start. I was travelling with Billy Ibadulla and Albert Wright, who was no sort of bat. We got there OK and at 11.15 Closey knocks on the door and says we have to toss up. There's nobody there except the three of us. We had to do something otherwise Closey would have claimed the match. We went out to the middle and fortunately I won the toss and chose to bat because there was only the three of us there. Part of my cricket kit was in AC's car so I had no bat, pads or gloves. I went into the Yorkshire dressing room and borrowed Dougie Padgett's pads and a pair of right handed gloves. I picked up a bat and said "I'll have this" and Ray Illingworth says, "You're not taking my bloody bat". Billy and I opened the innings and if we'd lost a wicket Albert would have had to bat and it would all have been over. Fred of course sets an extreme Carmody field with everyone in a huge arc from point to square leg with four slips and two leg slips. He comes charging in and I started slogging him, making Fred absolutely furious because there was no one in front of square. We batted for about twenty minutes before the rest of the side got there. Fred was incensed because he couldn't get a wicket and Illy was seething because he thought I was ruining his bat and I just said, "It's the first time the ball's ever hit the middle of this bat all bloody season". Eventually I said to Don Wilson to get hold of the ball because I wanted to get out and I didn't want to give my wicket to any of those other miserable buggers.

Bob had made 61 out of a total of 77 before he was caught by Richard Hutton off Wilson. Ibadulla, who carried his bat for 109, must have stood at the other end and watched open mouthed as Bob carved the Yorkshire bowling to all quarters of the ground, knowing that if he got himself out early his adventurous batting had cost Warwickshire the match. In the second innings, he got another rapid hundred before, yet again, he decided he had had enough and, as his friend Don Wilson was bowling, he decided to charge down the wicket; the ball turned past the outside edge and Jimmy Binks stumped him with his usual quiet efficiency. The relieved Yorkshire bowlers must have been sick of the sight of Barber carving them to all corners with impunity. His new England opening partner must have wondered what had happened at The Oval if Bob Barber could play like this. In fact, it was a good job that Bob had come off because as soon as the rest of the team arrived and Bob had duly got himself out, MJK and John Jameson were both dismissed by the enraged Yorkshire bowlers for ducks.

It was hilarious but if it had been Lancs it would have been all over the press; the two Birmingham fellows, even if they had found out, would never have said anything. They'd have tried to cover up for us.

This was another reason why Bob found the atmosphere in Birmingham so much more congenial than he had in the more fervid atmosphere of Manchester. Jim Stewart speaks with great fondness of the two Birmingham-based cricket correspondents.

When we went to away games, I used to travel in the same car as Ray Hitchcock for about fifteen years and we would take with us the cricket correspondent of the Birmingham Post and the cricket correspondent of the Birmingham Mail. John Solan of the Post was a brilliant writer, more than a journalist. Both were good men and you could trust them. Nothing would appear in the paper that would embarrass us and in return we gave them information that helped them in their jobs. Bob would have no trouble with them.

At Lancashire the cricket correspondent of the *Manchester Evening News*, who might well have had the best interests of Lancashire cricket at heart, nevertheless had a brother who sat on the Lancashire committee. When problems arose after the Kent match at Old Trafford in 1960, he had been busily stirring the pot. It can be argued that he was only doing his job but it certainly didn't help to create a warm relationship of mutual support between the captain and the local paper as he saw was in evidence at Edgbaston.

The local reporters in Birmingham were very different from John Kay but in Manchester you had the national press. I liked Eric Todd very much but generally those Manchester-based journalists appeared to be trying to do people down all the time. John Solan and Bill Wanklyn of the Birmingham Mail weren't in competition with the national press so the lads were happy that John and Bill travelled on the coach with us, came into the bar and had a drink with us. If one of them started to make things awkward for anyone he would have been frozen out, but it never happened so it was always a friendly atmosphere. John Kay's brother was on the committee and he always had the ear of Tommy Burrows and so on. It was very different at Warwickshire. I didn't trust any journalist in Manchester apart from Eric Todd. Liverpool was friendly, like Birmingham, but Manchester wasn't.

The 1964 county championship season ended with Warwickshire as runners up but a significant 41 points behind the winners, local rivals Worcestershire. Bob's ambition of playing for the county champions had still not been realised but the season did not end in anti-climax and personal recrimination as it had in 1960 when Lancashire lost out to Yorkshire. 1964 was the second season in which domestic cricket reached its climax not with victory in the championship but with the final of the Gillette Cup played in front of a full house at Lord's. After their victory over Lancashire, Warwickshire were eagerly anticipating a first cup trophy and M.J.K. Smith was keen to pit his wits against E.R. Dexter, the acknowledged master of innovation in the tactics of one day cricket.

Dexter was, not for the first time, late to turn up and when the umpires called the captains to go out to the middle to toss up he was nowhere to be seen in the Sussex dressing room. As vice captain, Jim Parks was on his way through the Long Room to meet Mike Smith

and Ted catches me as we're walking down the steps of the pavilion towards the gate. Now we always batted first and Ian Thomson put the squeeze on to get them behind the rate so that's what I was going to do, despite the overhead conditions and the early start – I think it was 10.30. Anyway, Ted catches me but he loses the toss and MJK decides to bat and Tommy runs through them – I think they were 95 for 7 at lunch something like that and it was all over. Bob was always vulnerable to Ian Thomson's inswing which was an outswinger to him and I think Tommy got him early.

Barber fell when the score was only 9 and he had made just 3 – caught Parks bowled Thomson who completed his 13 overs taking 4-23. Seven of the players on view in that Gillette Cup Final would make up almost half of the MCC touring party to South Africa that winter. In addition to the captain and Bob Barber, Warwickshire provided the young fast bowler David Brown and the reliable Tommy Cartwright, whilst from Sussex, Jim Parks and Ian Thomson would eventually be joined by Dexter, provided he was not required by the voters of Cardiff South-East.

Smith had taken over Cowdrey's party on the previous winter's tour of India when the Kent captain dropped out. The selection of Brown and Cartwright demonstrated that this touring party to South Africa was going to be significantly influenced by the new captain. A dithering selection policy in the summer of 1964 meant that twenty players had been involved in the Ashes series which had been lost. Finally, with a captain who could communicate with his players, MCC stood a chance of winning against a major Test playing country for the first time since victory in the Caribbean in 1959-60.

Ian Wooldridge, writing in the *Daily Mail* when the tour was two months old, spotted a significant social change.

If there is anything that will confer permanent historic significance upon this winter's MCC tour of South Africa, it is the loss without trace of that most noble of English anachronisms, the amateur gentleman cricketer. For a while, the resilience that brought him through one social revolution, two world wars and a dozen attempts to tax him into more productive employment, saw his spirit live on. David Sheppard saw out his sabbatical as the glamorous cricketing parson. Ted Dexter continued to captain England from a white charger so high that it was hard for him to consult colleagues during times of Test crisis. Colin Cowdrey went on leading Kent across England in a Mark Ten Jaguar, without accepting a salary. English cricket has now passed for better or for worse into the hands of the complete professional. Such a man is Mike Smith, Oxford Blue and relentless tactician.

Although MJK was an amateur, he was not amateur in the style of P.B.H. May, M.C. Cowdrey or E.R. Dexter. He was much closer to his men, which pleased professionals like Murray J.T. who summed up the difference even more pithily.

MJK would come out to dinner with you in the evening and have a laugh and a joke. I can't remember Colin or Dexter ever doing that. Cowdrey and Dexter were both rotten captains. If Plan A didn't work that was it, Dexter was chipping onto the eighteenth green at St. Andrews.

For Bob Barber, it meant a tour against tough opposition under a captain who was prepared to give him his head. After the misfire at The Oval would cricket lovers finally see for themselves the sort of batting at Test level of which he knew he was capable but which he had never yet demonstrated?

CHAPTER TEN

E.R. DEXTER'S ATTEMPT to wrest the constituency of Cardiff South-East away from the incumbent Labour candidate L. J. Callaghan in the autumn of 1964 was no more successful than his attempt to wrest the Ashes from R.B. Simpson had been during the summer. He lost to the future prime minister by 8,000 votes and was roundly booed on some appearances during his election campaign – presumably for his support of the unpopular Sir Alec Douglas-Home and his discredited policies rather than his inability to know when to bowl a leg spinner. Among the Conservative Party's other failures that year was "Professor" Jimmy Edwards, who failed to win the seat of Paddington North by a similarly large margin and was forced to deliver his political philosophy alongside Ted Ray and Arthur Askey from the panel on the Light Programme's popular *Does The Team Think?* Ted Dexter, meanwhile, flew to meet the rest of the touring party in Rhodesia.

Bob Barber voted in the 1964 election for the first of two occasions in his life. Fifty years on, it is perhaps possible to reveal without controversy that he voted Liberal before joining up with the rest of the tour party. By the time the plane had landed in Africa the world had changed. It wasn't just that boxes of H.P. sauce would now be transported to Downing Street as the Conservatives left government after thirteen years to be replaced by a supporter of Huddersfield Town and Yorkshire CCC. In Moscow, Nikita Khrushchev was removed from power in a way that was both mysterious and unexpected. It made the "Magic Circle", the method by which the Conservative Party chose its leaders, look transparent and democratic. On the same day, China announced it had detonated an atomic bomb, making the world feel considerably more insecure and the constant news from the Olympic Games in Tokyo ensured that little space in the newspapers was granted to the arrival of the MCC touring party in Bulawayo.

During the 1963-4 Southern Hemisphere summer, South Africa had gone to Australia and played out a hard fought 1-1 drawn series. After their disastrous tour of England in 1960, which had seen Bob Barber's Test match debut, it had taken some time for South Africa to identify a new crop of young players and bring them through to Test match level. The side now boasted the talents of Eddie Barlow and the brothers Peter and Graeme Pollock, together with the Rhodesian batsman and outstanding fielder, Colin Bland. They all knew that waiting in the wings was a teenager, who was expected to rival Graeme Pollock as a batsman of the highest class, called Barry Richards whose appearance could not be delayed much longer. The home supporters felt they were now in a position to beat England at home, especially since England were coming on the back of two disappointing and losing series against the West Indies in 1963 and the Australians in 1964. The fearsome bowling attack which had troubled South Africa in 1956-7 – Tyson, Loader, Laker, Lock, Bailey and Wardle had all gone. The medium pace of Ian Thomson and Tommy Cartwright, the leg spin of young Robin Hobbs, the inexperience of the openers Boycott and Barber held no terrors for the South Africans and contributed to this air of burgeoning self-confidence.

Back in Yorkshire, F.S. Trueman, holder of the record for most victims in Test cricket, sat fuming at the insult of having been left out. It was felt that he probably would not make the Test side, in which case he would prove a disruptive tourist. John Murray, who went as deputy to Jim Parks, remembers that

Fred only did four tours – he did two to the West Indies and two to Australia. He desperately wanted to go to South Africa and he certainly thought he should have gone. A few years ago, Warwickshire had a celebration for MJK and they wrote to Fred inviting him. Fred said, "No I won't be there, I'll be at home. Just like I was in 1964."

Mike Smith ignored it all and concentrated on giving all his players a good work out before the first Test which did not start until nearly seven weeks after the party had arrived in Southern Africa. Bob set out his stall in the very first match, scoring 108 in the second innings and guiding MCC to a five wicket win over Rhodesia in Salisbury. It was "a superb century" according to Denys Rowbotham in *The Guardian* who had not been an unequivocal fan of Bob Barber during his Lancashire days.

What Rowbotham wrote in praise of this innings, however, is revealing in that it does not suggest that Bob's new-found success was the result of blind slogging – hitting the ball on the up and hoping it missed the fielders, just "giving it a whack" in the vernacular employed by cricketers.

The secrets of Barber's authority were judgment, footwork and such disciplined eschewing of risk as permitted him only two dangerous shots. Scarcely once today did he miscalculate a ball's length or line. Always before moving forward to push or to drive, his back foot was unerringly behind the ball. Always he met the ball with the bat's full face. Never did he allow a chink of daylight between a defensive bat and pad.

The Rhodesians who had the good grace off the field not to mention the acronym UDI to their guests did not display quite the same civility on it, deciding to call for a second dilatory drinks interval in the space of an hour when MCC needed ten runs to win with five wickets left but with thick black storm clouds hovering overhead. The clouds burst in torrents of rain twenty minutes after Barrington and Parks had run the winning leg byes which, wrote Ron Roberts in the *Daily Telegraph*,

> *underlined the fact that Barber's aggression in the context of the event alone made victory possible.*

Roberts was reporting for the *Telegraph* alongside Michael Melford because Jim Swanton had taken a principled stand and refused to go on the tour – as had John Arlott who had been there in 1947-8, seen the initial impact of the Nationalist government on South African society and decided not to accompany the MCC tour in 1956-7. It is interesting how often that E.W. Swanton, easily categorised as a blinkered Southern right wing reactionary, appears liberal and progressive on the issue of colour amidst the sea of racism that swirled around him.

Bob was well on the way to satisfying the first of his two reasons for going on the tour. His century in Salisbury was a foretaste of plenty of innings to come on this tour and that of Australia the following winter. The other reason Bob was keen to go on the tour was that it would offer him a first hand view of *apartheid*. Although Rhodesia would not make its infamous Unilateral Declaration of Independence until November the following year, it was clear that tension between Ian Smith and Harold Wilson, the new prime minister, was already growing and the MCC party was inevitably caught in the crossfire. The possibility that the socialist anti-colonial Wilson would send British forces to crush "our kith and kin", as the Rhodesians were termed at the time, was anathema to many white British people. Ian Smith, after all, had been an RAF pilot during the Battle of Britain.

The right-wing instincts of the MCC at Lord's could not be seen to find expression in such a volatile political environment and the players were told firmly to keep their minds on the business of cricket. For the vast majority of the party this was no sacrifice but for two of them, being in Southern Africa in 1964 represented an opportunity to inform themselves about *apartheid*, that they could not possibly pass up. The two Cambridge graduates, R.W. Barber and J.M. Brearley, decided not to tell their Oxonian captain what they were getting up to.

> *We arrived in Southern Rhodesia in October 1964, just as the Labour government was being voted in and Labour were much more likely than the Tories to take a*

England in South Africa 1964/65.

Bob Barber, right, and a relaxed group of players at a South African gold mine.

Boycott, Parks and Barber do a spot of snake charming in South Africa.
The snake has chosen its victim.

The England team set off for Australia above and, below, Barber shows his intent for the tour by smashing Doug Walters for six during the first Test in Brisbane. This is the pose the Australian public most typically saw Bob in during the 1965/66 tour.

"They're making my runs" time. Boycott was paranoid he would not get his place back in time for the first test after leaving Ceylon late because of illness.

Relaxing with the family in Australia.

Despite the pressures of an Ashes series, there was plenty of time for other pursuits. Right, Barber accompanies Ken Barrington in a round of golf and, below, the other England players keep their distance as he tweaks the Aussie wallaby by the tail.

Above, Barber strolls out to practise with his opening partner Boycott, and, left, 3rd Test first day at Sydney January 7th 1966. Bob Barber in punishing mood during his innings of 185.

A new England team for the final test against the West Indies at The Oval in 1966.

On tour in East Africa.

With Geoff Edrich. Edrich had been a rival for the captaincy of Lancashire but had been dismissed at the end of the 1959 season.

stand against Ian Smith, so the pressure for UDI was building up and we got a fair amount of stick from the crowd about it. I wanted to go because I wanted to see for myself what conditions were like in South Africa. Even in those days I was cynical about organs of propaganda. Mike Brearley was very conscious of the politics and on two occasions, once in Cape Town and once in Durban, we got one of the black drivers of the Rothman's cars to take us out into townships at night. It was dangerous. You could end up in prison for doing that sort of thing. I suspect the instigation came from Brearley. Mike and I said to the driver, "Stop the car!" We got out and knocked on someone's door and asked to come in. Very nosey but everyone was very polite. What surprised me was that the properties were built out of breeze blocks and I expected much worse. I've seen worse in India and South East Asia.

The entire MCC party was invited to meet with the Prime Minister of South Africa, Dr Hendrik Verwoerd. As with Mugabe in 2003, there was much discussion in the team about whether they should shake hands with him. Bob was keen to learn about the reality of life in South Africa and understood the view of the country generally afforded to the cricket tourist would be partial and distorted. Tom Cartwright, he felt, was also interested in the politics of the country but his Warwickshire team mate didn't accompany Barber and Brearley on their adventures.

There were road signs saying Cattle Crossing and Natives Crossing. I felt terrible looking at things like that but I wanted to learn something about it. Going back to my schooldays, my oldest friend was Jamaican and there was Robert Aiyar, with whom I played so much cricket, and he was Anglo-Indian. Shutting the door and just saying, "I don't want to know what's going on behind the fence over there" wasn't an option. I wanted to know.

Mike Smith knew nothing of these nocturnal excursions. Bob, who was such a close friend, would never have wanted to have embarrassed his captain in this manner and his captain was grateful for the courtesy.

Personally, I decided that I would disregard the politics in South Africa. We were out there to win a Test series. The political shit hadn't quite hit the fan. I knew Brearley had gone into the townships but I didn't know Bob had. That might have turned out to be a very difficult situation. The feeling was that if you wished to get involved in politics you shouldn't go on a cricket tour. What Brears and Bob did was off their own bats and if they wanted to see what was going on and did it in a responsible fashion that's fair enough with me but it would have been very difficult if the news had got out.

It didn't. Again, there is something in Bob's behaviour that calls to mind what Michael Atherton might have done in similar circumstances.

The tour, nevertheless, progressed satisfactorily for the MCC. Bob Barber made a sparkling 59 against Transvaal before being unfortunately run out (not by Boycott) and then took four wickets as MCC won by an innings and plenty. He batted well too against Natal as MCC won by ten wickets, so Smith could afford to rest him as his side went to Port Elizabeth to play Eastern Province, in order to give the two young openers Boycott and Brearley a chance to find their feet. Although Bob wasn't playing, it turned out to be a defining moment in the Barber/Boycott relationship as Boycott well remembers.

I was still trying to find a bit of form as a young kid. I was about 190, trying to make 200 around lunchtime on the second day. Peter Pollock bowled bouncers over my head and then beamers three times at me. Then he bowled down the leg side to stop me getting to 200 by lunch. That night in the bar, I'm not a drinker but I was told about it, Peter Pollock was laughing about the beamers. Bob had had a whisky or two and Bob said to Pollock, "If you bowl one at me, let me tell you, you'd better f***ing hit me because otherwise I'm coming for you with the bat. And if you bowl another one at him again, when I'm at the other end, you're for it." He was like my older brother. I realised immediately that he was more experienced, more mature; everything about him was like an older brother. He was very good to me that way. He was a very powerful man, Bob Barber. People might not realise that but he was physically fit, 6'2" and very imposing.

In later life, Peter Pollock became an evangelical Christian. Geoffrey Boycott has neither forgotten nor forgiven the treatment he meted out and believes that it was really the least he could have done to compensate for the batsmen he had targeted. The Yorkshire opener who was left stranded on 193 hasn't yet absorbed the Christian principle of turning the other cheek.

They tell me Peter Pollock's become religious. He f******g needed to. He was a shocker. Bouncers and beamers and laughing and thinking it was all right. He was a shocker.

It was always going to be Boycott and Barber to open the batting in the Test matches because Brearley with no Test experience was in wretched form. It looked briefly, however, as if "The Refugee" as he was amusingly termed because of his dirty T shirt, Sixties student's hairstyle and generally unkempt appearance, might have to take Bob's place when, in the time between the province and the Test matches, Bob broke two bones in his right foot tackling Brian Johnston in a bizarre accident during a game of football.

We were playing barefoot on the beach against the press. I tackled him, saved the goal but broke two toes. I was pleased Johnston didn't score but I was taken to an orthopaedic clinic who said the best thing I could do was to bathe the foot in the sea. I had to cover it up because I had to play Peter Pollock for the rest of the tour with two broken toes on my front foot and we had to make sure he didn't know. Pollock wasn't Wes Hall but he was an aggressive bowler.

As Geoffrey Boycott had already discovered.

Boycott prepared for his first Test innings like a professional. Bob prepared in a way that would have made headlines in every tabloid in today's environment.

Before the Durban Test, we had to go to a function the night before at a country club. When I walked in I saw the manager Donald Carr at the bar with one or two locals and I said, "Hello, 'Ger, I'll have one on you." He said, "What would you like?" I said, "I'll have a scotch" and he got hold of a bottle and said, "You can only have a scotch if you drink the bottle" so I said I would but I paid for it next day when I was cramping with exhaustion and got out [for 74]. Finishing it took me till 3 o'clock in the morning, when an aggressive South African came up to me and told me I was drunk. Scotch doesn't affect me so I said I wasn't drunk. I said I'll go on the dance floor and do the Muffin Man so I went onto the dance floor with a glass, went down backwards and came up again without spilling a drop. "I'm not drunk and don't say that again". Next day however, I really felt it. I was determined not to get out cheaply but by the time I got out I was finished. That was a happy tour and that's why I played well. I was just happy.

However happy he was, however successful he was and however protective he was of young Boycott, the first Test match at Durban brought the matter of running between the wickets to a head in the most dramatic manner. When Bob had informed the Yorkshireman that he wanted half the bowling, Boycott believes he responded by saying,

"You're going to have to learn to be a better counter." He nearly did me at Durban because he wouldn't move.

There is no dispute between the two of them as to what happened. Bob recalls that it was as early as the first over of the first innings at Durban.

I let him take strike in the first Test at Durban and he did it to me at the end of Peter Pollock's first over. It could have been a two if I'd wanted to run, it was so fine of long leg. He got down my end almost into my crease before he had to turn round and go back again. He was furious and I said, "I told you. I am not running on the sixth ball just for your benefit. If you want to run yourself out you can do so because I don't give a damn." After that I think we ran together quite well.

Fifty years on, Boycott ruminates over being made to run twice the length of the pitch and receiving nothing for it in the scorebook. *Yes. He was a bugger like that, was Bob.*

The two of them put on 120 for the first wicket before Bob on 74, limp with exhaustion from the humidity and with his body starting to respond to the bottle of whisky he had consumed the previous night, brought his bat down too late to deal with a slow yorker from the South Africa captain, Trevor Goddard. He had already made his feelings clear about the quality of the South African bowling both in the manner in which he had played it and in what he said to his opening partner after the first over from Kelly Seymour. The young off spinner had made his debut the previous year on the South African tour of Australia and had bowled tidily but Bob Barber was not impressed. He played out the first over and then marched down the pitch to pronounce judgement to his opening partner.

He said to me, "This guy can't bowl. I think I'm going to slog him". Now, I'm a young lad from Yorkshire and I'm thinking, "Hang on, this is a Test match!" I was brought up to play proper cricket, keeping the ball on the floor. One day cricket had only just started. If you tried to hit the ball in the air in Yorkshire you got into trouble and here I am playing in a Test match in front of a full house because it was a Test match and a Test match was a big deal in South Africa in those days – they only played us, Australia and New Zealand - and Bob Barber is going to start slogging.

In fact, Bob had made the decision after Seymour's first ball. The second disappeared into the grandstand. The next over, two fours crashed into the boundary boards, one behind square off a strong sweep and the other straight behind the bowler. By lunch on the first day of the first Test, Bob was already 52 not out and young Seymour, whose eight overs had cost 35, was holed beneath the water line for the rest of the series. Bob had done exactly what he had set out to do – play aggressively and score quickly, damaging the confidence of the opposition bowlers.

The Test match at Durban produced an almost perfect performance from England. Boycott was out for 73 and Peter Parfitt followed for a duck. After MJK Smith was dismissed for 35, England were wobbling slightly at 279 for 5, but Parks and Barrington both made centuries in an unbeaten stand of over two hundred, allowing Smith to declare at 495 for 5. David Allen took 5-41 and Bob 2 for 48, as South Africa folded for 155 and, following on, performed not much better second time round. This time Fred Titmus was the principal destroyer with 5-66 as South Africa lost the Test by an innings and 104 runs. The home country's perception of England as an easy victim had proved drastically wide of the mark. Mike Smith remembers

The difference between the two sides in South Africa was very simple. We had a high class spin attack and they didn't. We were brought up on wet wickets and we could play spin.

Over the six weeks of games against the provinces, it seemed that the whole team appeared to be in some sort of batting form, but what gave Smith enormous confidence was the success of the opening partnership. He was particularly pleased that the two different personalities of Barber and Boycott seemed to mesh so perfectly even if that first over from Pollock had given the dressing room some concern.

Boycott had written to me when he was 16 about wearing specs and becoming a professional batsman. I just wrote the standard letter back telling him my eyes were 100% but he told me later it had helped and he appreciated it. Anyone would have done the same. I always got on well with Geoff Boycott and if you wanted someone to bat for your life on Day 1 of a Test match Boycott would be high on your list. You can criticise him and say he didn't always play according to the requirements of the team and that was true but you want a batter who will bat all day. Geoff was different because he would happily bat for two days. Having Bob at the other end, it was like Amiss and Jameson. It helped Boycott because he would never have to worry about getting on with it. He could just concentrate on playing.

The relationship between Barber and Boycott developed off the field because Bob deliberately set out to bring the young introvert out of his shell.

He was an instinctive loner but I remember going to his room and saying, "Come on, we're going out". I took him off to see the sights, safari parks, stick fighting and so on. Stick fighting involved two people, women as well, smashing each other with sticks. I've got Geoffrey on film with my father, my brother and one of his friends; it was like an afternoon's football. It was important that Geoffrey and I got on. To me he was a good chap to run with. I knew where I was with him. I had time for Geoffrey. We went off to see rhinos with our cine cameras. We'd been told rhinos were blind and if you stand still they can't distinguish you from trees. Our guide was Gary Player's brother. He was going to get the rhino to charge at him and we could take film of it at right angles, safely out of the way. So the rhino charges and suddenly turns straight towards us. The native was the first one up the tree. Those rhinos really move quicker than a horse. Geoffrey moved pretty fast I can tell you.

Geoffrey, perhaps unsurprisingly, has a slightly different version of these events, though he remains grateful that Bob took the time and trouble to look after him in that caring way, because he is ready to admit that his dedication to making it as a Test opener was such that it tended to cut him off from the japes that a touring party thrives on.

I liked Bob a lot and he was always good and straight with me. I was a very introverted lad about my cricket. I had blinkers on, very focused on my cricket and trying like hell to make something of myself. At that time I wasn't at all sure I was going to make it. To get to me wasn't easy but Barber did it. He took me off to Hluhluwe Game Park near Durban. We had the Sunday off in Natal – they were very religious and they all went to church. We got up and left Durban at 4am and travelled about two or three hours to see these rhinos – there was a big white one and a little black one. The guy who met us at the park was Ian Player, Gary Player's brother. He took us round the park and we came across this little black rhino, walking. "Shit, stand still! He's looking at you, pawing the bloody ground, he's getting ready to charge. Shit!!!" It was fun walking round the park looking at the antelopes. When the rhino starts looking you in the eye from forty yards away it wasn't funny then. I was shit scared. I turned round to find Bob and he was halfway up a tree. I'm still on the ground and I ask Ian Player if he has a gun. He says he doesn't. He says, "Just stand still because they can't see very well. They're short sighted so they respond to movement. If you move, they'll charge and they weigh about a ton." So we stood still, till it buggered off. That was very scary.

Whoever it was who made it up the tree first, it is clear that facing that black rhino was distinctly more terrifying than facing the bullying Peter Pollock. At Johannesburg, Barber confirmed for all to see that he was an outstanding Test match opening batsman with an innings that lived in the memory of all who saw it. It was to be superseded only by events at Sydney the following year.

England held the ascendancy for the first four days of the second Test at Johannesburg, and most of that was due to Bob Barber whose innings of 97 dominated the first day's play. Again Mike Smith called correctly and Barber and Boycott set forth to face Pollock and his opening partner, Partridge. Each batsman found the boundary in his first over but Boycott added no more before being caught behind off Pollock. Dexter then joined Barber and together they took the score in no time at all from 10-1 to 121 for 1 at lunch. Dexter had made 42 off 93 balls: Barber had faced 92 balls and was already on 75. He speeded up after lunch, crushing Pollock off successive balls for four to square leg, four to extra cover and an off drive which stopped just short of the boundary. Boycott, watching from the balcony of the pavilion, like everyone else, could only stand and admire what was happening in the middle. Understandably, he particularly enjoyed Barber's duel with Pollock.

He took the piss out of Peter Pollock because he started bouncing him. He turned his cap around and he got down on one knee and pretended to sweep him like he was a slow bowler. He kept doing it, which enraged Pollock who bounced him even more and Bob just let it go and then he would get down on one knee and pretend to sweep again. When Pollock pitched it up Bob would smash him through the covers for four because he was a wonderful off side driver. He wasn't a slogger at all; he was a beautiful classical driver of the ball through the off side.

Brian Johnston, grateful that he hadn't permanently incapacitated England's star batsman, described on the radio with relish Barber's approach to his maiden Test century, but as the end of the over came with Barber on 97 not out, he was instructed to hand back to the studio in London. As he was doing so and the fielders changed over, Bob met Dexter in the middle of the pitch saying to him, "It's going to be six or out". Boycott might have had heart failure. Even Dexter said "Don't be so daft" but Bob could not be dissuaded. "I mean it", he told the former England captain. He saw the ball in the hands of the nervous Kelly Seymour and decided that the first ball was going into the stand at wide mid on. He launched an enormous cross-batted swipe at Seymour's gentle off spin....

It was a bit of a wallop, yes but it was wide outside the off stump. The ball hit the inside edge and I dragged it on a long way. In that innings Kenny Barrington, who came in after me, got to 94. He scratched a new guard, looked up at the pavilion and I thought he was looking at me. Anyway, the bowler ran in and delivered and Kenny hit the ball straight back over his head and over the sightscreen for six. Then he looked up at the pavilion again as if to say, "That's how to do it".

Every Englishman was disappointed for Bob except Bob, who has never placed great credence in the acquisition of three figures, unlike most other batsmen. As far as he was concerned, he'd enjoyed the innings, England were on top and the South African bowlers were crushed so he had done his job successfully. If that ball had gone for six and he had been bowled the following ball, it would not have helped by a significant measure England to win the match so getting out for 97 instead of 103 by his standards made very little difference. Barrington came in and made 121; Dexter went on to make 172 and England were safe from defeat by the close of he second day, when South Africa were 9 for no wicket in reply to England's 531 all out. There was no way England could lose the match and that was due in no small measure not just to Bob Barber's 97, but to the way in which he had made those 97 runs.

When he returned to the dressing room there was no criticism of the shot he played to get out in that manner. Even fifty years later, Mike Smith remembers shrugging his shoulders and recognising Bob for the free spirit that he was.

As far as Bob is concerned if he's on 97 he's had a good day. You can rest assured though, that if the situation had been different and he needed to stay there he wouldn't have played that shot. He had a very off beat sense of humour.

The only thing that would have disappointed Bob was that his father and his brother Tony were flying out for the Third Test at Cape Town and had therefore not only not been there in Johannesburg to see his highest Test score to date, but had been subject to the moment when Brian Johnston had returned listeners to the BBC studios in London with Bob on 97. There was no television, no internet, not even Ceefax to stare at until Bob had safely passed into three figures. Nevertheless, the arrival of his family was an enormous fillip to him.

My father encouraged me all my life. He was a great supporter of me playing cricket. In about 1956 I was thinking of giving up cricket in favour of athletics. It was the one time I saw my father break down in front of me and say "You mustn't do it". I think he thought I would come to regret it. He was an athlete himself.

I had always had it in my mind to finish playing cricket at about 28. I was just turned 29 when the South Africa tour began. We had dinner together before I left and that was when he said I should consider my future and perhaps stop. I said that I was very keen to go to South Africa and he just said OK but remember you have a life to live afterwards. He was still supportive enough to pay for Tony and his friend for them all to fly out to South Africa just before the New Year's Test at Cape Town.

South Africa had saved the second Test at Johannesburg after being made to follow on again, but this time Allen and Titmus, who had bowled nearly eighty overs between them in the first innings and nearly a hundred in the second, could not force a win and South Africa escaped with a draw, thanks to a big hundred by Colin Bland on the last day. Although the build up to the Tests had been leisurely, the gap between the second and third Tests was just three days, including the flight of a thousand miles from the heights of Johannesburg to the coastal city of Cape Town.

To make matters worse, Smith now lost the toss and the tired England bowlers had to take the field and start all over again. This time, the South Africans made them pay and at the close of the first day they were 252 for 1, with Eddie Barlow on 138 not out. As far as England were concerned, he should have been back in the pavilion when he had made 40, because it was then that he chopped a ball from Titmus onto his foot, whence it lobbed in the air to Parfitt in the gulley who caught it easily. If they expected Barlow to walk they were disappointed. If they expected the home umpire to give Barlow out they were even more disappointed. The Middlesex off spinner let Barlow know exactly what he thought of his decision to stay there knowing perfectly well he was out. Eddie Barlow was no wilting violet. At the end of the over he walked from his crease and let Titmus know what interesting anatomical exercise he could perform on himself. From that moment on, Titmus's hold over the South African batsmen began to lessen. Bob had made a good catch at short leg off bat and pad in the previous Test which the umpire had not upheld. Now he joined in the chorus of resentment.

I said to Barlow that he was an effing cheat because he wouldn't walk. He was a pugnacious man, a non-walker but this was a fairly blatant catch that went off his boot to Parfitt in the gully. You have to remember the Jo'burg Test when we made them follow on. They really gave us a grinding, scoring 700 runs in their two innings and then we came to Cape Town and they were on their way to 500. So we had been fielding what seemed like a week and South Africa had scored 1000 runs for very few wickets and I think all 10 outfielders bowled in their second innings. When the incident happened, morale was not at its highest. We were frazzled and when somebody doesn't walk when it's obviously out and the umpire doesn't give it, that's the background. The f word was certainly floating around. [On the 1955-6 MCC tour of Pakistan] Donald Carr was involved in a major incident, when an unpopular umpire in Pakistan was drenched by a bucket of water deliberately set up to give him a good idea of what the English players thought about his umpiring. Now there's this incident with Parfitt and Barlow and Donald is getting a little anxious about his reputation back at Lord's but I must say that, in my opinion, Carr and Billy Griffith were the two best managers on a tour that I played under.

South Africa declared just before the close of the second day's play and on the Sunday that followed, Donald Carr called a press conference in which he tried to pour oil on troubled waters, although English dissatisfaction with the standard of umpiring continued to rankle. Titmus was told to apologise to Eddie Barlow, which must have required some moral contortion. Upon receipt of the apology, presumably made through gritted teeth, Barlow asked, "Did someone make you apologise?" Titmus nodded assent. "I wouldn't have" said Barlow bluntly and walked off. Perhaps coincidentally, perhaps not, but it became apparent with hindsight that Titmus's dominance of the South African batsmen disappeared at that moment.

Even in the midst of the hulabaloo, Mike Smith believes that the relations between the two sides were fine and certainly nothing like the poisonous atmosphere we are told exists between England and nearly every other Test playing nation today. Sledging in the manner we have come to expect it was minimal in 1964. People generally walked and those who didn't were quickly identified. Perhaps if Test cricket in 1965 had been played in the full glare of the media spotlight that is currently exerted on England's cricketers, if Eddie Barlow's "catch" had been shown to the world in super "slow-mo", if England had had the benefit of recourse to DRS to cope with some of the more contentious umpiring decisions that upset them so much.....They didn't. It was a different world and a different time and no good will come of judging yesterday's world by today's standards.

Bob Barber's South African trip had peaked with that innings in Johannesburg and for the England party generally their best performances were behind them, as the third and fourth Tests disintegrated into boring draws. The South Africans were frustrated because there was pressure on them at home to beat an England that no longer contained May and Cowdrey, Statham and Trueman, Lock and Laker and they couldn't recover ground after their defeat in Durban. England, pleased to be still in the lead going into the last Test, knew that they were struggling to keep their hold on the series and the South Africans had regained some of the initiative.

Bob made 58 at Cape Town, desperate not to get out early after his father had paid £1000 for three air fares, and 61 back at Johannesburg for the fourth Test, but in the second South African innings of that match Bob rather awkwardly caught Trevor Goddard at long leg off John Price and in doing so shattered the lowest joint of his right hand. It was bad enough for him to have to abandon the tour. England recognised that he wouldn't be able to play again for the rest of the tour and, with some misgivings, sent him home which left them without a partner for Boycott in the last Test.

For most of the professionals MCC had only themselves to blame for this situation. It wasn't so much that Mike Brearley and Robin Hobbs had been brought out as youngsters who might appear in future Tests but were unlikely to play in this series, but that the obvious third opener was not The Refugee but the more conventionally dressed John Edrich who was in the country coaching, as so many English professionals did during the winter months. Brearley was, like Steven Finn on the recent Ashes tour, "unselectable". The man who walked out to bat with Boycott in the last Test match at Port Elizabeth turned out to be England's reserve wicket keeper, J.T. Murray.

I played in the last Test and opened the batting. Bloody idiots. John Edrich was sitting in Jo'burg playing club cricket and they didn't pick him. Brearley was technically the other opener but he was a disaster, so they picked me and made me go in first. I was a 7 an 8 or a 9. If I was batting, we were either in the shit or we were slogging for a declaration in three day cricket. I never concentrated on batting. Jim Parks was a proper batter. I didn't get enough big scores to dislodge him.

It wasn't just Barber who was missing. Tommy Cartwright and John Price were also unavailable and England were forced to call up Ken Palmer, the Somerset seamer, who was also coaching in South Africa. Only a painstaking innings of 117 by Geoffrey Boycott rescued England after the Middlesex trio of Murray, Parfitt and Titmus had all failed. England conceded a small lead but, thanks to Boycott and Barrington, they had batted for most of the third and fourth days and in the end they clung on to win the series by virtue of that early victory in Durban.

Meanwhile, Bob Barber had flown back to England having scored 290 runs in four innings at an average of 72.50. He has never set any store by averages but it does give some confirmation to the idea that he had been one of the big successes of the tour. The South African commentator Charles Fortune had written after his innings of 97 in the second Test at The Wanderers

From first ball to finish this was an innings brim full of character and competence: the sort of export that would soon cure Britain's trading deficit. Its immediate effect was to give an enormous stimulus to bookings for the remaining days of the Test and go a long way towards assuring MCC of a credit balance on the tour.

It was exactly the judgement Bob had hoped to provoke. He returned to the British winter with the grateful thanks of team mates, crowds and MCC ringing in his ears.

He was still uncomfortably aware of what his father had said to him about not delaying a full time business career too long, but when he arrived back in England at the start of February 1965, he was very conscious that it was only nine months until the next MCC party left Lord's. This time the destination would be Australia. Tom Pearce had scuppered his chances of selection for the 1962-3 Ashes series. In the days when sometimes there were three years between Ashes tours and sometimes four or five Bob knew that the next tour was due to take place in 1970-71 when he would be thirty-five years old and certainly unlikely to be picked, even if he made himself available. This time round, he would be one of the first names on the team sheet but at the same time he knew that Anne, who was raising their daughter Sandy, needed him at home. He knew that his father had reservations about the amount of time he was dedicating to cricket and he knew that the longer he delayed his entry into the business world the harder it would be for him to catch up with those who had been forging ahead since graduation. But still....Australia....it would be his last chance to make the trip that all cricketers dream about. If ever he was to play the one innings of his life that would define his time as a cricketer it would have to be in Australia.

CHAPTER ELEVEN

WHEN HE GOT home from South Africa Bob Barber was a star. It wasn't like 2015 and nobody asked him to advertise anything with his shirt off. His cricket performances were reported exclusively on the sports pages and it was his performances on the field that had made him a star. Despite his well-intentioned plan to play less cricket rather than more and to give due time to his young family and to his father and their business, the fact was that in the English summer of 1965 he played all six Test matches against New Zealand and South Africa, a full season of county cricket for Warwickshire and finished off with two matches at the Scarborough Festival. For a man who was constantly attempting to back away from full time cricket, he gave a good impression of a man still besotted with the game.

Oddly enough, although his form in South Africa had been outstanding, not for the first time he failed to demonstrate to England fans in England the quality of the form which he displayed on overseas tours. With film of those performances pretty much non-existent, England supporters could have been forgiven for wondering if the newspaper reports of his batting in South Africa had been somewhat exaggerated, although to be fair nearly all England's batsmen struggled for fluency that summer.

He made very few runs for Warwickshire in May but was chosen to play for MCC against New Zealand, who had arrived as the first tourists of the summer. 1965 was the first season in which the experiment of having two touring sides visit during the English summer was tried. In the MCC match, Bob tried to play in the manner that had been so successful in South Africa. It was applauded by John Woodcock in *The Times*

Barber attacked as intrepidly as he did in South Africa, and in half an hour with effortless pushes, deflections and lissom straight drives and cover drives, made 26 of MCC's first 41 runs before he attacked Motz viciously once too often.

It was a tale that was endlessly repeated. Half a dozen boundaries and glorious strokes and then an ill-advised one followed by dismissal. It might have frustrated his supporters but he refused to mope. It was the way he believed the game should be played and he would not revert to his Old Trafford persona now.

Fortunately, he had a captain who knew what he could do and showed unswerving faith. When the Test series began, he and Boycott resumed their successful opening partnership. Barrington, Cowdrey and Dexter provided the underpinning of a nine-wicket win at Edgbaston in the first Test. New Zealand's batting folded in their first innings when Bob took 2-7 in the three overs he was allowed but, following on, the Kiwis put up sterner resistance. Over the two days of their second innings, Titmus bowled 59 overs and Barber 45, by far the most he had ever bowled in England and was rewarded with four wickets for 132. Denys Rowbotham in *The Guardian*, however, expressed in print exactly what Bob had long felt.

> *One thing that helped New Zealand was Smith's failure to persist with Barber and Titmus after the former had drawn forward and bowled Dick with a beautifully flighted and pitched leg break after only 12 minutes. Barber's figures at the end of this successful spell were 4-3-1-1 and his length and direction had proved as taxing as his spin. Smith unaccountably decided to dispense with both in favour of Trueman and Cartwright with the new ball.*

In character, when he and Boycott set out to chase the 95 required to win, Bob drove Morgan for four to bring up his half century and to bring England within a couple of runs of their target. He then tried to repeat the stroke next ball and was caught by the substitute fielder in front of the pavilion. The batsmen crossed and Boycott acquired the necessary runs off the next ball. Bob had barely taken his pads off when his partner returned with a highly prized not out to add to his average. He wondered why Bob had thrown his wicket away. Bob didn't feel he had thrown his wicket away. He had played quite nicely and his dismissal in no way affected the result which was a foregone conclusion. England had won the game and he had contributed to that victory. How could he possibly have been said to have thrown his wicket away? The two men espoused such widely differing cricketing philosophies it is fascinating that they made such a successful opening pair.

MCC were taking seriously the general demand for England to play the so-called Brighter Cricket, beloved of newspaper headline writers. To that end, during the summer of 1965, the most reliable batsman in England, Ken Barrington, was dropped after making 137 in the first New Zealand Test but taking seven and a quarter hours to do it. Two years later, when Boycott took all day to crawl to 106 not out against India at Headingley, he met the same fate. Barrington was restored for the third Test and responded by making 163 in five and a half hours but his innings was overshadowed by John Edrich's 310. Smith declared the innings closed after lunch on the second day with England on 546 for 4 so presumably the warning had been heeded. Bob contributed just 13.

His form did not improve when he returned to Warwickshire to play county cricket throughout a cold and cheerless summer, although he did not change the way he played nor did he suffer the sort of criticism he had experienced at Lancashire. Even the prospect of the Gillette Cup failed to rouse him to anything like the form he had displayed in the winter. Having overtaken Cambridgeshire's total of 86 in just over an hour in the first round, Warwickshire were drawn at home to Lancashire in the second. There was to be no repeat of the previous year's fireworks. A weak Lancashire batting line up, including Peter Lever at 7 and Brian Statham at 8, managed only 166 which Warwickshire knocked off for the loss of four wickets. Bob made a breezy 33 out of an opening stand of 47 with Billy Ibadulla and Warwickshire progressed easily past Hampshire in their quarter final, despite Bob's dismissal by Shackleton for 0 in the first over. Yorkshire, however, beat them by twenty runs at Edgbaston in the semi-final and went onto the final in which Boycott made his famous 146, having been warned by Close at the other end to get on with it or face the consequences.

The second tourists of the summer of 1965 were the South Africans, who arrived determined to eradicate the memory of their home series defeat earlier in the year. They knew all about Bob Barber now and were determined not to let him get the innings off to the flying start he had managed in all four of his Test innings the previous winter.

In this they mostly succeeded although in the first innings of the first Test he still made a rapid 56 and left with the total on 88. Thereafter, he never really got going. He made 41 and 1 in the defeat at Nottingham which owed everything to Graeme Pollock's now legendary innings of 125 and in the final Test at The Oval, where he was joined by a "new" opening attack of the recalled Brian Statham and the surprised debutant Ken Higgs, he made a painstaking 40 in the first innings and a cameo 22 in the second. England had been set 400 to win but had gone about their task in such a way as to arouse expectations of a remarkable victory. Eric Russell, the Middlesex batsman who opened with Bob, made 70, the chastened Barrington 73, Parfitt 46 and Cowdrey was on 78 and had just been joined by Smith when the rains came. England had needed just 91 more in 70 minutes of playing time with the doughty Parks to come in next when the clouds that had been hovering over The Oval deposited their contents with such venom that the match was soon abandoned. The South Africans took the abbreviated series 1-0 and went home in triumph. England did not play South Africa again for nearly thirty years.

Barber finished sixth in the Test batting averages, below Titmus but above Smith and Boycott, the latter of whom averaged a mere 18 which made his inclusion for the coming tour of Australia by no means certain and possibly stimulated his reaction to Close's threat in the Gillette Cup Final that year. In the event, MCC chose four openers. Boycott made it onto the plane but he and Bob were joined by Eric Russell as well as John Edrich who would not miss out this year. The inclusion of the extra opener incensed Boycott. He knew exactly what the selectors were saying and he was determined to respond with runs that would make it impossible for them to drop him from the Test team. E.W. Swanton warned against accommodating the plethora of openers by dropping Barber into the middle order.

In England where the ball does more, his quickness in going into the attack sometimes costs him his wicket. In South Africa, however, he never failed to reach 50 in his four Test innings and his enterprise is a necessary foil to Boycott's slowness. They have on the whole been a successful and dependable partnership.

Bob believed that the end of the 1965 season pretty much meant the end of his career in county cricket. The tour to Australia was going to be the grand climax to his life in cricket and to come home to a cold damp English spring and try to motivate himself for matches against counties he had been playing for over ten years was going to be difficult. In addition, a further winter tour would mean that by March 1966, he would have been away from home and the family business for two years with scarcely more than a few weeks off between engagements. Anne was pregnant again and they were expecting the baby to be born around the time the tour finished.

Bob informed both Leslie Deakins, the Secretary at Warwickshire and Doug Insole of MCC, of his inclination to retire and received appropriate letters of understanding from both. He had told Warwickshire when he joined them in 1963 that he intended to play only three summers of county cricket and, true to his word, he politely declined the offer of a contract for the summer of 1966. He wrote

I've always regarded cricket as a game and it must therefore always come second to the more serious aspects of life. Once it becomes sufficiently professionalised to become my main interest, both mentally and commercially, the game for me as a person would suffer. It is not possible for me to lead a normal home life by being away from home so much. By next March (after Aus) I shall have been away from home for two years with only fleeting visits. Playing cricket has of course brought me much to compensate and believe me I do not want to fully cut myself off from the game. It may be that I shall find myself able to play some cricket in the future more than seems possible at the present, particularly if the structure of the game changes.

MCC had indicated that they might rearrange the county cricket fixture list for 1966 to include Sunday play, which immediately attracted Bob's interest. He would be able to play cricket without feeling badly that his indulgence was interfering with the working week. Warwickshire were very happy to take "perhaps" for an answer. When Bob set Australia alight with his batting, emptying bars and being widely acclaimed as the most attractive batsman to play for England since the glory days of Denis Compton, Deakins wrote to him again.

There is no doubt that in the minds of the public you represent a new image and your approach to cricket has caught the public imagination. There is nothing more natural in consequence than that they should be looking forward more than anything to seeing you, in the van of England's efforts this season, defeat the world champions, the West Indies. You may be sure that everyone here is appreciative of your difficulties and also very understanding. I attach a fixture list.

The plea clearly fell on fertile ground because the fixture card is decorated with ticks beside the names of the matches in which he thought he would, after all, be able to play.

MCC was of a similar opinion, hopeful that a successful tour might change his mind but, in the autumn of 1965, it was agreed that the decision to withdraw from full time play should be kept private as the press might have something acerbic to say about MCC picking a player who would have no future in international cricket. Bob Barber himself left England that October with the intention that this tour of Australia would be his swan song as a cricketer and he was determined to ensure that the song would be heard by all and sundry.

The MCC party arrived in Australia under orders to play the sort of bright, attractive cricket that Bob had practised as well as preached. To enforce their orders MCC had for the first (and subsequently it transpired only) time invested in their manager the authority to dictate tactics on the field. Fortunately, the man so charged was Billy Griffith whom the players all liked enormously and even more fortunately, Mike Smith appeared not to resent the new order which meant that the players were not split between obedience to an employer's wishes and co-operation with a well-liked and much respected captain.

There was an understandable feeling that, in an era of declining attendances for Test cricket, what could not be tolerated was another series like the boring 1-1 draw of 1962-3 or the even more boring series in England in 1964, the apogee of which was the deathly high scoring Old Trafford Test. Griffith did not wish to give the impression that he would dictate tactics against the wishes of a captain who was violently opposed to his suggestions. Although he retained the ultimate power in the relationship, he hoped he would always be in agreement with the captain and that it would never become necessary to use it.

After a diplomatic couple of games in unwelcoming weather in Ceylon, during which Bob scored with a freedom unmatched by any other batsman, the MCC party arrived in Australia to a chorus of indifference. The party of David Brown, Jeff Jones and Mike Smith seemed to Australians a far cry from that which included Hutton, Compton, Tyson and Laker. It was immediately categorised in traditional Ashes fashion as "the worst English party ever to arrive in this country". As far as *The Australian* was concerned, England arrived "with all the prestige of a team that was picked by prodding a pin into the telephone directory."

Such denigrating comments had no impact on Bob Barber who started the tour as he meant to carry on. He won the first upcountry match with his bowling, taking five wickets for eight runs in the space of twenty-five minutes to give MCC victory with five minutes to spare. Against Western Australia, he walked out with John Edrich to open the innings in the first state match and remarked just before they split up to take their ends that he intended to hit the first ball of the match for four; probably over mid off's head. Edrich had been wrongly omitted from the party that toured South Africa so, like Boycott had been a year earlier, he was taken aback to be informed so bluntly that his partner was going to take the attack to the opposition literally from the very first ball. Mike Smith, if he didn't know at the time, showed no surprise when informed fifty years later.

The idea that Bob would set out deliberately to hit the first ball of the first state match at the WACA over mid off's head for four comes as no surprise to me. The fellow was a one-off. You either accept the peccadilloes or you don't pick him but don't forget Bob had the same attitude as the rest of us – namely that we're here to win the game. He had a perverse sense of humour and he enjoyed being a little bit different.

In fact, the ball glanced off a thick inside edge for three runs square of the wicket on the leg side, but the statement had been made. He scored 23 of the first 26 runs made, reached his fifty in fifty-five minutes and converted it into a century just after lunch.

Barber's was the batting which made everything possible. His recipe was the same as on the good pitches of South Africa. He took the fast bowlers' first eager aggressiveness as his chance to drive every ball slightly over-pitched and then thrived gloriously off the back foot on the shortness which he inevitably persuaded.

When he was eventually out for 126, made out of 197 for 1, he had given the watching Don Bradman, Australia's Chairman of Selectors, plenty of problems to think about, as the spearhead of his attack, Garth McKenzie, finished the day with 1-76 off 16 overs. The first day ended with MCC on 332 for five, made at a run a minute and fulfilling all the hopes that Smith's side would play positive cricket.

In the following match against a Combined XI also in Perth, Barber continued in similar vein, racing to 113 made out of 149 in just 105 minutes. If there was any realistic possibility of dropping him into the middle order in order to accommodate Boycott, Russell and Edrich at the top, these two innings made plain the folly of such a move. It was a whirlwind, somewhat agricultural display of hitting but played in the interests of his side as they chased quick runs to set up a declaration. All the bowling disappeared as his bat swung with powerful determination. Terry Jenner, later to become instrumental in the development of Shane Warne's command of the leg break, was hit for fourteen and fifteen an over and conceded 63 in seven. Even Tony Lock, who had so bamboozled Bob when the two had first met over ten years before, was treated with no respect, although Bob gave the former Surrey spinner his wicket five minutes before close of play when he skied yet another boundary attempt.

The cricket correspondents, who had seen him struggle through the damp English summer, could only marvel at the transformation that appeared to come over Bob Barber as soon as his feet touched foreign soil. In the brighter light of South Africa and Australia, he appeared to find it much easier to pick up the flight of the ball. His left eye had always been weaker than his right, which is why he always batted left handed although he is predominantly right handed in everything else. Standing side-on in his crease, a batsman's leading eye is usually the stronger. Many English grounds were not easy to see on, particularly Lord's which had at that time no sightscreen at the pavilion end and distracting dark trees at the nursery end. Somehow, in foreign climes where the light was brighter, Bob picked up the flight a fraction earlier, allowing his feet to be in the right position for an aggressive stroke when the ball arrived. The harder pitches too, favoured a batsman who was prepared to hit on the up through the line of the ball. At home, he would hardly be the first batsman to be tied down by the subtle variations of swing and seam purveyed by the likes of Derek Shackleton and, when he was on the opposite side, Tom Cartwright. If the bounce were consistent, he could drive with confidence but, on the softer wickets in England where the ball might stop after he was committed to a shot, he was not able to play those attacking shots with the same assurance.

Before the first Test at Brisbane, MCC played all the state sides, beating South Australia, Western Australia and New South Wales, losing to Victoria and drawing with Queensland. With only one opening place now realistically available,

Boycott was having a terrible time. He fell ill before the team arrived in Perth and remained in bed in Singapore as the party flew on. When he rejoined his team mates, he was distraught to see both Edrich and Russell in form. "They're scoring my runs", he moaned. He eventually recovered to make a fine 94 against South Australia, batting in what was now the prescribed MCC manner, but he failed in both innings against Queensland when Russell and Edrich made centuries.

Having suffered through illness, he now benefited through injury when Cowdrey was ruled unfit for selection for the first Test and Eric Russell split his right hand whilst fielding, so Boycott, who had been included at number six, moved up to resume his partnership with Bob Barber. The match was ruined by rain with Australia stranded on 79 for 1 at the close of the second day's play. Bill Lawry who went on to score 166 had been caught by Jim Parks down the leg side off David Brown before he had got off the mark but he stood his ground and the catch wasn't given. Nobody complained. It was in a sense only to be expected. It was unfortunate in that the winning momentum, that England had built up going into the match, seemed to come to a crashing halt in Brisbane.

Doug Walters also scored a century in his debut Test and England were forced to follow on after lunch on the final day but it was only ever going to be a psychological defeat because there was no time for the Australians to bowl England out a second time. Barber went for five in the first innings, caught at slip in Neil Hawke's first over which must have relieved the Australians who were genuinely starting to fear the damage this man with the flashing blade might do to their bowlers. In fact, so excited had the travelling British press become by the performances of Barber and MCC in general that when they closed the fourth day on a disappointing painstaking 197 for 5 they ripped into the England side. Mike Smith makes no apology for his negative tactics that day.

We got criticised in that Test but we saved the game. You try to win a match and, if you can't, you make damn sure you don't lose it and that's what we did with no regrets.

In the second innings, when the draw was inevitable, Bob decided to give the crowd value for money. He had not been thrilled to see young Walters take runs off his bowling with such disdain and resented the fact that his first five overs in a Test match in Australia had gone for 42 runs. When Walters came on to bowl in that meaningless second innings, England's premier opening batsman resolved to extract revenge much in the style of his big hitting in the match against a Combined Western Australia team. He wound himself up as he had done against Kelly Seymour in Johannesburg and clubbed the ball to all parts, missing as many as he hit. He clouted Walters's first two balls for six and three, giving the strike back to Boycott who played the next four balls quietly before taking his traditional single off the penultimate ball. Barber told the Australian close fielders exactly where the next ball was going, probably onto the Great Barrier Reef. The huge slog unfortunately simply sent the ball gently up into the air where it was easily caught by Tom Veivers, much to the amusement of the Australian fielders. Their sniggers were to have a most unfortunate consequence a few weeks later but the mood of the dying Test match had been significantly lightened.

The second state match against South Australia was played over the Christmas period, although in 1965 both Christmas Day and Boxing Day were holidays and no cricket was played. Anne had brought Sandy out to join Bob so they could have some semblance of family life during the long separation and so happy was Bob, and so confident had he become that he had the measure of the Australians, that he rang his father and suggested that he fly out for the Test match in Sydney starting the second week in January. He had an inkling that if he were ever to play that one life-defining innings it would be in Sydney which, at the risk of offending all Victorians, he had always regarded as the heart of cricket in Australia.

He had had this feeling for some weeks. After the whirlwind 113 in Perth, he had ridden in the hotel lift with Denys Rowbotham of *The Guardian,* Crawford White of the *Daily Express* and Ian Wooldridge of the *Daily Mail.* They had complimented him on his two centuries and it was then that he confided his feeling about the special innings he knew he would play at some point on the tour. It is tempting Providence to confide this sort of deep feeling to men, whose living is made by revealing those thoughts to a gawping public, if the following matches produce nothing more than a string of low scores. It is a tribute to the strength of Bob Barber's self-confidence at this time that the possibility of subsequent humiliation never occurred to him.

Meanwhile, there was the New Year's Test Match to be won at Melbourne. England, after their unspectacular showing in the first Test, started as second favourites but they kept a lid on the Australian first innings by dismissing them for 358 and then, after an opening stand between Boycott and Barber of 98 made at a fast clip, centuries by Edrich and Cowdrey gave England what should have been a winning first innings lead of 200. When Brian Booth was bowled by David Allen, Australia were 176-4, still 24 behind England with only six wickets left. Peter Burge, who had made 160 at Headingley that won the only Test in the 1964 series of draws, was still there and England would not feel they were on the road to victory until he was dismissed. Barber had already taken the wicket of the Australian captain Bill Lawry, whom he had caught at short leg and his turn and bounce were clearly troubling all the Australian batsmen. Bowling in tandem with Allen, the two

England spinners looked as though they would slowly but surely work their way through the lower order and leave England a modest total for victory.

The score had reached 204-4, effectively 4-4 when Burge gave Barber the charge. The ball turned past the outside edge with the batsman well out of his crease but the ball had bounced as well as turned and it hit Jim Parks on the forearm. Burge gratefully regained his ground. Three balls later, he swept Barber to long leg but the ball dropped fractionally short of Jeff Jones. Burge went on to compile a stand of nearly 200 with Doug Walters. The game died. Bob feels Jim should have taken the ball that turned past Burge's bat cleanly because he was so far down the pitch. Mike Smith is more tolerant.

I always thought that Jim Parks was under-rated as a keeper. Missing chances are always going to happen. Especially to keepers. They're like goalkeepers. One mistake and that's it. Apart from Burge at Melbourne, when the South Africans came over in 1965 we lost the second Test at Nottingham and Jim dropped Pollock early on standing up to Tommy Cartwright. There is no way anyone is going to be infallible and if you're a keeper, you'll get more catches than anyone else, you'll get more chances than anyone else and it stands to reason you'll probably drop more than anyone else.

It is surely possible to see from this reaction why players loved playing under Mike Smith. He was a superb manager of the men under his command even if he never really understood how best to utilise the talents of Bob Barber, the spinner. Bob would only ever have one game as an international bowler under a captain who understood him, but it wouldn't be on this tour.

Jack Barber arrived in Sydney early in the morning of Friday 7th January 1966. After a relaxing swim in the hotel pool, Bob picked him up at the airport and together they drove to the SCG. Bob had arranged a ticket in the stand but for Jack Barber, that doughty Yorkshireman, there was only place from which to watch his son open the batting in a Test match at Sydney. He duly took his place on the Hill, as Bob went back to the dressing room.

The curator had left the pitch well grassed to prevent it from crumbling but both sides thought it would take increasing spin as the match progressed and both sides chose two specialist spinners – Allen and Titmus for England, Philpott and Sincock for Australia. Mike Smith called correctly and elected to bat. At eleven o'clock on that Friday morning, Bob Barber strode out with Geoffrey Boycott to open the England innings. By 5pm that day Bob Barber would have achieved everything he had hoped for in his cricketing life and shown the world the ultimate fulfilment of that magnificent talent that had begun to emerge twenty years earlier on the playing fields of Ruthin School in the late 1940s.

If there was one England batsman the Sydney crowd might reluctantly have wanted to do well, it was Bob Barber. He had made a sparkling 90 in the state match against New South Wales at the end of November. He and Eric Russell had put on 151 in 103 minutes off just 22 overs until Bob was run out by Brian Booth just before lunch, looking for the century that nobody on the ground would have begrudged him. Back on a Sydney pitch that was expected to play well on the first two days but take significant spin as the match progressed, Barber and Boycott were determined to take advantage of the toss.

Neither batsman tried anything flamboyant early on, as both McKenzie and Hawke extracted lift from the pitch, but Bob stroked each bowler sweetly to the square cover boundary to reassure himself that his timing had not deserted him. Boycott was struggling and was hit painfully on the forearm by McKenzie but gradually the batsmen weathered the early storm and began to impose themselves. Sitting on the Hill, Jack Barber's attempt at anonymity was soon exposed and he revelled in the applause that greeted his son's arrival at 50. The Hill was a challenging place in front of which to fail but in those days, when abuse was less drunken in character and more verbal, there was invariably a good acknowledgement of fine cricket. The Hill knew its cricket and could be generous in its recognition as Barber Snr. and Jr. would discover before the end of the day. In accordance with tradition, David Sincock was brought on for the last over before lunch but failed to pitch his left arm googlies and Bob finished the morning session by smashing him to the boundary. At lunch England were 93 for 0 with Barber on 59 and Boycott on 34.

There was a feeling in certain quarters that Boycott's tendency to hog the strike made him the wrong partner for Barber who, when in the mood as he clearly was this day, just needed to be let off the rein and given his head. Jim Stewart certainly understood that the best thing he could do was to play into the V and let Bob take the bowling. On the other hand, Boycott and Barber maintained a strong professional respect for each other. For all of their striking differences they were compatible in other areas; they were each obdurate, singular men. Bob was clearly the better team man but the cussed Northern streak was strong in both of them. Bob liked Geoffrey and respected the Yorkshireman's fanatical dedication to making the best of his talents. Did he wonder what he might have achieved at Lancashire with a character like Boycott in his side?

At the start of the Sydney Test they were averaging 48 together as an opening partnership which, at the time, was the highest in the post-war era by any two batsmen apart from Hutton and Washbrook. Bob's driving and the use of his feet to come down the wicket and loft the slow bowlers straight induced all the bowlers to drop short which benefited Boycott who was always particularly strong when cutting and pulling.

After lunch Barber cut loose. Just as at Johannesburg he had targeted poor Kelly Seymour so at Sydney another slow bowler was on the verge of being hit out of Test cricket by Bob Barber. Geoffrey Boycott remembers it well.

They had a left arm wrist spinner called Sincock and his nickname was Evil Dick. Aussies always have nicknames but I have no idea why he was called Evil Dick. Anyway, he bowled like he was tossing hand grenades. Again Bob comes down the pitch and tells me he's going to start slogging. To a Yorkshireman – I mean, Arthur Mitchell - can you imagine his reaction? But he did. He put his knee down and slogged him over mid-wicket. When Evil Dick eventually put a man out there for the slog Bob just started laughing, telling the Aussies they hadn't got a man at long on so he started hitting him there as well. The Aussies thought he was crackers but the fact is Evil Dick just couldn't bowl at him. It was a marvellous innings, one of the very best you could ever see. I'll never forget it. Magnificent.

Evil Dick sounds more like an eighteenth century highwayman who has wandered into the SCG from *The Beggars Opera* than a left arm chinaman and googly bowler. He was, however, regarded as someone who could spin the ball on any wicket and he had already claimed eleven MCC wickets in the two games they had so far played against South Australia. He wasn't getting any wickets at all in this match as Bob Barber cut and drove his way towards his first century in Test cricket. This time there was to be no repeat of the "failure" when he got himself out for 97 at Johannesburg. On 99, he off-drove Cowper easily for one to reach his century.

The Hill rose to acclaim an outstanding innings that had mixed mature watchfulness with entertaining aggression. Jack Barber rose, along with the rest, luxuriating in the compliments for his son he was hearing in every direction. It was, as his opening partner has always said, a magnificent innings and it wasn't yet over. This time Bob decided not to give it away on 103 even though Edrich, Barrington, Cowdrey, Smith and Parks were still to come to the wicket. He called them in jest "the run accumulators" but this time he decided to do some run accumulating himself. Boycott was worried that there would be another "six or out" scenario in the offing and was relieved to see that Barber intended to stay in the middle for a while.

Now Evil Dick stood exposed before the full force of the Barber hurricane. The loop of Sincock's wrist tossed the ball up high enough for Barber to get to it on the full and place it wherever he wanted. This is when he started to tell the bowler and fielders where the next ball would be going and he did it with ease. Psychologically, he was crushing the Aussies and handing them his wicket now would be letting them off the hook. In three overs after reaching his century Bob claimed 23 runs and together they raised the partnership to 200. Soon it had passed every other record for the first wicket against Australia, save for Hobbs and Rhodes who made 323 at Melbourne in 1911-12 and Hobbs and Sutcliffe who batted all day at the MCG in 1924-5.

Barber hit both Cowper and Sincock out of the attack but Boycott proceeded on his stately way always displaying the caution that his partner respected but rarely emulated. Playing for tea with the score on 234, Boycott pushed forward at Philpott's penultimate ball before the interval but failed to kill the spin.

Bob must have been 140 when I got out the last ball before tea for 83, the muppet that I am, caught and bowled by Peter Philpott.

Boycott remembers all his dismissals and his scores, revealing a frighteningly impressive memory.

Edrich came out after tea to watch Barber in the first over reach 150 but he contributed 20 to the second wicket stand of fifty which arrived when Bob was on 172, the total being 284, made off just 65 overs, admittedly of eight balls in duration. Hawke and McKenzie came back to take the new ball and now it was a question of who was the more tired, the Australian bowlers and fielders or England's opening batsman, who had been there since the first ball. It appeared to be the former as the latter clipped McKenzie off his legs for four and then cut him beautifully away to the point boundary. He was into the 180s. He had never been there before. This was the innings that he had dreamed of all his life. He might as well go on to 200 now. The chance would almost certainly never come again. England passed 300 with just one wicket down and the clock ticked towards five o'clock. There was plenty of time to get there before the close. He wished desperately that he wasn't starting to feel so tired. It had been a draining innings, played out in the full glare of an Australian summer sun.

The first ball of Neil Hawke's second over with the new ball was a wide long hop. This would take his score to 189. He hammered it away through the offside but he was tired, the bat was fractionally late through the air, the ball deviated slightly off the pitch and from outside the off stump he got an inside edge. He heard the death rattle, as every batsman has always heard it, as a funeral knell to his hopes. He swung round at the end of the shot to look at the disturbed wicket. The photograph of his face as he sees the displaced bails is one of infinite sadness.

The magnificence of the innings and the sorrow of its demise briefly united batsman and crowd. Bob Barber walked back to the old green pavilion at the SCG, raising his bat to acknowledge the warmth of the crowd's applause. Kenny Barrington who came out to replace him could never have felt a more irrelevant figure on a cricket ground. Bob Barber had finally played the innings of his life, justifying all the many compliments he had received since that 41 not out on a cold Monday morning at Old Trafford in May 1954. Nearly eleven years later, this was the innings he knew he had been born to play.

Fifty years later, Geoffrey Boycott, Mike Smith, Jim Parks and John Murray who were all there to watch it at first hand still recall it as not only Bob Barber's finest innings but one of the finest innings in the history of Test cricket, a judgement passed at the time by the watching press and never revised over the passage of the years. Murray, whose memory at the age of 79, is outstanding, recalls watching from the balcony and wondering what happened to the batsman he first knew playing for Lancashire.

When Bob got that hundred against McKenzie and Hawke at Sydney he just stood there like he had contempt for the bowling. From the bloke who batted at 6 and used to nudge it to third man, this was a different bloke altogether.

The statistics are impressive but not germane to the judgement. He made 185 out of 303 runs scored whilst he was at the crease. He batted for four minutes short of five hours, without giving a chance. He hit 19 fours and the last 85 runs had been made out of 129 in 108 minutes; perhaps more to the point, he had done it in a Test match in the middle of a decade in which Ashes Tests in particular were regarded as extended wars of attrition. He didn't need Billy Griffith or the MCC to tell him how to play. Bob Barber's 185 at Sydney was the ringing manifestation of the philosophy he had long espoused but never been able to put into practice with such devastating effect. He fears he might now be known as "a one innings wonder" but if that is indeed the case, what an innings it was to be known by.

It was a good job he had not thrown his wicket away when he got to a hundred because Neil Hawke with the second new ball brought Australia back into the game. Barber was dismissed with an hour of the day left. By the time the umpires removed the bails, England had collapsed from the unparalleled prosperity of 302-1 to the more mundane level of 328-5. Barrington was caught at short leg for one, Cowdrey was caught by Grout off Hawke for a duck and the captain went the same way for six in forty minutes of mayhem. The night watchman, David Brown, was immediately dropped at first slip by Cowper off McKenzie and the wisdom of sending him in with twenty-five minutes to go was questioned. He survived the night but was also out caught Grout bowled Hawke in the first over of the morning so it appeared that much of Bob's hard work had been wilfully jettisoned.

The newspapers, the day after the innings, were naturally full of praise. One compared it to the historic 187 Stan McCabe had made on the same ground against the full fury of Harold Larwood and Bill Voce in 1932. John Woodcock in *The Times* called it one of the great Test innings of all time.

In every line of Barber's remarkable innings there showed an independence of character; there was also judgment tempered by aggression. In the early stage of his career as a first-class cricketer Barber was tediously introspective. Yet this evening, when he was out, he returned home to a salvo of cheers.

The story of Bob telling the Australian bowlers "You need a man at long on" before depositing the next ball precisely there was seized upon eagerly by the English press who didn't wish to linger too long over the four wickets Hawke collected in the penultimate half hour of the day's play.

It was tempting fate but it was fun. After all, it might be Test cricket but it's still a game. Ian Wooldridge wanted to interview me and I told him that there was no essential difference between playing Test cricket and playing cricket on the beach. Anyway he thought I was taking the piss – which I wasn't.

Barber Joins The Immortals was one of the headlines to cherish.

Few Englishmen in history have been accorded such an ovation as that which the Hill, for all its xenophobic prejudice, gave Barber as he walked stiffly and unsmilingly back to the pavilion. I have called his innings of 185 the innings of a lifetime because in the limited amount of time he has allowed himself to continue playing big cricket I doubt whether he will ever surpass it.

One of the delights of the day indeed was to hear that his father had arrived from England only this morning in the quiet hope of seeing the family name written into the records. It was. Alongside the immortals.

Twenty years later, looking back on that January day in Sydney, E.W. Swanton wrote in his memoirs

Often in bleak moments do I cast my mind back to Bob Barber's 185 in front of 40,000 on that sunny Friday in January 1966. He batted without chance for five hours, starting decorously enough and then hitting the ball progressively harder and with a superb distain to every corner of the field. One recalls the exceptional vigour of his driving and how he brought his wrists into the cut, making room for the stroke. It made blissful watching to English eyes – to one pair in particular, for by a wonderful chance father Barber had flown in from home that very day.

It is always assumed that Bob's innings paved the way for the innings victory that followed but, from the slightly awkward situation of 328-6 when Brown was dismissed at the start of the second day, the match had still to be won. Fortunately, the tail wagged, David Allen made a valuable 50 and England were eventually dismissed for 488. Evil Dick and Cowper on a pitch that favoured spin had failed to take a wicket though Philpott claimed two.

As in the Brisbane Test, Bill Lawry was caught by Jim Parks in the first over but this time the umpire's finger was raised and, though Titmus and Allen bowled tightly, the honours went to David Brown who took 5-63 as Australia were bowled out for 221. Bob Barber was brought on to break the tenth wicket stand which he did by finishing McKenzie's 85 minute stay at the crease when he had him caught at slip by Cowdrey. With an analysis of 2.1-1-2-1 it was Barber's match all right. Following on, Australia's batting folded again. Titmus and Allen took four cheap wickets apiece and England won the match by an innings and 93 runs, two hours into the fourth day. It would be impossible to imagine a more satisfying victory in Australia and the English press who had waited eleven years for a repeat of Hutton's famous win on the 1954-5 tour were quick to predict a similar result.

It was a blow to the cricketers as much as to the Press when the following Test at Adelaide turned out to be a mirror image of the one played at Sydney. The demon Barber, as he was now called in the popular press, was bowled third ball by McKenzie. It was one of the few times he stewed over his dismissal for, even before he reached the dressing room, he was already feeling that his over-confidence had cost England the Test match and therefore the Ashes. He had such a hold psychologically over the Australians that getting out in the first over, playing a loose shot, gave the opposition a lift they utilised to the full.

Jim Parks isn't quite so hard on himself and certainly doesn't believe Bob's dismissal was responsible for the generally poor showing of the team.

The defeat at Adelaide was shocking. It was such a good hard wicket and we should have made the most of it but we got ourselves out. We thought we were going to make a lot of runs and we didn't.
Geoffrey Boycott has a different interpretation. He has someone to blame.

We all felt badly about losing at Adelaide. It was the only tour when MCC gave the manager authority over the captain. The reason was that Lord's was obsessed *with us having to play brighter cricket. Billy Griffith was a lovely man, secretary of the MCC, but captains had always been in charge of the cricket on the field and this was the first time the manager was. All that crap about playing Brighter Cricket. What a terrible word. Cricket is not a f***ing comedy show. Of course you want to play good positive sensible winning cricket. We were one up in the series. I have no criticism of Billy Griffith as a person because he was a very nice man but he said in a nice way that we had to carry on playing attacking cricket and at Adelaide Bob and I both got out attacking the new ball. Bob was bowled and I was brilliantly caught at third slip by Ian Chappell. He still remembers it and so do I. Kenny Barrington was quietly doing his head in. We lost the Test but we certainly contributed to our own downfall with some of the shots we played. It was a good pitch, flat, and all we had to do was bat well because we'd won the toss and had first use of the pitch. We should never have lost that game. It doesn't mean batting slowly but if we had put a decent score on the board, we would have controlled the game because it would have taken them so long to equal or pass our total we couldn't have lost. But we lost the match and couldn't regain the Ashes.*

Australia passed England's first innings total of 241 without losing a wicket as Lawry made another century and Simpson made a double. Second time around, Barrington fought hard and long for a painstaking 102 but England lost by an innings and nine runs in the middle of the fourth day. After the euphoria of Sydney, the England party left Adelaide feeling utterly deflated.

Before the final decisive Test back in Melbourne the MCC party returned to the SCG for the last state match. It seemed at first that their poor form of the last few weeks was pursuing them as they were forced to follow on yet again but thankfully in the second innings the batsmen rediscovered their touch. Barber and Boycott put on 120 for the first wicket when Bob was out for 75 made from 64 balls with only twenty-nine of them scoring shots. It was an appropriately sparkling way in which to say farewell to a ground that would always be associated with his supreme triumph as a batsman.

Back at Melbourne, Billy Griffith used the power he had been granted by Lord's much to Boycott's contempt, to issue another call to arms. England had to regain the Ashes by playing attacking cricket or leave them behind with honour, he told a press conference on the eve of battle. It may have accounted for Barber and Boycott yet again.

They had reached 36, relatively untroubled by Hawke or McKenzie, when Boycott, forgetting what Bob had done to him in Durban, pushed the last ball of the over down the pitch and started to run. A loud peremptory "No!" was ignored. Boycott kept running. Ignoring his previously stated position, Bob began the pointless race to the other end. Walters ran from leg slip to take the return from the bowler and gleefully removed the bails with Bob still half way down the pitch. Bob returned to the dressing room fuming. Jack Fingleton called it "sheer cricketing lunacy". "It was a very bad call" said a smiling Jim Parks, "and Bob was absolutely livid." Boycott's attempts to stay out in the middle until the demon Barber had calmed down were foiled when he was caught by Stackpole off McKenzie twenty minutes later. History does not report the exact details of the conversation that followed and your correspondent decided that, since the tenor of it was predictable, a cross-examination of the involved parties was unnecessary. Barber contented himself with the typically generous observation

To me, he was a good chap to run with. I knew where I was with him. The only time I had a big problem was the last Test in Australia when he ran me out by the length of the pitch. Because of the weather, it turned out it made no difference but it could have affected the match. I had time for Geoffrey.

Ken Barrington was the man who rescued England with a Barber-esque innings of 115 but, though they declared at a more than respectable 485, they knew and Australia knew that a good long Australian innings would draw the match and the series and retain the Ashes. What happened was exactly that. Bob Cowper, coming in when the score was a promising 36-2, stayed to compile 307 in nearly ten hours. It became, disappointingly, a re-run of Old Trafford 1964 which MCC had been so anxious to avoid and had spent much of the tour ensuring it didn't happen. When Cowper was eventually out on the fifth day, Australia were 55 runs ahead and only seventeen overs remained to be bowled in the match. Boycott did less damage this time round, trapped lbw by McKenzie for 1 and Bob, having made 20 out of 21 at a run a ball, went to the same bowler.

So ended Bob Barber's tour of tours because Anne who was due to give birth in April had had an accident and it was advised that she return home and that Bob forego the New Zealand leg of the trip and accompany her.

After we came back from Oz, she never went in a plane again. In Adelaide, she was expecting our second child and, to amuse Sandy in the playground, she got on one of those circular rides about two metres in diameter that kids push around. She was sitting on it gently rocking the baby when a boisterous Australian boy jumped on it and started rotating it very fast. Anne fell off onto the hard ground and she retreated to bed in the hotel, terrified that she was going to lose the baby. Billy said I'd better take my wife home. We got on the plane and a tropical storm started. We got to Fiji and she had to rest up for three or four days in bed. I told Janny she was lucky she wasn't born in Fiji. Anne was six or seven months gone. We got to Hawaii and again she had to go to bed. We got to Vancouver and we ran into a snow storm in Calgary. She never liked flying to begin with so by the time we got back to England she said that was it and that she was never going to fly again.

Bob was now thirty years of age. The innings at Sydney was the statement he had always wished to make to the world. Repetition was pointless unless he believed in the primacy of runs and records. The sadness was that England had played poorly at Adelaide and failed to regain the Ashes but he would be too old to make the next trip so there was nothing to be done in this regard. A new baby and a long prepared for career in business awaited him on his return to England. Both Warwickshire and MCC knew that he was fading out of the game and that cricket was no longer his primary focus. It would have presumably come as a surprise to him if he had known on that anxious plane ride home that, when Warwickshire took the field at Fenner's to play Cambridge University in the traditional chill of an English May, R.W. Barber would be opening the visitors' batting with R.N. Abberley.

CHAPTER TWELVE

THERE IS INVARIABLY some kind of sadness in the diminution of the powers of an elite sportsman. There comes a time in every sportsman's life when the impact of age starts to take its toll in the level of performance. Danny Blanchflower, the great Tottenham Hostspur wing-half and captain, claimed he decided to retire in the middle of a tackle he failed to make cleanly. At the moment that Andy Murray passed Tim Henman in the ATP rankings for the first time, it was clear that the Scot might win Wimbledon but the Englishman never would. David Beckham resigned the England captaincy in tears after defeat in the 2006 World Cup. Michael Vaughan did the same after defeat by South Africa in the home series of 2008.

It doesn't always have to be like that. Nasser Hussain scored a century at Lord's to help win a Test match against New Zealand in 2004 and retired a couple of days later. He was spared the public humiliation experienced by Beckham and Vaughan but he made the decision because he recognised the signs. Andrew Strauss had hit an outstanding century on his international debut in the first innings of that match at Lord's and would almost certainly have made another one in the second innings if Hussain hadn't run him out when he had reached 83. Michael Vaughan had already made a success of captaining the one day side and was ready to step up. He had been injured for the match at Lord's but was bound to be recalled for the second Test. Strauss was going to be a fixture in the side for years to come and the rest of the batting order was solidly in place. Hussain was the logical candidate for exclusion so he took the decision out of the selectors' hands.

For Bob Barber, it was not proving so straightforward. He felt obligations towards cricket and pressure from the game's administrators. Unlike those other sportsmen on their retirement, he felt no decline in his powers and the glorious 185 was still fresh in everyone's memory. Warwickshire and England both wanted and needed him. Perhaps he could, by being quite selective in the choice of his matches, continue a little while longer. His father Jack, who had supported him so whole-heartedly all his life, would never presume to tell his 30 year-old son that he had to retire. He knew that Bob knew perfectly well that his future lay in the world of business not the world of cricket but the West Indies were coming in the summer of 1966. They were by common consent the world champions and Bob was always tempted by the prospect of pitting his wits and his skills against the best. He decided to give it a whirl.

After Australia, it was agreed that I would play 30 days cricket and according to my records I actually played 32 days in the summer of 1966. It was fortunate that they changed the system so that some matches were played Saturday, Sunday and Monday that year so if I played in that match it only counted as one day. I tended to play groups of matches. It didn't seem sensible to me to play one three day match and then go back to Chester and not come back to Birmingham for two weeks. I certainly would admit to preferring to play at Harrogate rather than Middlesbrough. Jim might have been joking about how I picked my matches but there was probably an element of truth behind it. I never asked for any sum of money from anyone in the cricket world but they started paying me on a match basis. If I played in a Test match I got £100 or maybe £110 but that was for a five day game. If I played a three day game for Warwickshire I got paid £75 plus expenses for travelling from Chester – £25 a day. I was better off playing for Warwickshire than for England. If you took that £75 and multiplied it by the number of first class matches Warwickshire played in a season I was getting paid more than anyone else. Jim would say jokingly that I was the best paid player in England and I was supposed to be an amateur.

The situation at Warwickshire started to become uncomfortable for Bob. It would never get as bad as it had been at Lancashire (that would have been almost impossible) but it was starting to affect the dressing room adversely. It is difficult even at the moment of triumph to create a dressing room in which harmony is total and where each player's contribution to that victory and the reward he gets from it is exactly equal to that of every other player. Always, someone somewhere feels that somebody else is getting a better deal and although in a winning dressing room the momentum of victory is sufficient to obscure the resentment, when defeats mount the bitterness bursts forth in all its unpleasantness. The summers of 1963, 1964 and 1965 had been a golden time for Bob at Warwickshire, the resplendence polished by the contrast with what he had left behind at Old Trafford. On his return from Australia Bob Barber was hailed unanimously as the most exciting batsman in England with Dexter effectively in retirement and Colin Milburn not yet the figure of public affection he became during the summer of 1966.

I had always said to everyone that, after what happened at Lancashire, I was not interested in playing cricket unless I was enjoying myself. I was on the horns of a dilemma. There was pressure from the Warwickshire club and from Lord's who wanted me to keep on playing because they were telling me that I was the player that the crowds wanted to see. I should probably have called it a day then but that's looking back at it now. I felt pretty good about my cricket when I came back from Australia.

And so on 14th May 1966, Bob Barber took the field at his old haunt of Fenner's cricket ground to watch Cambridge University captained by Derryck Murray bowled out for 36 before lunch, Rudi Webster taking 8-19. He made a composed 43 and Warwickshire won by an innings after lunch on the second day. He then opened a letter which made him wonder why he had been wasting his time at Fenner's.

> *I got a letter from Doug Insole saying they weren't considering me for the first Test against the West Indies because I hadn't yet played enough cricket but I was in their thoughts. I was actually ready when the Tests started, so the longer I didn't play the further away from Test cricket I would get. That's what I felt though I didn't say that to anyone. I still felt in good nick; it wasn't long since Australia but they were probably right. However people didn't communicate very well in those days and nobody said I had to play a certain number of games or I should have a net against Fred or anything like that. That letter was all anyone said.*

In fact the selectors were trying to see if Colin Milburn might be Bob's long term replacement, to which end he was chosen to play for MCC against West Indies at Lord's when Bob was shivering in the Cambridge cold. Naturally, Bob had no inkling of the selectors' intentions. Milburn made a rapid 64 opening with Eric Russell and both clinched their places for the first Test at Old Trafford. West Indies were in devastating form, particularly Garry Sobers, whose all-round skills dominated the summer. However, although Sobers made 161 in the tourists' only innings, Milburn was run out for a duck (which doesn't really count) in his first innings but hit a sparkling 94 in a losing cause in the second.

The hero of Sydney in January was now bizarrely relegated to the county circuit. He played a match against Middlesex but not another one for a month. He played only twice in June but in July, presumably under instructions from the selectors, he played a full month as the West Indies took a stranglehold on the Test series. Mike Smith had paid the price for defeat in the first Test and had been replaced as captain by Colin Cowdrey, who had not been comfortable as Smith's vice captain. Bob explains why that was the case.

> *He was not happy to play under another amateur like Ted or Mike because he saw himself as the senior amateur so he should be captain.*

Smith, however, had no complaints. "I hadn't made enough runs" he says bluntly and that generally was the accepted reason for the change in the captaincy. Bob though sniffed something slightly more malodorous which he thinks emanated from Gubby Allen, although by the time Smith was relieved of his post, Doug Insole was the Chairman of Selectors.

Mike knew that the first chance Gubby had, he would campaign to have Mike sacked. Gubby preferred Ted and Colin Cowdrey. Mike's lifestyle was not Gubby's style. If Mike doesn't want to buy a new carpet or new curtains or a scrubbing brush in the kitchen, I couldn't give a damn. That's Mike's choice. Colin of course managed to marry a Duke's daughter and Ted certainly lived in a certain style as well. They were very different from Mike. That's how the world was.

Cowdrey's first Test in charge at Lord's should have been memorable for Milburn's exciting 126 and for an England victory because when David Holford came out to join his cousin Garry Sobers, West Indies were only nine runs ahead of England with just five wickets left. Instead, the principal legacy of the match was Sobers and Halford who proceeded to save the match with an unbroken partnership of 274 and secure the momentum for the series. West Indies won the third Test at Trent Bridge comfortably and Cowdrey's captaincy was under threat after only two games. The public call for the demon Barber was irresistible and when it was answered positively John Clarke wrote in his book about the West Indies tour of 1966.

Barber's recall was greeted as ecstatically by the cricket writers as England's World Cup victory had been hailed by the football writers. In Australia he had been dubbed the "Demon Barber". England certainly needed a demon at Headingley.

Bob drove to Leeds for the fourth Test of the summer to resume his international career but found on his arrival an astonishingly different dressing room from the one he had left in February.

I thought it was a mistake to sack Mike and I have always said I don't think Kipper should ever have been captain of any team. It was such a different atmosphere in the dressing room compared with the tour of Australia. I felt too many players were thinking that they could lose inside three days and they could all go home. It was just dreadful in there. Colin should never have captained a club side.

The West Indies were of course an extremely fine side but it doesn't quite explain how England's performances had deteriorated so badly in such a short time. Tom Graveney had been successfully recalled and had batted well and Basil D'Oliveira had made an impressive start in the Lord's Test but Bob found an England side that felt defeated even before Sobers won the toss, decided to bat and then made

174 in a West Indies score of 500 for 9 declared. Sobers was eventually bowled by Barber but the dismissal was at the end of a tortuous road.

It was the usual Cowdrey thing. When West Indies reached 250 for 2 he'd say, "Come and have a bowl, Bob". I got Garry out but really the only question was whether he would get 100, 200 or 300.

His treatment by his captain did not go unobserved. John Clarke noted shrewdly,

Cowdrey's reluctance to employ Barber stemmed, I think, from the defensive complex he and other county captains had acquired in county cricket. Pitches are so bad in county cricket that it is far more economical to use seam bowlers to get wickets at a reasonable cost than use wrist spin bowlers who can prove expensive. So the Barbers of the cricketing world only come on as a last resort, when wickets have to be bought.... Barber had a long (for him) spell and was the only bowler who looked capable of getting Nurse or Sobers out.

Bob then renewed his partnership with Boycott, as Milburn dropped down to number three, but Hall and Griffith soon made inroads with the latter getting him caught behind for 6. John Clarke thought he was out of practice and as outclassed as Brian London was to be by Muhammed Ali later that same day. Sobers then claimed five wickets and England were following on before the end of the third day. D'Oliveira made a bold 88 but England's next highest scorer was Ken Higgs. The dressing room was a depressing place to be and Bob felt the atmosphere acutely. Second time round he top scored with a sound 55 but West Indies had won well before the scheduled close of play on the fourth day.

The astonishing Sobers was the focal point of that side but in the days before helmets and arm guards, when thigh pads were just rolled up towels thrust down the facing trouser leg, the impact of two extremely hostile fast bowlers could not be overestimated. The bounce of Hall's silver cross against his chest as he ran in like an Olympic sprinter was mesmerising enough but Charlie Griffith was feared for reasons other than sheer speed.

*Charlie decided to bowl Tom a beamer early on, at which point Basil called Charlie a "black bastard" which would have made a bit of a splash in the **Daily Express**. There was no doubt it was deliberate on Charlie's part. Tom is 40 years old and he's just come in. It went just past his nut. Ted and Kenny Barrington I remember were concerned about Charlie when he first turned up and wondered if* *we had to wait till somebody was killed for anyone to do something about it. Of course he had nearly killed Nari Contractor in India a couple of years before.*

The public clamour for some fight by England resulted in the selectors – Insole, May, Kenyon and Bedser – making five changes for the last Test, including the sacking of Cowdrey and the consecration of Brian Close as captain. Inevitably therefore, Ray Illingworth replaced Fred Titmus as the off spinner, Edrich batted at three instead of Milburn, Murray took over from Parks behind the stumps, Amiss replaced Cowdrey in the batting order and Close thought he had enough bowling at his disposal to do without the young Derek Underwood who had been hit in the face by Griffith.

Of course I was happy when Closey got the job for the next Test. It started the previous night. The form was that we had dinner as a team with the selectors, then the selectors would leave and we'd have a tactical discussion but it rarely happened like that till Closey took over. He started off by saying, "Some of you booggers probably think I'm not good enough to be here and maybe I'm not but I am. Now how are we going to stuff the booggers?" Then there was a long silence and Closey just said, "Well what about this boogger Sobers? Does he fancy it?" I can see Ken Higgs and John Snow finding something very interesting to look at on the floor because neither of them had anything to say. "Well", said Closey, "Whichever of you boogers is bowling when he comes in, let him have it. None of us likes it, especially first thing." Closey made it clear that we were there to win the match.

The Oval Test of 1966 became one of the strongest memories of England test cricket in the 1960s and it shows exactly what can happen when a dressing room is strong enough to recover from the inevitable reverse of fortune. West Indies won the toss and batted first as every team did in those days. This time they were facing a captain who knew when to bowl an attacking leg spinner.

We were only an hour into the game when Closey called me up to bowl – totally different from waiting till the opposition are 200 for 1. It was August at The Oval, so the ball would be turning and I turned it a lot. I went with the Swanton team to the Windies in 1961. I was bowling to Basil Butcher and Joe Solomon and, when I tossed it up, they would come down the wicket and try to whack you into the stand so you always had a chance against that sort of batsman. Garry doesn't like it being said and he gets defensive about it but the Windies batsmen were not very good players of leg spin.

Bob bowled well, taking three wickets for 49 runs in fifteen overs. All six England bowlers took wickets and West Indies made only 268, despite a century from Kanhai and 81 from Sobers who clearly withstood Close's Plan A before he was caught by Graveney at midwicket off Barber. That 268, nevertheless looked a decent score early in the afternoon of the second day when England were tottering on 166-7. Bob had gone at the start of the day, caught at slip off a Sobers googly for 36. At the fall of the seventh wicket the recalled John Murray came out to join Tom Graveney who yet again was showing that he was in the form of his life at the age of 40. Together they put on over 200 before Graveney was unfortunately run out when he had reached 165. Murray passed his century too and when the last wicket pair of John Snow and Ken Higgs came together, England already had a healthy first innings lead of 131. Oddly enough, the Graveney-Murray stand was then outshone by one of the great tenth wicket partnerships in cricket history. Snow and Higgs, neither of them renowned as a batsman, made 128 together, falling two short of what was then the all-time record for an England last wicket partnership. It was shattered by Root and Anderson on the dead Trent Bridge wicket in 2014 but that stand never compared to the delight engendered nearly fifty years earlier by the unlikely partnership of the unpretentious Snow and Higgs, genuine tail enders both, against the finest attack in world cricket, albeit one with the series already well won.

The momentum of the game had shifted, and when the seemingly invulnerable Sobers came to the crease early on the fourth day, his side was still 122 runs behind the England first innings total.

When Sobers came in, Snow was bowling and I presume Close said, "Let him have one" again. I'm at backward short leg so you can't see the edge of the bat. I can see John Snow stuttering up to the wicket and Closey's so close. He finished up bowling a medium pace long hop, which so surprised Garry that he'd gone through his swing and Closey almost picked the ball up off Garry's pad when he under-edged it. He would have been killed if Garry had made contact but instead he just picks it off Garry's pad and he's out first ball.

From behind the wicket, John Murray had a slightly different view, rather more complimentary to Snow.

The dismissal of Sobers in that second innings was planned. Snowy was bowling well and when Garry came to the wicket Brian said, "First ball bouncer but I want it straight" and he went and stood three feet from the bat. Snowy bowled the perfect ball - exactly what the captain had asked for – straight, quick, Garry went for it, got a bottom edge, the ball went onto his chest and it bounced up. Closey from three feet away was moving in and just took it off his chest but that was planned.

The key point was that Close, no helmet or shinpads, crouching low to the ground and with his arms stretched out menacingly in front of him, did not flinch as the world's most feared batsman threatened to pull the ball straight at his face. It was because he did not move that he was in the right position to pluck the ball off Sobers's thigh/box/chest – delete as remembered.

With the dismissal of their Goliath, the demise of the West Indies was only a matter of time. Quarter of an hour after lunch, Bob Barber caught and bowled Lance Gibbs, his future county team mate. Now it was England celebrating an innings victory on the fourth day. It wouldn't be the last time that victory at The Oval offered some solace in a summer of misfortune but under Close the England side was to experience something of a rebirth. They wouldn't be outplayed in a series again as they had been in 1966 until the West Indies returned in 1973.

The 1966 season had one more triumph in store for Bob Barber. It was generally thought that Bob would take to one day cricket like a duck to water because his forceful attacking style which went after the bowlers from the first ball would be perfectly suited to the limited overs game. In fact, he never quite fulfilled that expectation, except in the summer of 1966 when he won two Man of the Match awards in the four games they played.

After a thumping win in Swansea, Warwickshire were drawn at home to Gloucestershire in the quarter final. The away side made a respectable 193 but were blown away in 38 overs as Barber made 113 and got himself out with the scores level, trying to hit a boundary to win the match when there were singles to be had all over the field. That wasn't the Barber way and the crowd must have smiled tolerantly as an irritated Ibadulla made his way to the crease and hit the next ball for four. Bob made a rapid 45 out of 60 in the semi-final, as Warwickshire eased past Somerset by five wickets and then, to his surprise, in an eagerly anticipated final against Worcestershire, the local rivals won the toss and batted first.

There wasn't an instant clatter of wickets which sometime ruined the Gillette finals but Worcestershire struggled to 155 in their 60 overs only courtesy of Norman Gifford who swung agriculturally but to some effect at the end of the innings. MJK maintained the defensive field settings which had so enraged Clayton and Grieves in 1964 by having six men on the boundary and three half way back whilst A.C. Smith also stood deep behind the wicket. Bob made a more than usually sedate 66 but, when he was out with the score at 95 for 2, Warwickshire had the match effectively won. The batsmen who followed him, however, made hard work of their task and in the end Warwickshire won by five wickets but with only a couple of overs to spare. Of the four finals that had so far taken place, this was considered to be the most exciting.

E.W. Swanton in the *Daily Telegraph* was always a Barber supporter.

Where the scales were so delicately balanced one performance was always likely to be decisive. In the view of the adjudicator P.B.H. May, the man of the match was Barber and nobody could begrudge the prize going to the one high-class innings played.

Victory at Lord's was some consolation for Warwickshire after yet another failure to win back the championship they had last claimed in 1951. Warwickshire won only six of their 28 matches and finished seventy-one points behind the champions, Yorkshire. Bob had played only 23 first class innings and, though he had averaged a respectable 30.14, he had made fewer than 700 runs and had failed to score a century for the first time since 1956. One assessment of his year's achievement, including the tour of Australia, rated him as the top professional sportsman in Great Britain.

For sheer brilliance of individual performance….he thrilled a continent with his stroke play and warmed those early winter mornings for those of us who followed every ball on the radio. Typical of a man who seems to have stepped down from a bygone age, he declined to play full time cricket in 1966 and the game was the poorer for it.

The implication that Barber had wandered into the Swinging Sixties from the era of the horse and buggy must have come as a surprise to a man who was working hard to discover the route to success in a competitive business world as well as honouring a commitment to Warwickshire. In 1967, he played a dozen county championship games for which he had warmed up by agreeing to fly out to the Caribbean to play for the Rest of the World XI against Barbados in a first class match played to celebrate the island's independence from Great Britain.

It was a signal honour, shared only with Tom Graveney, J.T. Murray and Basil D'Oliveira from English cricket. It meant of course another confrontation with his old enemy Charlie Griffith.

It was great fun and I couldn't wait to get after Charlie Griffith. I went for him that match. I went into the tea room and I could see Charlie looking at his reflection in the window and I said "Hello, Charlie . I see you're still looking at yourself in the mirror. I was saying to someone only the other day I think you're the ugliest bugger I've ever seen!" So when we went out to bat shortly afterwards, I think Wes bowls the first over to Bill Lawry who was at the other end and then Charlie comes on to bowl at me. Five of the first six balls he bowled were aimed at my head. I would always try to gee Charlie up. It was easier for me than for the right handers. When Charlie bowled his bouncer he got very wide on the crease and it went away from me. He never went round the wicket.

Lawry went in Hall's first over and history does not record Rohan Kanhai's response to the revelation that Barber had been up to his old provocative tricks again. What Bob does recall from that match was that it was Kanhai and Lance Gibbs, the two players from Guyana on the Rest of the World team, who were most delighted by the result in which Barbados were defeated by 262 runs.

England were due to play in the Caribbean the following winter and Bob was made aware that he would be chosen if he indicated his willingness to go.

I was asked to go on the 1967-68 tour of the West Indies but I turned it down. Doug Insole wrote to me with the dates saying it was fourteen weeks, which was longer than he had originally said, and that payment would be in the region of £900. He then apologised for telling the press all about my reservations. I simply could not take the time off to play the cricket they all wanted without jeopardising the development of my business career. I told Doug Insole that I didn't think it was good for me or for the England side that I should get picked. Insole was very understanding and said it was a blow to cricket if I wasn't going to be available to play in the West Indies but he understood my reasons and he wanted me to be available for Australia in the summer of 1968 and possibly be available to be flown out to the Windies if someone got injured.

Inevitably somebody did get injured. It was Ken Barrington, England's rock throughout the 1960s. The call went out to Barber but by this time Bob had decided to widen his qualifications by taking a diploma in Business Studies at what was then called Liverpool Polytechnic. He wanted to be a serious student of business and not the man who had made 185 at Sydney, so he didn't call himself Bob and he wore a pair of plain glasses that would have aided his deception. It lasted as long as Barrington stayed fit.

One day the chap running the course came to tell me he was puzzled because he had had a phone call from Lord's. They said there was a famous cricketer on this

course and he wondered if by any chance it was me. I said it was and would he
mind keeping the information to himself?

As it turned out Barrington recovered to finish the series which England, now led yet again by Cowdrey after Close's refusal to apologise after time-wasting at the end of a county game at Edgbaston, won 1-0 to the surprise of most people, particularly Garry Sobers.

The 1968 season saw the return of the Australians and hopes were high that, on the back of the excellent win in the Caribbean, England would finally manage to recover the Ashes they had lost ten years before. A squad of 13 was announced before the First Test at Manchester, but the day before the match Bob was issued with an emergency summons, when Barrington announced that the condition of his back would not allow him to play through a five day Test.

The England selectors told Bob that he wouldn't be playing but that it would be a good idea if the Australians were to think that the demon Barber of Sydney might slaughter them afresh. On that basis, Bob made the drive north to Manchester. Ian Wooldridge in the *Daily Mail* understood why the selectors had doubled back on themselves.

They did so because, rightly, they continue to rate him the big occasion player,
whose blistering batting, leg spinning, close fielding and nerveless arrogance can
still upset the Australians.

He had not been at all surprised to have been left out of the original selection. He had played precisely three county matches so far that summer in which he had scored a total of 54 runs and taken exactly three wickets. His contribution to the MCC match against the Australians in May had been one innings of 9 and nine wicketless overs. He was in no sort of form at all but he agreed out of politeness to be a mute but unused threat to the old enemy.

It was Alan Knott's first game with me and of course he'd never kept to me. He
asked me to go down to the nets and bowl at him but I knew I wasn't playing so
I wanted to say there was no point but I couldn't say it to anyone. I said I was
stiff or had a bad back. In fact I'd been using a scythe on my small holding and
I had a red raw back and shoulder. I was so embarrassed about it, I got changed
in the toilet. I'd played two innings that year and I must have used different
trousers because when I took my whites out of my bag they had been there since the
previous August so you can imagine how I looked.

Then Alec Bedser, the Chairman of Selectors, and Cowdrey the captain, went out to look at the wicket. When they returned to the dressing room, to Bob's complete surprise, Bedser told him he was playing. For a moment he didn't know what to say.

I could hardly start an argument saying, "You told me I wasn't going to be in the final eleven!" in front of the rest of the team just before the Test match was due to start. Three quarters of an hour later I was bowling and Knotty was keeping wicket. He wasn't pleased.

It was a good old-fashioned omni-shambles. Bob bowled neatly enough taking three wickets in the match for 80 runs and scoring 66 runs in his two innings which, in a poor England display, was no disgrace. The match, however, was one-way traffic in the Australians' direction and they soon took complete control. England's meagre total of 165 saved the follow on by eight runs but, set 413 to win in the last innings, they subsided quietly. Only D'Oliveira with 87 and Barber with 46 held up the Australians' progress and both men were dropped for the next Test, one with dramatic public consequences to come, the other with the recognition that perhaps it would have been better if his Test career had come to an end at the end of the trip Down Under in 1966 or perhaps after the triumphant Oval victory over the West Indies later that same year. This experience at Old Trafford was one he would try to forget as soon as possible.

I had no wish to be playing with people like Kipper. The only part of the England experience I enjoyed was when Mike was captain and that match at The Oval under Closey. I had to be part of it and enjoying it. Mike might have been a defensive captain but he created the right spirit and we were all happy. Kipper never did that.

Still England were not prepared to let go of the demon Barber without a fight. On 1st July 1968, Doug Insole wrote to him from his offices at George Wimpey & Co in Hammersmith in a supplicating tone that would have made Kevin Pietersen, not to mention most other cricketers who have ever played for England, green with envy.

I can foresee a situation a bit later in the series when we might wish to call upon you – especially if you manage to strike a bit of form – and I wonder if before announcing the fact that you are out of the running, I could suggest that if a Test match covers a period during which you are already committed to first class cricket, you might be prevailed upon to play.

Bob replied to Insole immediately upon receipt, declining with thanks.

I can assure you that I would dearly have loved to play on a winning side against Australia, not only in England but, if it could have been possible, in Aus[tralia] as well. However one cannot have everything. I have been lucky.

Across his copy at the bottom of the handwritten letter he has scrawled poignantly THE END!

Barber was now caught on the horns of a dilemma. Even if he had burned the bridge to Test cricket because he had found the England dressing room an unwelcome place to enter, he still retained a love for the game and above all perhaps, he still wanted to win the County Championship with Warwickshire. However, he also wanted to pursue his business interests and believed that he had developed a philosophy that would allow him to do it.

I did not think it was necessary to have to play 32 three day games to be up to scratch to be able to play to the best of your ability. If I wanted a game of cricket, I would go and play for Boughton Hall. I wanted to devise something between practising in Chester and Birmingham and playing with a restructured game.

In the winter of 1966-7 Bob, and presumably other players, knew that MCC was discussing a number of alternative ways of changing the structure of the game. One suggestion was a county championship of 16 matches of 3 days duration with a possible 16 days of another one day competition.

That would have suited me perfectly. It was thought that such a decision would bring talented players back into the game. And in the end it took over twenty years for that to happen. I could possibly have played on and I genuinely believe the game ought to be played in a particular way and I was trying to do that.

The Middlesex left arm spin bowler Phillippe Edmonds made a similar case in the 1980s. He too no longer enjoyed the grind of county cricket but he still wanted to play for England, so he proposed to play for his local club Finchley at weekends which he believed would prepare him for bowling at Viv Richards and Clive Lloyd in Test matches. In their desire to balance business and sport, in their thoughtful approach to the need for radical change in the structure of domestic cricket, these two Cambridge graduates had much in common.

Bob never went as far as demanding to be selected for England if he made runs playing for Boughton Hall in Chester but he was certainly now picking his matches carefully. It amused Jim Stewart to see his friend studying the fixture list from an original point of view.

> He'd look at the fixture list and tick off the matches he fancied playing in. If it was Yorkshire, he liked playing in Harrogate but he wouldn't be so keen to go Hull or Middlesbrough. He liked Scarborough and the seaside places and he liked Taunton. He didn't pick the weak sides or anything like that. He just picked the games where he fancied staying. When you teased him, he just said "Business meetings".

Bob Barber returned to county cricket after the debacle of his last Test match at Old Trafford, but Warwickshire was no longer the same county side it had been when he had first arrived and his chances of securing that coveted county championship winner's medal seemed to be receding. At the same time, a resurgent Lancashire with a new captain and a new committee were now heading in the opposite direction. In 1967 Warwickshire had dropped to tenth, just one place above the slowly recovering Lancashire and in 1968 the two counties accelerated in their respective directions. Lancashire under Jack Bond, and now boasting the significant influence of Farokh Engineer with the prospect of Clive Lloyd to come the following summer, finished sixth whilst Warwickshire continued their decline to eleventh.

Bob had known all about these two fine overseas players because, to his astonishment, Lancashire had approached him before the start of the 1968 season to ask if he would consider returning to Old Trafford as captain. Brian Statham had indicated that, though he would play one last season as a bowler, he wished to be relieved of the captaincy.

The intermediary was Arthur Booth, who had written that glowing letter of recommendation for Bob as long ago as 1951. Tommy Burrows had given way as Chairman of the committee to Tommy Higson, who was in turn poised to be replaced by Cedric Rhoades, the new Emperor but just as dictatorial in his own way as the men he had ousted. What was apparent to Bob in the way negotiations were handled, was that nothing had really changed. John Kay, who lost out in his bid to be elected onto the committee, had also been making overtures to Bob, unknown to Arthur Booth, so the chairman seemed to be sending two emissaries, deliberately attempting to disguise the fact from each of them that someone else was doing the same job. It made Bob's refusal very easy.

Arthur Booth wrote plaintively to him after Bob intimated politely that he wanted nothing more to do with a county run by that sort of committee and chairman.

All I wanted was RWB playing for Lancs again, though I did not want to give the Press any idea what I was doing. It was, as I have repeatedly said, a private matter which I had undertaken for the chairman… I had in mind Bob Barber as captain and I had therefore to put the committee in the picture. They were delighted at my progress and swore to keep it all secret (some hope!)… Still that is how the world goes.

Bob also made it clear that, in his opinion, Lancashire already had the perfect captain on their books in Jack Bond and further searching was a pointless exercise. Bond knew that the summer of 1968 might be his only year as Lancashire captain because he was initially appointed merely as caretaker after the Lancashire committee had approached and been rejected by R.W. Barber of Warwickshire, G.S. Sobers of Nottinghamshire and probably U.T. Cobbley of Allshire. Eventually, when Lancashire started moving up the table and winning trophies, they agreed to make the appointment permanent. Jack Bond remains forever grateful for Bob Barber's support at that difficult time.

In July 1968, five weeks after the less than glorious end to his Test career, he was batting against the unthreatening medium pace of Graham Burgess in the second innings of the match against Somerset in Taunton, when he was hit painfully over the eye. He missed the next match against Middlesex at Lord's but returned for the next two matches at Edgbaston, against Lancashire and Glamorgan. When Malcolm Nash bowled him for 4, he berated himself for having played down the wrong line and walked back to the dressing room to find the Warwickshire and England physiotherapist Bernard Thomas, waiting for him.

I was already thinking if I am getting bowled like that, I'd better pack it in, when Bernard asked if I'd seen the ball that bowled me. I said, "I missed it, I don't need an excuse, I was bowled." He said, "I am asking a serious question. I was sitting behind the line of the bowler's arm and I don't think you saw the ball. You played six inches inside it. You have to get your eyes checked." He sent me to see a specialist in a hospital in Birmingham who told me I had a detached retina. I had to go and lie down and was told not to move from this darkened room, lying completely still for about two or three days.

His eyesight in English conditions had never been particularly good, which was why in the bright sunlight of Australia and South Africa he succeeded consistently. He was off for a month but returned to play in two county matches before the 1968 Gillette Cup Final. In the second match against Sussex at Hove he made a scintillating 125, his last first class century. It was the perfect preparation for the big showpiece one day final against the same side at the end of the season.

Warwickshire (along with Lancashire) became, in the late 1960s, an outstanding one day side. Rohan Kanhai and Lance Gibbs signed on and both were playing at Lord's in September 1968 in the revenge win over Sussex, who had beaten them four years earlier. Strangely, Sussex won the toss and did the reverse of what they had done in 1964, when they had won the game by sending Warwickshire in to face the new ball in seamer friendly conditions. They certainly made a better fist of it this time, reaching 214 in their 60 overs but Warwickshire reached their target with three overs to spare.

It was rather sad that Ted Dexter failed on the big occasion making only 8 and Bob too failed to contribute much more than 15 runs at the top of the innings. Jim Stewart top scored and A.C. Smith, captaining in place of his namesake, received the Man of the Match award. Dexter and Barber had been such dominant figures in English cricket only a couple of years earlier. Indeed, Dexter was recalled for the last two Test matches against the Australians that summer, but his time had come and gone. Was Barber going to accept that his powers too were fading? It was already clear that he was having continuing problems with his eyes and he was at least six years past the time when he had always supposed he would call it a day.

One reason he might have continued to play cricket was the memory of his father's final words. Bob and Jack Barber were extremely close. His father had always encouraged his son's desire to play cricket and enjoyed the success that followed without ever getting, as he had so delightfully termed it, "swelled-headed". He had also quietly reminded Bob that he would be a long time retired, so that he had better take steps to ensure he had a career after he had packed away his flannels for the last time.

Jack Barber's health had never been robust and Bob had been concerned about it for most of his own life. Jack's presence at the Test matches in Cape Town in 1965 and Sydney in 1966 had been deeply satisfying occasions for both men but by the end of the decade, although only just past his sixtieth birthday, Jack was dying. Bob returned home frequently to be with him.

Because of where he came from, he knew how to work very hard. His final words to me, he was very sick and he'd drifted off under morphine, so I was going to go downstairs to sit with my mother and I'd got as far as the end of the bed when he opened his eyes and said to me, "Don't do what I've done, Bob. Don't work all your life until it's too late" and then he died. I'm not sure I've paid enough attention to that but I know he was right.

Maybe that was why at the end of June 1969, Bob Barber returned to play in fourteen first class fixtures and the inaugural season of the John Player League, which was known at that time simply as the Players County League. He played his last matches against Lancashire at the end of August, losing the Sunday afternoon match by a distance to a Lancashire side on the verge of clinching the trophy. Warwickshire made a better fist of it in the three day match and were in a position to push for a win at the end of the second day but the last day was washed out and the match ended in an unsatisfactory draw. Bob Barber was bowled by Barry Wood for 25. The Warwickshire team looked strong on paper – Barber, Kanhai, Ibadulla, Jameson, Amiss, Brown, Cartwright and Gibbs – but it lacked the motivation that Mike Smith had given them earlier in the decade and although they finished a more than respectable fourth in the table, they were a long way behind the eventual winners, Glamorgan.

Bob Barber's last first-class match was a friendly at Edgbaston against the New Zealand tourists. He was trapped lbw by Cunis for 0 in the first innings but managed 18 in the second before falling in the same way to Dayle Hadlee. He was still expected to display his talents to the Sunday crowds who took immediately to the John Player League. He played in ten of Warwickshire's sixteen matches but failed to make a significant contribution.

He now recognised that he was barely contributing to the team with his runs and this, combined with his anxiety to immerse himself completely in the anticipated second career, hastened the contemplation of a life without cricket. Besides, perhaps most important of all, the joy of those first three or four seasons at Warwickshire was starting to diminish.

One reason why that was happening was that he had returned partly to please the administrators at Warwickshire, who thought his presence at these games would increase crowd attendance figures rather than because he had an overwhelming desire to test his talents in this new forty overs format. Another reason was that he was being paid relatively well but that too had a negative side. By turning up on Sundays to please the crowds and the Warwickshire committee, he was, to his own embarrassment, behaving in a manner that he knew that professional cricketers had long resented. He would breeze into a dressing room that was managing perfectly well without him and take the place of someone who was slogging it out six days a week on poorly attended county grounds. Sometimes, that place was that of his best friend, Jim Stewart and the situation got even trickier when the

Professional Cricketers Association, which had been founded in 1967, started to grow in strength. The Warwickshire representative was W.J. P. Stewart.

I'm not particularly a union man but I represented Warwickshire and we had a problem with Bob and Mike [Smith] coming back, after they had both retired, to play the John Player Sunday League. Our boys said it wasn't fair that they should waltz back in and take their places. The result of it all was that I had to represent these lads. It was awkward because Bob and Mike were my close friends. I told the chairman that I would play Sunday League cricket for nothing if he went back and asked Bob and Mike if they would play for nothing. I knew at that point that that was me finished. I went home and my wife typed up the letter, putting it all in writing. I couldn't accept what was happening but, at the end, I think I was the only cricketer to get twelve months salary as a redundancy package. Fortunately, it never affected my friendship with Bob. We always used to stop in the Red Lion pub in Henley in Arden on the way back to the house from Edgbaston when he stayed with me but it was a major thing at the time.

Jim's final year contract after nearly twenty years with Warwickshire was £1295. He wrongly suspected that Bob was getting nearly that amount in about six games. In fact, as his participation in county cricket declined so did Bob's income from it. In 1965 he estimates that cricket provided him with 80% of his gross annual income. During the next three years the percentage was never higher than 40% and dropped as low as 20%. The players who made way, Jim is anxious to emphasise, had no problems with Bob personally. They all liked him but they didn't get their match fees if they had to drop out. They received a basic salary but appearance money was worth an extra five pounds and if the team won, they wouldn't get the win bonus either. Suddenly 20% of their anticipated weekly wage was disappearing.

Bob is quick to acknowledge the problem which the PCA's attitude exacerbated.

The problem came when they formed the players' union and Jack Bannister and Warwickshire were central to it. Jack was in charge of the national body so Jim Stewart became what I called the shop steward and what he called the players' representative. They had a meeting during pre-season training with the chairman, Edmund King. I suspect it was Jack Bannister who complained that it was unfair for me to swan in and play a game and for Neal Abberley to get left out to accommodate my wishes. I was reticent about Jack Bannister. I felt he was a bit too keen to bowl out 9, 10, Jack. Albert Wright, who was a good bowler, would flog his guts out getting them down to number 8 or 9 and then Jack would start waving his arms about, indicating to Mike that he was ready to come on and bowl. I didn't take to that. After the year of living with Anne and Sandy at Ladbroke Hall in Tanworth, I stayed with Jim when I played and he might be the one who was dropped to make way for me and there I was accepting his hospitality. "We gave you a bed, we feed you and I get dropped and lose my appearance money."

With the aggravation levels rising, it was perhaps unsurprising that Bob played no county cricket at all in 1970. What is surprising to find is that in 1971, approaching the age of thirty-six, now eight years after he had initially planned to retire, he actually returned to play for Warwickshire, although only in the Sunday League.

On May 23, in a match reduced by rain to an 11 overs-a-side thrash, he went in at number nine to be dismissed caught and bowled by Tony Greig for 0. Warwickshire lost by two runs. Was his journey from Chester really necessary? He was at Swansea the following week, batting at three, but Warwickshire lost again. He took three weeks off and then came back to face Middlesex in a match in which he was bowled by Keith Jones without scoring. The following week he was bowled by Vanburn Holder for a duck.

He made a couple of respectable scores against Leicestershire and Nottinghamshire but at Edgbaston on Sunday afternoon 25th July 1971, Bob Barber walked out to bat for the last time for Warwickshire. Tom Cartwright, now playing for Somerset, was probably salivating at the prospect of claiming his old colleague's wicket. He never got the chance. Brian Langford, the veteran off spinner and now in his testimonial year, caught and bowled Bob Barber for three. He walked back to the pavilion, acknowledging whatever smattering of applause the family crowd gave him, and said his farewells. It was, after seventeen years, the end of Bob Barber's career in county cricket.

It is not given to many cricketers to leave the stage for the last time like Nasser Hussain at Lord's or Steve Waugh at the SCG. Success or failure isn't really the point at such moments. "Bradman bowled Hollies nought" probably lingers longer in the memory than "Bradman bowled Hollies 59" might have done. The man who broadcast the last two balls that Bradman faced in Test cricket, bowed out in similarly minimalist fashion. "And after Trevor Bailey, it will be Christopher Martin-Jenkins" was his famous last sentence. What John Arlott left behind is immortal. Bob Barber left cricket the richer for his contribution to its history. Sometimes, that is all that matters.

CHAPTER THIRTEEN

"WHATEVER HAPPENED TO Bob Barber?" "Didn't he make a big score against the Aussies?" "Who is Bob Barber?" These are the questions that are prompted when his name is mentioned. It should be clear by now from the preceding pages that Bob Barber deserves a higher standing in the history of English cricket than he is generally given and one of the reasons why he doesn't have it, which should also be clear, is that he has never sought it.

If you Google the name you will see a three minute clip of the Third Test at Sydney but astonishingly the only images of Barber are of his walking out to bat with Boycott and letting a ball go outside the off stump. If there is a reason for the existence of Sky Sports it is that such historic moments as his 185 will now no longer be allowed to disappear without trace. There are also some standard references to his statistics and then to a chain of Bob's barber shops in the USA and even one to Fat Bob's barber shop in Bournemouth.

Bob's modesty and charm may give some indication of why and how he struggled in the Lancashire dressing room in which, for much of the time he was there, he felt like a fish out of water. His success in the world of business is also not a matter for wide proclamation and the generosity of his donations to worthy causes, though considerable and significant, is not a matter of public record because he has no wish for it to be so.

There is of course the other side. No shrinking violet is going to approach Peter Pollock and threaten to wrap the bat round his head if he bowls any more beamers. No one short of considerable physical courage is going to call Charlie Griffith an ugly bugger to his face and then go and stand twenty-two yards away as he runs in and aims a hard cricket ball at his head. No one gets to the top of international sport without an inner core of steely resolve. "You don't mess with Barber", noted John Murray wisely.

Bob Barber is an easy man to like on a superficial level. He is quietly spoken, quick to smile, a delightful raconteur, a generous host as the postscript to this book details perfectly. The stories pour out of him but none of them are boastful, none of them are designed necessarily to reveal himself in a heroic light. He has reservations about certain people, (which one of us does not?) but his accounts of them are invariably tinged with a generous reappraisal. He wrote to Peter Marner's widow telling her how much he admired Peter's talent. He has entirely obliterated from his mind whatever it was that Jack Dyson said to him that caused him to be sacked in 1960. He feels Chimp Clayton was unfairly scapegoated when he too was sacked four years later. He made a point of tracking down Geoff Edrich who had been treated so badly by Lancashire and offering support towards the end of his life when he was suffering from throat cancer. It made him sad to learn after Tommy Greenhough had died that Greenhough had always wished they had bowled more in tandem.

The initial conversations about the difficulties he faced in that Lancashire dressing room of the late 1950s and early 1960s were notable for Bob's admiration of everyone in it. It was only much later that the problems started to emerge. In the end, he concluded that he really didn't have much in common with any of them. He is certainly only too ready to acknowledge that he was culpable too. He should have built bridges to the men he had been asked to lead. Maybe they thought he was too aloof – it was a common accusation made by professionals of university educated amateurs in the 1950s.

There is some comedy in this aloofness because Bob (and nearly everyone else) thought that Ted Dexter, who shared a similar educational background, was too aloof. It was only many years after they had both retired that he realised that Dexter's apparent social disdain was the result of a painful shyness. Bob certainly acknowledges that he himself was very shy as a young man. It is entirely possibly that it was this shyness rather than alleged aloofness that was at the root of his difficulties as Lancashire captain. What do you do with a very young captain who needs to build trust with his senior professionals if you are the committee that has appointed him? Why, of course, you make him stay by himself in a separate hotel. A coconut for Chairman Burrows, if you please.

In those last, rather desultory, seasons for Warwickshire, Bob spent a year at Liverpool Polytechnic preparing for his business career. At the end of it he was awarded a distinction. Unlike Dexter, Cowdrey and a few others it would be easy to mention, Bob Barber had been admitted to Cambridge on academic merit rather than sporting prowess. In 1968, Nicky was born and now there were three Barber girls under school age. In 1969 he turned his diploma into a full MBA from Liverpool University and, following his father's sad death, he took a job working for the British Institute of Management in London and went to live just outside Princes Risborough.

What they wanted was someone to computerise all their information services. That wasn't my field but it would get me to London and it would get me into the centre of the BIM and I thought that would produce some useful contacts. Within three weeks of starting, I got called in by the director I reported to and he asked me if we were going with IBM or some other firm to install all the computers. I said "I don't think it should be done at all. As far as I can see there is only one place that's done what you want to do and that's the University of Wyoming and it hasn't been successful." I felt we should do a lot more thinking before making a big decision like this and he blasted me. "The committee of the BIM have already taken the decision which we have employed you to carry out". I said, "If you give me an instruction to commission one of the big computer firms, I will do as you say but I am not prepared to take the responsibility for it because I don't think it will work." The Director General of the BIM, a nice fellow called Marsh, told me that Shell and ICI and the leaders of British industry had decided this is the best thing to do. I still demurred, pointing out it would cost a quarter of a million which might be lost entirely and I queried if the BIM could afford to do that. The result was that I pretty much talked my way out of a job. I decided I would learn what I could for a year and then give in my notice.

Within months of starting his new career, Bob Barber's steely resolve to do things his way and not be swayed by external pressure was abundantly clear. Frankly, facing Trueman and Griffith and Hall at Lord's in fading light with no sight screen at the pavilion end, being castigated in the press for losing a cricket match, being sacked by telegram by men he didn't respect in the middle of a badly appointed hotel in Pakistan, these were life shaping moments. A reprimand from the British Institute of Management held no terrors for him.

After leaving the Institute, Bob went to work for the management consultancy Collinson Grant. Bob had known James Grant from Cambridge because they had been on the athletics team together but as ever there was a snag.

Len Collinson wanted to use my name as a sportsman but I didn't like that at all. I wanted to be standing on my own two feet. I recognised that my name had a commercial value but would the CEO of Tesco take me as seriously as one of my competitors because I had opened the batting for England. [If it was Lord McLaurin, undoubtedly!] Much better if it never crops up. Anyway I joined them for three years, but I didn't like the idea of constantly having to sell myself to get the next job because I felt that it led to a lack of integrity on the part of the consultant.

After Collinson Grant, Bob went into partnership and bought one of the companies that Jack Barber had introduced him to. It was called Sanoda which he knew very well from the inside. Jack had regretted that much of his efforts had gone into running companies for others who then enjoyed the profits created by Jack's hard work. He warned his son against repeating that mistake and his son had listened. He took over Sanoda on the understanding that if it were successful he would have a share of the equity. It was to be the start of an extremely successful business which would make him wealthy.

The early years involved as much travelling as cricket had demanded, so although he wasn't spending winters on tour and summers on county grounds, he was still away from his growing family but the business demanded total commitment and he was not prepared to offer it anything less. He enjoyed building the business as much as he had enjoyed playing for Warwickshire in his first three or four years at Edgbaston.

You win some and you lose some, but you try to come out ahead and the success of Sanoda owed a lot to team work. I avoided in business a lot of the things I had been appalled by when playing cricket. It was fun getting the company to break even and then forging ahead. One day, I got back from lunch to be told that someone from an arm of Shell was desperate to get hold of me and I thought that I must have made my mark somewhere.

Sanoda made things that sniffed and foamed in the bathroom and kitchen. They were competing with Reckitts and Airwick and companies of that nature so it was a major triumph when Sanoda turned out to be one of the first to get Tesco onto a non-foods private label.

Sanoda had been making few products and were losing money. The first thing I did was to sort out the cost structure and see how much more cheaply I could make things for. We expanded into Europe and the US. We had a distribution company in Florida, but the goods were being manufactured in the UK, mostly in north Wales. We benefited from government development grants so we never owned a factory as such. We would get the Wales Development Board to build it for us so we never had to capitalise in that way. When I was working with my father I had something to do with construction and I was very conscious of the amounts of money you would have to borrow and interest rates were much higher. I wanted to explore and build the market base for our products slowly so that I hadn't ploughed in vast sums building up a business that wasn't there. I built the company up out of internally generated funds and no borrowings. Our compound growth rate was about 34% compounded over seventeen years. You didn't get many companies moving at that pace but we were starting from a very low base. In our market place Sanoda was the lowest priced and highest margin company. We could do that because I did not think it necessary to spend a lot of money on marketing, particularly when you are doing things like private label. Now they hire a star to hit a tennis ball. We didn't spend a postage stamp on that sort of marketing.

The success of Sanoda under Bob's guidance came as little surprise to Bob's friends. David Bray, who had been one since their undergraduate days at Magdalene, joined Bob to work as his Commercial Director.

Knowing Bob as sober and well balanced and thoughtful and dedicated and persevering, I knew he would succeed because he can be very single minded.

Mike Smith and Jim Stewart who remain close friends to this day also freely confess that they were unsurprised that Bob had made such a success of his business career. It rather followed the lines of an innings – a slow careful assessment of pitch and bowlers, an understanding of where he could profit from a perceived weakness, followed by a ruthless demolition of the opposition. For all his charm and softly spoken gentleness, it is not difficult to imagine that in business negotiations Bob Barber very rarely came out as anything but a winner. There must have been a few battered Kelly Seymours and Evil Dicks in the world of chemical hygiene.

Bob and Anne decided to send Sandy, Janny and Nicky to Howell's School in Denbigh and moved house to a village called Bodfari just outside of Denbigh in Clwyd, only a few miles from Ruthin. For all the business success and the comforts of country living, pressures were beginning to mount on both the business and the marriage.

Whatever I did to try to delegate some of it, it never succeeded because I always ended up with more work than before. I was working longer and longer and getting more and more stress. I didn't want to go public because if I'd done that I would have been in the same position but I would have had to report to the shareholders.

David Bray, from his privileged viewpoint as Bob's Commercial Director, was very aware of the physical impact of this pressure.

Bob was overworking and he nearly had a stroke. He told me that his head had an iron band round it. I didn't know about it until after the event because he was a strong fit guy always playing squash and tennis.

The medical scare and the constant pressure of running Sanoda eventually caused a mid-life crisis. In late 1986, after twenty-five years of marriage, Bob and Anne separated. The girls were 24, 22 and 20 years old and had their own lives to lead. Bob had had enough of the business and two years later demonstrated that he had also had enough of England. He moved into a new flat in Valais, two hours out of Geneva where he sat for six months and stared at the magnificent panoramic view of the Alpine range outside his living room window. Six months of relative inactivity after a lifetime of frantic action was all he could take. As carefully as he had built his second career he built a third, this time as an investor particularly in South East Asia where he spends his winters. At the age of 79, he is working as hard as ever.

He played his last game for Warwickshire in 1971 but a couple of years later the siren song of a game of cricket was heard again. He was in the bar at Lord's after play when he was accosted by the MCC Secretary, Jack Bailey, who had been on the tour of Canada in 1959-60. As the country groped its way through power cuts and the three day week, MCC offered Bob the chance of sunshine.

Jack asked me what I was doing at Christmas and persuaded me to go on this trip to East Africa. We shut down at work for a fortnight over Christmas and I was probably out there for three and a half weeks. It was great fun and [two winters later] they asked me to go West Africa. I got a hundred in Nairobi on the first trip and another one against Nigeria in Lagos on the second, which thrilled me because I hadn't played for so long. Ted Clark captained one of the sides and Kipper joined us for a while. He'd been sent over by his employers, Barclays Bank. We started off in the Gambia; we had New Year's Eve dancing with the President and his ladies in a tin hut with holes in the roof. We went to Ghana and Sierra Leone and Nigeria. The only place I haven't played cricket in is South America. I wrote to Jack Bailey and said I wanted to go to Brazil but there wasn't a tour there planned for years and I didn't please them by turning down the chance to go to Bangladesh. I had no wish to go back there again.

Despite his self-imposed exile, Bob never lost touch with the game and in 2005 as his seventieth birthday approached, he wondered what he could do to mark the occasion that would give pleasure to others as well as to himself. He decided to invite men from every part of his cricketing life to join him at the cradle of cricket, Broadhalfpenny Down, the home of Hambledon Cricket Club in Hampshire. It was appropriate that there was a William Barber who became landlord of the Bat and Ball Inn immediately after Richard Nyren.

Lance Gibbs flew in from Florida, Jimmy Binks from California and Ian McLachlan, his old Cambridge team mate, from Adelaide and they were only three of the many who travelled great distances to be with Bob on a day in September when the sun shone and ghosts walked abroad on Broadhalfpenny Down. Stephen Chalke wrote a delightful article on the day for the magazine *The Wisden Cricketer* which is reproduced in the Post Script.

He also never stopped thinking about the game and, as might be expected of a thoughtful and singular man, he has very pronounced ideas about the game which he has been developing for fifty years.

Cricket is measured in irrelevant numerals. There are three sorts of averages – mean, median and mode – and they all provide different measures of a group of figures. When cricket statisticians speak of an average they refer to the mean but because not outs are not counted as completed innings within the total their statistics are skewed or false. Hundreds were not important to me but they were to other people. Once you got into the 90s you might as well go on and get it but to score at the rate I liked to do, things had to be going your way and the statistics they use don't take that into account.

If he won the toss as captain of Lancashire, he wanted to see 300 to 350 on the board by 5.30 so he could have fifteen overs at a tired opposition before the close. He didn't care who got the runs or if a batsman made 20 or 120 but if the match was won the task had been achieved by the team which was all that mattered.

He believes strongly that averages mean little and personal scores mean even less.

Maybe when I was young I took the figures seriously but as I got older I felt someone has to make this point. You will find somewhere in Wisden a game where there was the Lawrence trophy for the quickest 100 in the season. We were playing, I think Glamorgan, at Nuneaton which is a long narrow ground. The umpire said to me you're easily going to get the fastest hundred of the season. I think I was on 94 so I said the next one's going for six, just like I did at Johannesburg. I think Jim Pressdee caught me by the sightscreen on the long-on boundary. Now any idiot could have nudged for a few runs to get to the hundred but I honestly wanted to give the impression that it wasn't important to me and that I didn't give a damn. I'm not saying that because I'm 79 and going ga ga. I believed those things then and I believe those things now.

His point is perfectly valid and a number of star cricketers of the current generation should be reminded that if they make 200 but their side loses the game what is the point of it? It is particularly the case if the 200 is made in a style and at a rate that positively repels potential spectators and the match ends in a desultory draw. He then posits a match in which each of the first three innings has produced 100 runs and nobody has scored more than 10. Then it rains and his side is left 70 minutes to score 101 to win the match. Bob bats at number 8, scores 20 in ten minutes but then gets out. The match is won in the last over with the last pair at the crease. "Which runs have greater merit?" he asks. "Which set of spectators have enjoyed the match more?" he wonders rhetorically.

Bob Barber's career averages give no inkling of his impact as a player or his worth as a cricketer. He averaged 35 in his 28 Tests with one century; as a bowler, his 42 wickets cost 43 runs each. In all first class cricket he made 17,631 runs at under 30 with 17 centuries and 90 half centuries, a conversion rate that would rouse today's commentators to a fine fury. He took 549 first class wickets also at just a fraction under 30. He has no time for averages, not surprisingly, because they do not reflect a cricketer's true worth. How can taking the wicket of Don Bradman on a featherbed pitch in the 1930s be rated as exactly the same as taking the wicket of Monty Panesar? - Cardiff 2009 notwithstanding.

Committees look at the statistics of a player's season before offering him a contract for the following year. Whatever the benchmark figure is to get that contract renewed, that is what the batsman will primarily be aiming at. The result of the match and his county's standing in the championship become subservient to that end. The lunacy is, in the opinion of Bob Barber, that the judgement of the committee is actually based on false statistics because the statistics that are used and have been used throughout the history of the game are fundamentally skewed. He is almost certainly right but I suspect he won't be invited to speak at the Annual Dinner of the Association of Cricket Statisticians and Historians. More's the pity.

Barber's career as a cricketer and a businessman coincided with the social revolution of the mid-twentieth century. When he made his county championship debut against Glamorgan in 1954, British schoolchildren still celebrated Empire Day. When he walked off the field at Edgbaston in his last John Player League match in 1971 the Prime Minister, Edward Heath, was on the verge of taking Britain into the European Economic Community. When Harold Macmillan, the British Foreign Secretary in 1955, was asked by the six European countries who signed the Treaty of Rome whether he wished to attend their preliminary meetings, he told his deputy to inform the Europeans that he was far too busy dealing with the problems of EOKA in Cyprus to spare the time. Britain was a different country in 1971, with a very different focus.

The new Britain, forged in what Harold Wilson called the white heat of a technological and scientific revolution, took some time to materialise. The old attitudes towards class still permeated social and labour relations. The increasing power of the trades unions tended to solidify traditional suspicions of science and technology. These suspicions were by no means confined to labour versus management battles in factories or humorous barbs cast by satirists. In 1962, F.R.

Leavis intemperately attacked C.P. Snow's earlier Rede Lecture in Cambridge on the two cultures, a talk in which he famously argued that the application of science and technology, and the prosperity that was presumed to follow, offered the best hope for meeting mankind's fundamental needs, but that this goal was being frustrated by the gulf of ignorance between the two cultures and the educational arrangements in Britain that perpetuated this divide. For Bob Barber, this public controversy had a very personal impact because he was exactly the sort of natural scientist that Snow had in mind.

Bob Barber played as an amateur in the last days of that social anomaly. He was educated at public school and Cambridge University. He quickly became a favourite of the cricket establishment, men like Harry Altham, Jim Swanton and Billy Griffith. To be fair, his extraordinary talent as much as his educational background earned him that distinction but it would be true to say that he moved easily in a world that Colin Hilton and Billy Ibadulla might have found alien and intimidating.

What makes Barber so interesting is that he was in that world but not of it. His brain worked like that of a professional cricketer and a professional scientist. He played the game for enjoyment but he played to win. He did not care to expend his energy in a losing cause and shrug off the defeat as a matter of no consequence. As a result, it became easy to see why so many of his colleagues used the word "perverse" when describing him. There was nobody quite like him in the game. He was ruthlessly determined to achieve his aims in business and cricket and nobody could intimidate him for all his charm and inbred civility.

Perhaps he didn't achieve all he could have done or should have done when he entered the game with all that potential. He certainly feels like that but without exception the players who played with him, men of character and substance like Jack Bond and Jim Stewart and Mike Smith, all said in their own ways and with some poignancy, "I wish I'd had his talent". His success in business and finance indicates a man of vision and meticulous planning. They were qualities he brought to his cricket too but cricket was not necessarily always ready to acknowledge them. He is a singular man with a bright incisive mind. If he didn't make the most of what he brought to cricket it wasn't necessarily entirely Bob Barber's fault.

You never know what your childhood heroes will turn out to be like when you meet them in later life. The image of Bob Barber clattering down the steps of the pavilion at Old Trafford ahead of Statham, Grieves, Higgs, Wharton, Marner and the rest remains as strong as ever after nearly fifty-five years. I have learned a great deal of what it took for that tall, lissom young man in the cap crested by a red rose to walk onto the field and captain Lancashire. I was fortunate in many ways because at the time I first approached him, Bob was particularly receptive to the idea of recalling many of the disappointments he had suffered, particularly during his time as captain of Lancashire. On the night before his seventieth birthday celebrations, in the Bat & Ball pub across the road from Broadhalfpenny Down, Bob had dinner with Roy Collins. "Why", asked his old friend, "have you never been willing to talk about what happened at Lancashire?" Bob mumbled a reply but the question had struck home. Just over a year before Bob and I first met, Roy Collins died. When I started to talk to Bob about those difficult years of 1960 and 1961 I was surprised at how open he was about the hurts he had suffered. Learning much later of the conversation with Roy Collins, I realised that I had been extremely fortunate in my timing.

It was no wonder then that Bob Barber turned out to be a fascinating subject for biographical research. He might have spent seventeen years as a cricketer and fifty years as a businessman, but it is the memory of the upright, beautifully correct left-handed batsman, the quirky, bouncing rhythm of the right-handed wrist spinner and the predatory, superbly athletic fielder that will always come to mind when the name Bob Barber is mentioned. He graced and enriched the game he loved. Who could ask for anything more?

POSTSCRIPT

BOB BARBER CELEBRATED his threescore and ten with a match at Broadhalfpenny Down between friends and playing contemporaries. **Stephen Chalke** *secured an invitation*

Saturday, September 17, 2005. Not since the 1770s, when the great Hambledon club took on and beat an All-England XI, when John Small the elder's batting triumphed over the bowling of the broad-shouldered Lumpy Stevens, has Broadhalfpenny Down seen a gathering like it.

For Bob Barber's 70th birthday his son-in-law Simon Smith had organised a cricket match between the Gentlemen of RW Barber and those of MJK Smith, and the players arrived from all parts of Bob's life and all corners of the globe. There was his Warwickshire team-mate Lance Gibbs, all the way from Miami: "Man, if Bob Barber invites me to play a game of cricket, I'll be there." His university friend Aizaz Fakir, complete with family, from Karachi: "I couldn't afford it work-wise but Bob's such a lovely person - and orders are orders." Another Cambridge colleague Ian McLachlan was over from Adelaide and the Yorkshire keeper Jimmy Binks had flown in from California.

The day was blessed with sunshine, with just a hint of an autumnal chill in the air. The ancient ground sported a marquee alongside its wooden pavilion, with the downland fields of the Meon Valley rolling away in the distance, all harvested and ready for winter. With match rules that required each batsman to face 18 balls and a loss of five runs whenever they were out, the day's hardest task was that of the scorers, among them Bob's accountant Robert Godfrey. "They're hoping for a tie," it was explained, "so we need somebody who can be creative with figures."

How the years rolled back! With Donald Carr and Jack Bailey the day's first umpires, Fred Rumsey and Ian Thomson took the new ball. It was hard to visualise the menace that Rumsey once possessed but the 76-year-old Thomson still displayed a high arm and good control of length. "Is that really Tommy?" David Allen - sitting comfortably beyond the boundary - asked, breaking off his reminiscences about MJK Smith as a fine England captain. "I'm sticking to a turn of umpiring," he explained, "I'm afraid my bowling mechanics have completely gone."

First to take strike was Glenn Neil-Dwyer, a friend from Bob's Ruthin School days. The son of a Jamaican airman, he is now an eminent neurosurgeon and, before the first ball was bowled, he turned to the tall figure of Peter Walker standing perilously close to him at backward short leg. "What on earth are you doing there?"

Back came the reply from one of cricket's greatest close catchers: "This is where I always field." Behind the stumps, impressively low, crouched Binks: "Getting down wasn't the problem," he said. "It was coming up again afterwards."

At the other end McLachlan, a former Australian Government minister, clipped his second ball for four over John Jameson's head at mid-wicket. Then, just as Neil-Dwyer was finding his touch with a four through mid-on, the scorer's voice came over the Tannoy: "Come in, No. 1, you've had your time."

Fakir, in his Pakistan top, batted with sweet timing, and several eyes were caught by the confident swing of Harold Rhodes' bat. "They didn't want me to bat at Derby," the one-time fast bowler explained. "They said that, as a tall man, I'd use up too much of my strength." Top score of the day, however, with 31 off his 18 balls, was the MCC secretary Roger Knight but then, at the age of 59, as the watching Alec Bedser put it: "He's a bit young to be playing this sort of stuff."

"I've just had my flu jab," Tom Cartwright said, "and I was looking round the field, wondering if all the others have had theirs. I've never thought about that on a cricket field before." Fakir flighted some lovely legbreaks and Robert Aiyar offered a hint of the schoolboy pace that meant that, for Barber, "I never had any fear of fast bowling again". But the pick of the bowlers was inevitably Cartwright, immaculately turned out and still leaping, crossing his legs and landing sideways on in his delivery stride. "He doesn't know how to bowl a bad ball," Carr said. In all his travels with the Old England XI, had Tom ever played here before? "Never, but I did visit here once. I went out on my own into the middle and I listened to all the ancient voices. And I knew which end I would have bowled. Uphill, into the wind, like Lumpy Stevens used to."

Mike Brearley arrived late. "I looked across the field, at all these old men playing cricket, and I thought it was a very odd sight," he said later in the day, "but now I've been here a few hours, it all seems quite normal." His own day was chequered: a dropped catch, a last-ball boundary that saved him from the ignominy of a minus score and a rare wicket, hitting the stumps of Bob's friend Owain Howell. Half an hour later the batsman was still full of delight: "Isn't it wonderful? I've been bowled by Mike Brearley."

The food and drink was plentiful, so too were the memories that flowed from early morning to midnight. The presence of the ever elegant Ted Dexter set off Rumsey: "He was such a fine player. I used to field in the gully and the way his bat came down, the noise it made, it frightened the living daylights out of me." Then there was Peter Richardson, telling of the encounter between the amateur Walter Robins and the sharp-tongued Roly Jenkins: "'That was a very good article on spin bowling, Jenkins; who wrote it for you?' 'I wrote it myself, sir. Who read it for you?'"

And in a wheelchair Gloucester's very own Bomber Wells. "Do come," Bob Barber wrote, "and add a little class to our day." Back in their National Services days, Colin Stansfield Smith told me, a brigadier opened the batting against them and Private Wells - standing in the gully - produced a red water pistol and squirted it at him. "Only Bomber could get away with that."

"It is going to take me weeks to get rid of the nostalgia," one old cricketer said. If you wanted to remember how they all used to play, you could sit in the pavilion and watch a film that Simon Smith had compiled of the players' glory days, featuring - above all else - the magnificent 185 that Bob Barber himself had hit on the first day of the Sydney Test in January 1966. It was one of the great Test innings, played by a free spirit - as cricket at its best is always played. As John Woodcock - himself a spectator at Broadhalfpenny Down - had written in The Times: "In every line of Barber's remarkable innings, there showed an independence of character."

The film was of another age. He reached his hundred with a push into the covers, made one wave of the bat, took his cap off briefly and settled back to his innings. His father had arrived in Sydney that day and he reported back the words of a man on the Hill: "Why can't we have a batsman like this Barber?" Until Virender Sehwag hit 195 on Boxing Day 2003 it stood as the highest score by a batsman on the first day of a Test against Australia. "Bob hit everything in the middle of the bat," Dennis Silk said. "That innings was sublime. It had the hallmark of real talent."

In later life Bob Barber has settled in Switzerland. Successful in business, he is too private to trumpet his support for various good causes. Among them is the Broadhalfpenny Down Association that works hard not only to preserve cricket on the historic field but also to provide playing opportunities for children from all sorts of backgrounds.

Batting one last time, Bob was desperately anxious not to fall victim to the bowling of his old Warwickshire keeper Alan Smith but he struck the ball with freedom.

The final over of the match arrived. RW Barber's Gentlemen had made 155; in reply MJK Smith's side stood on 144. And who else should bowl the last balls but Bob Barber himself? He tossed up his legbreaks to his old Lancashire team-mate Roy Collins, and - with a little help from umpire Allen, who somehow let the over run to 14 balls - the scores finished level and the players departed from the field to much applause. For most it was a last departure.

The sun dropped down the Meon Valley, leaving that chill autumnal breeze. Many of the players drove off to change for the evening meal, MJK Smith led a small posse to the Bat and Ball pub across the road and a group of wagtails took up occupation of the pitch. "You've caught the sun," somebody said as I set off for a quiet walk down a country lane. So much fun, so many friendships. It was a day to live for years in the memory. "This," said Bob Barber, "is the heart and the soul of the real game of cricket."

Among those present: DL Acfield (Essex), DA Allen (Glos, Eng), JA Bailey (Essex), RW Barber (Lancs, Warks, Eng), AV Bedser (Surrey, Eng), EA Bedser (Surrey), JG Binks (Yorks, Eng), SIA Bokhari (Lahore), JD Bond (Lancs), JM Brearley (Middx, Eng), DJ Brown (Warks, Eng), DB Carr (Derbys, Eng), TW Cartwright (Warks, Som, Eng), EA Clark (Middx), R Collins (Lancs), ER Dexter (Sussex, Eng), Aizazuddin Fakir (Khairpur, Karachi), LR Gibbs (Warks, W Indies), DJ Insole (Essex, Eng), JA Jameson (Warks, Eng), RDV Knight (Surrey, Glos), IM McLachlan (South Australia), MEL Melluish (Camb U), JT Murray (Middx, Eng), RJ Parks (Hants), JF Pretlove (Kent), JSE Price (Middx, Eng), HJ Rhodes (Derbys, England), PE Richardson (Worcs, Kent, Eng), FE Rumsey (Worcs, Som, Eng), WE Russell (Middx, Eng), DM Sayer (Kent), DRW Silk (Som), AC Smith (Warks, Eng), CS Smith (Lancs), MJK Smith (Warks, Eng), WJP Stewart (Warks), R Subba Row (Surrey, Nthants, Eng), NI Thomson (Sussex, Eng), PM Walker (Glam, Eng), BD Wells (Glos, Notts), OS Wheatley (Warks, Glam)

PPS writes the author, his eyes momentarily misting even though he wasn't there and knew nothing of the occasion until after Stephen's article appeared in *The Wisden Cricketer* in the autumn of 2005.

Is there anyone reading that who doesn't wish in his or her heart that they had been present on that occasion to celebrate the life of one of cricket's unsung heroes and to have revelled in the sheer joy provided merely by being in the presence of a scorebook with such names upon it? In the autumn of that year, in the autumn of his years, Bob Barber celebrated not just his landmark birthday but the very essence of why we are all drawn magnetically to cricket, the greatest of games.

APPENDICES

RW BARBER - CAREER RECORD

Test Career Batting and Fielding:

	M	I	NO	Runs	HS	Ave	100	50	Ct
England	28	45	3	1495	185	35.59	1	9	21

Test Career Bowling:

	Bs	Ms	Runs	W	BB	Ave	5wI	10wM	SR	ER
England	3426	101	1806	42	4-132	43.00	0	0	81.57	3.16

First-Class Career Batting and Fielding:

	M	I	NO	Runs	HS	Ave	100	50	Ct
Overall	386	651	52	17631	185	29.43	17	90	210

First-Class Career Bowling:

	Bs	Ms	Runs	W	BB	Ave	5wI	10wM	SR	ER
Overall	31604	1177	16176	549	7-35	29.46	12	0	57.56	3.07

List A Career Batting and Fielding:

	M	I	NO	Runs	HS	Ave	100	50	Ct
Warwickshire	37	36	1	977	114	27.91	2	4	7

List A Career Bowling:

	Bs	Ms	Runs	W	BB	Ave	5wI	10wM	SR	ER
Warwickshire	212	4	117	5	2-11	23.40	0	0	42.40	3.31

TEST CAREER SERIES BY SERIES

Batting:

Season	Opponents	M	I	NO	Runs	HS	Ave	100	50	Ct
1960	South Africa	1	2	0	9	5	4.50	0	0	0
1961-62	India	5	8	1	184	69*	26.28	0	1	4
1961-62	Pakistan	3	4	1	154	86	51.33	0	1	1
1964	Australia	1	2	0	53	29	26.50	0	0	0
1964-65	South Africa	4	4	0	290	97	72.50	0	4	6
1965	New Zealand	3	5	0	142	51	28.40	0	1	2
1965	South Africa	3	6	0	172	56	28.67	0	1	2
1965-66	Australia	5	9	1	328	185	41.00	1	0	4
1966	West Indies	2	3	0	97	55	32.33	0	1	2
1968	Australia	1	2	0	66	46	33.00	0	0	0

Bowling:

Season	Opponents	Bs	Ms	Runs	W	BB	Ave
1960	South Africa	96	2	55	1	1-29	55.00
1961-62	India	761	26	351	10	3-54	35.10
1961-62	Pakistan	474	10	315	4	2-70	78.75
1964	Australia	36	1	23	0	0-23	-
1964-65	South Africa	222	4	103	3	2-48	34.33
1965	New Zealand	600	36	236	9	4-132	26.22
1965	South Africa	363	12	193	3	2-30	62.17
1965-66	Australia	441	2	261	3	1-2	87.00
1966	West Indies	307	7	182	6	3-49	30.33
1968	Australia	126	1	87	3	2-56	29.00

SEASON BY SEASON FIRST CLASS RECORD - BATTING

Season	Teams	M	I	NO	Runs	HS	Ave	100	50	Ct
1954	L	9	13	2	172	41*	15.63	0	0	6
1955	CU & L	13	23	6	260	53	15.29	0	1	7
1956	CU & L	13	24	2	667	91	30.31	0	4	4
1957	CU & L	15	26	4	637	106	28.95	1	2	6
1958	L	25	39	1	986	115	25.94	1	5	10
1959	L & G	18	32	2	1104	121	36.80	1	7	5
1960	MCC, L, E & G	33	59	4	1386	146	25.20	1	6	8
1960-61	MCC	10	16	2	316	68	22.57	0	1	6
1960-61	EWS	3	5	0	254	83	50.80	0	3	2
1961	L & G	33	59	6	1572	175	29.66	2	5	14
1961-62	MCC & E	12	15	2	421	71	32.38	0	4	7
1961-62	MCC & E	5	7	2	179	86	35.80	0	1	2
1961-62	MCC	1	1	0	37	37	37.00	0	0	0
1962	L, MCC & G	30	51	5	1316	114	28.60	2	5	20
1963	W & MCC	29	47	5	1316	113	31.33	1	8	16
1964	MCC, W & E	31	54	4	1573	138	31.46	3	7	26
1964-65	MCC & E	11	14	1	595	108	45.76	1	5	14
1965	W, MCC, E & TNP	27	47	0	1266	94	26.93	0	7	17
1965-66	MCC & E	13	22	2	1001	185	50.05	3	3	10
1966	W & E	13	23	0	693	84	30.13	0	5	11
1966-67	RoW	1	2	0	36	30	18.00	0	0	1
1967	W	12	23	1	779	91	35.40	0	8	9
1968	W, MCC & E	15	24	1	507	125	22.04	1	2	6
1969	W	14	25	0	558	86	22.32	0	1	3

KEY: L - Lancashire, CU - Cambridge University, G - Gentlemen's XI, MCC - Marylebone Cricket Club, E - England, EWS - EW Swanton's XI, W - Warwickshire, TNP - TN Pierce's XI, RoW - Rest of the World XI.

SEASON BY SEASON FIRST CLASS
RECORD - BOWLING

Season	Teams	Bs	Ms	Runs	W	BB	Ave	5wI
1954	L	204	9	117	0			
1955	CU & L	226	5	195	2	1-13	97.50	0
1956	CU & L	258	9	154	5	2-74	30.80	0
1957	CU & L	548	21	319	11	4-41	29.00	0
1958	L	343	8	209	9	3-7	23.22	0
1959	L & G	876	35	432	13	4-48	33.23	0
1960	MCC, L, E & G	3056	126	1396	57	7-35	24.49	1
1960-61	MCC	2289	90	1070	45	7-89	23.77	3
1960-61	EWS	659	25	324	19	5-44	17.05	1
1961	L & G	2870	115	1467	46	5-74	31.89	1
1961-62	MCC & E	1019	36	479	12	3-54	39.91	0
1961-62	MCC & E	1598	56	890	22	4-66	40.45	0
1961-62	MCC	12	0	15	1	1-15	15.00	0
1962	L, MCC & G	2764	99	1524	38	5-68	40.10	1
1963	W & MCC	3048	127	1550	65	6-74	23.85	3
1964	MCC, W & E	2565	110	1174	51	5-56	23.01	1
1964-65	MCC & E	1122	43	605	21	6-67	28.80	1
1965	W, MCC, E & TNP	3029	126	1434	50	4-50	28.68	0
1965-66	MCC & E	1409	8	873	10	2-33	87.30	0
1966	W & E	1227	41	606	20	3-49	30.30	0
1966-67	RoW	126	9	36	2	2-36	18.00	0
1967	W	858	24	485	19	4-41	25.52	0
1968	W, MCC & E	846	38	403	17	4-28	23.70	0
1969	W	652	17	419	14	3-53	29.92	0